Living On A Fault

A JOURNEY TO JOY

Martha Sarkissian

This memoir dramatizes a cross-cultural love story that begins in the era when social and sexual mores restricted women's lives and choices. We follow the author as she copes with her alcoholic father, the crib death of her baby, and the mental illness of her son, at a time when the psychiatric world believed that mothers cause schizophrenia. Finally, we travel with the writer when she pushes aside superstitions, guilt and fears from the past and creates a life of joy in the present.

2nd edition, questions for discussion added
Copyright © 2015 by Martha Sarkissian

All rights reserved.
ISBN 0692238425
ISBN 13: 9780692238424

Blog: marthasheartbeats.com

Cover design by Martha Faghani

I want to thank Linda Joy Myers for developmental editing; Jeanne Fobes for line by line editing; my son Geoffrey Sarkissian for creating the website "Living on a Fault," formatting the document, and handling the publishing.

Special thanks to Betty Edwards, Dawn Thurston, and Linda Joy Myers, writing teachers who passed on some of the secrets of writing to me, and Linda Missouri for her caring.

The National Association for Mental Illness has enabled me to understand mental illness as a brain disease and helped me to be accepting of my afflicted son and others.

Contents

Part I: Family Portraits...1

   Chapter 1:   Good Night, Sweet Prince 3

   Chapter 2:   I Was Waiting for You 10

   Chapter 3:   "Love demands...." 20

   Chapter 4:   Our Lady Los Angeles 29

   Chapter 5:   The Broken Marriage Tie 38

   Chapter 6:   The Marriage Quilt 46

   Chapter 7:   Waffle Irony 57

   Chapter 8:   Artificial Brains Develop: 1951 64

   Chapter 9:   Tracing the Guilt 74

   Chapter 10: Taking Care of Daddy............................. 86

   Chapter 11: "Facing the Lion, Being the Lion." *Mark Nepo*.............. 96

   Chapter 12: Pinching Pain 106

Part II: Jennifer's Story **113**

   Chapter 13: A Scream Hung Over the Canyon 115

   Chapter 14: God in the Rose Trellis 124

   Chapter 15: A Heavenly Secret 132

   Chapter 16: The Little Armenian Man 141

   Chapter 17: Heroic Journeys 151

Part III: Mosaic Mind **171**

   Chapter 18: The Angels of Pierce County Jail 173

   Chapter 19: Ring the Bell.......................................184

   Chapter 20: The Escape...195

   Chapter 21: A New Marriage Contract.................... 203

   Chapter 22: "Ma'am, Is He Mental?".......................214

Chapter 23: Aloha to Paradise 223

Chapter 24: The Quest... 231

Chapter 25: Tough Love 239

Chapter 26: The Lost Tooth.. 244

Chapter 27: Return 250

Chapter 28: Going Home 258

Epilogue: A Journey to Joy 263

Questions for Discussion 269

The Guest House

Every morning a new arrival.
A joy, a depression, a meanness,
Some momentary awareness comes
As an unexpected visitor.
Welcome and entertain them all!

Jelaluddin Rumi, Persian poet, 1207-1273

PART I

Family Portraits

CHAPTER 1

Good Night, Sweet Prince

Hal, jaunty in a green polo shirt with an alligator logo, and I, disheveled and wet-eyed, leaned forward in the office chairs to hear Dr. Vandermolen's verdict. "Your platelets are normal. However, your heart is shriveled as a walnut. There is nothing more we can do for you." The words crushed our spirits like a bombardment of hail stoneshailstones.

I wrung my hands helplessly. Hal drew in enough oxygen to speak. His labored breathing filled the office. In the exploratory voice of an inventor, he suggested, "There must be some tests, some experimental procedures you can try."

"You need to understand our monoclonal experiment was successful and cured your lymphoma, but there is nothing we can do for your congestive heart-failure heart that hasn't been done. All the medical world can do now is drain fluids and supply oxygen. We can treat you in a hospital or at home. The choice is yours, Hal."

I waited while Hal's engineering mind weighed options. At last he spoke. "Every damn second of my life is important to me. If there's nothing more the medical world can do for me, I'll stay home to enjoy my remaining time. That is, if it's okay with Martha." He turned his head toward me. His eyes asked, "Do you want me at home?"

Leaning across our mahogany chairs, I managed to hug him. "Of course I want you at home. I never want to be separated from you. Every second of your life is important to me, too!"

His smell, a mix of Après Noir shaving lotion, Irish Spring soap, and sun-warmed earth meant love and security to me. He unwrapped my clutching

3

arms and gripped my cold hand in his warm one. At heart a shy man, public demonstrations of our love embarrassed him. He stared intently, trying to read my face. "Are you sure this is the right choice for you?"

Inside my brain, nasty gnomes hurled insults at me. *You don't have the guts to be his nurse. Bet you don't even remember how to administer CPR. You'll mix up medications! You'll fall asleep.* I ignored their sinister whisperings. "Yes, it is. As long as we are together, everything is all right. I'll be happy and take as good care of you as I can."

The doctor shook his finger at me. "You'd better! He's my favorite patient."

Decision made, our little yellow house and garden on Lido Isle became a small world encased in a balloon of light protecting us from the terrors of the hospital and death. My sweet Prince Hal, our two fluffy Siamese cats, Finch and Snowball, and I dwelt together in peace. Each simple task in our daily routine became a special ritual.

First, there was the Preparing of Coffee. The scent of French African beans and far off places filled our house as I ground our coffee. Next, came the Preparing of Grapefruit. With a sharp saw-toothed knife, I loosened each segment of the golden fruit so a weakened hand could dig it out. I held my breath waiting to see if it would be sweet and juicy to his satisfaction, or a miserable, dried-out third- rate bargain to place before him.

Then I announced, "Hal, breakfast is ready," and stood by as he began the daily Arising From Bed. The right leg emerged first. Then the left. I tucked my hands behind my back and stood at attention, trying to conceal the impatience simmering in me as he slowly, methodically gathered his energy. He stood! I almost cheered. Snowball and Finch, displaced from their master's bed, ran yowling to the kitchen. I grabbed the oxygen tank, which I privately called an ugly green dwarf, and walked behind Hal. We moved slowly to the dining table and to the joy of being alive for *one more day.*

Visitors and agency representatives and workers came and went, but we kept our eyes on each other. We noticed each down curving or up curving of the lips, each tear that appeared in the corner of an eye, each tremor of hand. We smiled.

"Coffee tastes good this morning," Hal said.

A little tremor of joy zigzagged through my body.

Then came the ceremonial Reading of the Newspaper. Solemnly, we traded sections. When his heart pumped enough oxygenated blood through his body, he'd comment on the politics of the day. And when, "shriveled as a nut," it failed to pump enough for speech, an excellent editorial to read aloud always lay nearby. He listened intently. We gazed in each other's eyes, knowing each other's exact viewpoints and sharing our indignation or hope or anger. In each small ritual of the day, we found happiness. Each meal and every cup of coffee and every piece of toast created a Holy Communion.

One day, while watching football on TV, Hal leaned over from his recliner to my grandfather's wooden-backed chair to take my hand. "Martha, I know you need lots and lots of attention. But I want you to understand. At this point in my life, I am very involved in processing what is happening to my body. I do not have the energy for other things. I know you are here and that my existence now depends on you. But I cannot pay attention to you." He closed his eyes. His breath did not permit any more of the electric conversations that had kept our love alive and flourishing for fifty-three years. Now I had to trust his wordless love.

In bed, our hands and arms and legs became too cumbersome and heavy to meet, but our toes liked to touch. Sometimes we shared the colors we saw with our eyes closed. "Blue, purple, and orange," he whispered.

Then I tried to persuade the colors to appear behind my eyelids. "Blue and purple coming, no orange."

"Think... orange."

And so we fell asleep.

February 13, 2001, our son Joseph, who suffered mental illness, moved in with us while his board and care home was fumigated. The same day, our granddaughter Julie, on a short vacation from her studies a Princeton University, surprised us by coming to lunch with Valentine presents. Hal presided at the head of the table, smiling and nodding to Joseph and Julie, but unable to speak. Still, he managed to kiss his granddaughter good-bye before she left.

That night, he sat in his recliner chair, fumbling with his medical stockings. I jumped to my feet. "I'll help you, Honey."

He frowned and whispered, "No you won't."

Joseph, shy and awkward, edged forward. "I'll do it, Dad." He kneeled at his father's feet and slowly, carefully drew off the socks.

Hal took a deep breath of oxygen. "Thank you, my son," he whispered.

That night Hal and I wriggled our toes together, then fell asleep, too weary to share our magic colors.

At midnight, Hal sat up on the edge of the bed and said, "Martha, call 911."

While I was talking to 911, Hal toppled off the bed and died when his head hit the floor.

A large pool of blood surrounded him. I fell to my knees on the floor and pressed my lips to his to administer CPR as the telephone operator directed. I heard the shrill scream of a siren, the rattle of the door as the paramedics broke in and the howl of our Siamese cats, the patter of Snowball's feet on the roof as he fled the scene. I felt the arms and hands of a young paramedic. Gently, he lifted me from my husband's body. "He is already gone," he said.

"I know." Only our spirits could touch now, not our toes. His spirit blew on me like a breeze from the sea. Like a feather. Like a dream. Before they carried him away.

Our half-Siamese cat Snowball lived on our roof for years and never returned to me, believing in his feline mind, that I had stolen his beloved master.

The next morning, I told Joseph, "Your father died last night."

"I didn't know. I heard the siren but he always comes back from emergency."

I hugged Joseph. A terrible fear filled me. When his father was hospitalized, Joseph often had to be, too. "Joseph, I know it's hard to believe he's gone, he's survived so many times. I'm sorry, dear."

Joseph pulled away and sorrowfully intoned, "I never loved Dad enough."

I pulled him back into my arms. "Joseph, none of us loved him enough, including me. But please remember, dear, you took off his socks for him the night he died."

"Yes, I did. I really wanted to do something for Dad." We wept together.

During the following two weeks, my loving family surrounded and comforted me like a warm quilt. Geoff, our oldest son, and Sarah, his wife drove from Modjeska Canyon to be with me on my first terrible night alone. Julie, our oldest daughter, her husband Ron and son Danny, flew in the next day from Seattle. Our youngest daughter Laura came, too, with her husband Bob and my new grandson, Jesse. Dear Hal had risked his life to fly to Oakland to see the precious two-pound preemie Jesse in his isolette. In the remaining six months of Hal's life, he often raised a hopeful thumb and whispered, "Atta boy, Jesse." As we planned the memorial service at Fairview Community Church, the presence of this chubby tow-headed baby reminded us there is life even in the midst of death.

The board and care home where Joseph lived found a sport coat and tie for him to wear, and a caseworker to accompany him to Hal's memorial service. Even in my grief, I felt proud as Joseph shook hands with old friends and thanked them for coming. But old regrets that Hal had soothed away arose as I watched my son. I recalled the words of a psychiatrist who, thirty years ago, told me that too much mother's love causes schizophrenia. Had I loved too much? Or not enough?

My family fended off my anxious guilty feelings for the next few days, but after they returned to their homes, and Finch died and his brother Snowball took up official residence on the roof, I felt completely alone. Hal's death expanded the fault line where I lived, fearful of each new emotional quake.

I studied myself in the mirror. Not a beloved wife, but a wrinkled widow of seventy-six stared back. I never felt old until Hal died. We saw each other and ourselves with our hearts, not our eyes. Wrinkles, trembling hands, growing waistlines—he never noticed them. Of course, the chandelier in our bedroom had a dimmer and he didn't wear his glasses in bed.

I wandered, lost, on the small island where we had lived for forty years. Like me, Lido Island had changed. The bay turned purple-gray. Trash littered the beach. A dead crow fell at my feet. Without Hal, I was a nothing. I thought of India, where I could have died on a pyre with the husband I had failed to keep alive. Why did I say he should stay at home? He would have lived longer in a hospital. Once, I had failed my baby, Jennifer. I failed Joseph daily. I was useless. The song my brother Ben once used to taunt me played over and over again in my mind, "You're nothing but a nothing, a nothing, a nothing, you're nothing but a nothing, and you're not a thing at all."

7

One Sunday evening when Geoff and Sarah came to dinner, Joseph begged, "Let's have family dinner just like this every week. Keep everything the same as it was."

"We'll try," Sarah, my daughter-in-law, answered. Her words trembled in the air. But Joseph looked satisfied and nodded.

At one such dinner, I told Sarah, "If I died, my children would inherit our Lido Isle house. Wouldn't that be a big help with the grandchildren's college expenses?"

Her voice, cool and calm as a mountain brook, washed me ashore. "Martha, my father died and now Hal, so don't you die, too. We couldn't stand the stress."

An honest reply from an honest woman. I wanted to reassure her, but as I drifted daily into a different consciousness where death loomed large and appealing. It became more and more difficult to project a positive attitude. I managed to say, "I'll try to live by the motto on the Coat of Arms of my grandparents, "We finish the race."

Sarah nodded. "That sounds good, Martha. Geoff and I are betting you'll live to be a hundred."

My eyes smarted. I dashed toward the kitchen, calling over my shoulder, "I've made a blackberry cobbler for dessert."

I knew how desperately Joseph wanted everything to remain the same, and how impossible that was. But I hoped the smell of the cobbler would evoke the happier past and let him experience it as real for at least a moment. I looked at mortality in a new and up-close way. If Hal could die, I knew I could, too.

The children and I worked to preserve family continuity. Our seating positions at the table had changed. Our oldest son, Geoff, held down the head of the table, his father's place. Sarah sat next to Joseph on the east side of the table so she could encourage conversation with him. Alone on the west side, I sat near the kitchen, where I could run for the odd spoon or two or escape for a few tears.

That night, after the family left, as I scraped and racked dishes in a silent kitchen, Death attempted to lure me. "What is the best way for you to die?" he asked. "Drowning in the ocean?"

"Not possible. My body would just keep on swimming and I'd be rescued."

"Pills? The left-over medication you hoarded from Hal could handle the job."

"That sounds like a good way to go, but it would reek of suicide. Not a good legacy for my children."

"Seal up your garage, turn on your car, and let the carbon monoxide end your sorrow."

"Choose life! Choose life!" I repeated, to drive away Death.

CHAPTER 2

I Was Waiting for You

The next day, a cream-colored envelope arrived in the mail. I didn't want new shoes or energy saving windows so I dangled the envelope over a trash can. Some force restrained my hand. Who would send me an ad in such expensive stationery? I worked open the envelope flap and pulled out an engraved invitation. "You are invited to attend a Grief Group for relatives of patients who died in Hoag Hospital. Time: Mondays 7 pm. Place: Hoag Conference Room." The words *choose life* still lay on my lips.

The following Monday night, my stomach felt queasy when I seated myself with other grievers around a mournful table. I breathed rapidly as I listened to the tragic stories of fellow sufferers.

A bride, Leticia, damp with grief, wept for her groom; a mother, Claire-Joy, elegant in pin-striped slacks, mourned the death of her fourteen year old son from cancer; a father, with cheeks swollen and red with rage, recounted how a drunk driver took the lives of his wife and children. My body contracted with the pain of each speaker. When the leader called on me, my every day ordinary grief felt out of place but I tried to cooperate. "My name is Martha. My hobby is writing. My story is insignificant compared to all of yours. I was married to Hal for 53 years. His doctor gave him only five more years to live, but he lived fifteen years after that and..."

A crystal bell voice interrupted, "How lucky you are, Martha. Imagine, happily married fifty-three years!" A gentle breeze of sighs agreeing with the speaker swept through the room. Their loved ones had been too soon ripped away. My tragedy didn't belong here. Once more, I didn't fit into a group. I had never fit in anywhere except with my husband Hal. The unity within the Grief Group magnified my feelings of loneliness.

When the discussion died down, I pushed back my chair and tiptoed from the room. Footsteps followed me across the dark parking lot. I speeded up. Someone grabbed my arm, startling me. Then, in the dim light of an eyelash moon, I saw that it was Claire-Joy, the mother in fashionable slacks who'd lost her fourteen-year-old son. Her fingers dug into my arm. "You need to belong to a group, Martha. Maybe not this one, but a group. You're too isolated."

"Of course I'm alone. My husband died. Most of our friends were really his."

She loosened her grip. "Don't worry about your husband's friends. What do you like to do?"

I growled, "I don't like to do anything."

"You just said you liked to write. Find a writing class. Meet some writers. Don't let yourself be isolated."

I thought, how can she reach out to me when her son has died? Perhaps, whenever she senses death on the prowl, she fights to save a life.

"It's not any use to write now," I whispered.

"Your words are precious. They can help you find yourself. Don't try to atone for your husband's death. His death is a separate issue. Find a writing class," she urged.

I dared not ignore the strong force, whether my own intuition or a spiritual power, that drew Claire-Joy's wisdom to me. I couldn't find a college that would admit me in the middle of a semester, so this force dragged me by my hair to a Life History writing class in a senior citizen center. I crossed the threshold into a lavender room full of oldsters. Although I prided myself on being an egalitarian, I felt a distaste for seniors—and I was one of them. No wonder I wanted to die. I opened my new notebook and scribbled away on the story of my mother's life.

After six months writing in this class, the teacher, Betty, invited me to McDonald's for coffee. Her tawny hair stood on end like a lion's mane. In an imperial tone, she told me, "You're a gifted writer, but you need to write about yourself, not your mother. This is a Memoir class. I want to hear *your* voice." The steam from her coffee clouded her glasses.

How could I explain my feelings to these women? Squirming in the hard-backed wooden booth and tearing at my cuticles with my fingernails didn't help. "Can't do it, Betty." I stared into my mug at the shimmering black. "Too much bad stuff in my life, too many times. Stuff went wrong because of me. Best thing I could do would be to die and let my family inherit my property."

Betty stood up abruptly. "I've got a sweet tooth. I'm going to get us some cookies—three for a dollar." She strode toward the counter while I rubbed my eyes with the backs of my hands.

She handed me a cookie in a parchment envelope. All at once, I was swigging coffee, chewing cookies and feeling better. Betty finished her cookie and wiped the crumbs from her mouth. She didn't hesitate, but looked straight into my eyes as she said, "I'm a recovering alcoholic. I've seen a counselor for ten years. I think you should see a counselor yourself. Soon."

"So you think I'm crazy! Well, I'm not. It's good common sense to die as soon as possible to help your children. There are too many widows cluttering up the world, anyway." I slammed down my coffee mug. A puddle of coffee splashed on the cream-colored plastic table.

She smiled and quieted the stormy waters. "Whether you do or don't go into therapy isn't my business. I'd like us to be writing buddies." Her lips cracked into a small smile. "Martha, let's make a deal. We'll each write three books before we die. Are you in?"

"Sure, Betty. Three books." I was humoring her. I didn't want to awaken her lion. But Betty started an emotional shift in my mind. Maybe I could write three books. Maybe I could make a good life for myself without Hal. Perhaps death was not the only alternative to losing a spouse and a happy marriage.

To ride an ocean wave, you must wade out until you reach the point where a wave curves upward. Then insert yourself at the top of the curve and you are joined to the ocean and you trust the wave as it races to shore. That inner wave of feeling that brought me to Claire-Joy and Betty carried me next to Linda. We met in a Senior Citizens' Water Aerobics Class. Words bubbled up as we jogged back and forth in the water. Linda's gray eyes held such understanding that I felt no one had ever listened to me before.

I told her, "Our second son, Joseph, has schizophrenia."

"Let's get out of this water and talk," Linda responded. We perched dripping and shivering on a wall by the pool, too involved in our conversation to even shower and dress. "Do you want to tell me about him?" she asked.

"I mentioned him because in a NAMI meeting for parents, I learned how much damage stigma and guilt causes parents of children with brain diseases. So my husband and I promised to be open and honest about this illness, hoping to diminish the stigma."

"What is NAMI? I've never heard of it and I'm a psychotherapist."

"NAMI stands for National Association for Mental Illness. We couldn't have lived through the difficult years of his breakdown without their help. Why don't you look it up on the internet?"

"I will. And I want to tell you something I don't usually mention. I have a mentally ill brother. That's why I became a therapist. I don't know where my brother is now." Our eyes filled with tears and our shared sorrow forged a strong connection between us. The following week, Linda enrolled in a NAMI family training group and the following October we marched together in the NAMI walk.

As the months passed, I decided to ask for her help with Joseph. The County Health system controlled his hallucinations but did not provide a therapist to assist him in improving his quality of life.

One night, strolling along the seashore waiting for grunion to roll in on a wave, I asked Linda, "Would you consider being my son's therapist? He could still use his county psychiatrist and case worker, but you could help him develop his creative talents and social abilities." Silently we scuffed through the sand and watched the waves hit the shore with little explosions of phosphorescence.

Finally, she answered. "Martha, I couldn't be his therapist and your personal friend at the same time, and I'd much rather continue developing our friendship than be his therapist. I couldn't be your therapist either. It's too difficult to be objective when a friend's involved. Would you be willing to give up our friendship if I worked with Joseph?"

I swallowed the lump in my throat. "I treasure our friendship, but Joseph's welfare comes first."

"It just wouldn't work." The angle of her chin and the tone of her voice made it definite. I stomped through the sand to the car. What's the use of counting on her! She doesn't care what happens to Joseph and me. We'll survive all right, but I so wanted a better quality of life for us. She's let me down.

A few weeks later, I stopped to rest on a bench on Lido Island. My collie dog, Kristen, lay down in the shade of a monkey-puzzle tree where herons nested. Sandpipers on the shore walked in pairs, he and she, poking their beaks in the sand to find clams. They reminded me I had no mate and walked the shore alone.

Sunshine spilled through a crack in the sea wall that held back the bay. I stretched out my hands to receive the rays of warmth, but I received much more. My emotions shifted. My heart cracked open and sunshine spilled inside. It wasn't Joseph who needed therapy! I was the one who needed to free myself from the guilt of Hal's death and tap into my own creativity.

A wild impatience overcame me. I had to find a counselor before I forgot the sunshine spilling in, changed my mind and gave up hope. I tugged on my dog's leash. "Come on, Kristen, let's go home." I wouldn't put my good brains in the hands of just anybody, but Linda could recommend a counselor. Whomever she selected would be right. There was an alternative to dying. The minute I stepped in the house, I phoned. "Linda, can you recommend a good counselor for me? I want an older woman, someone who has an office nearby—you know I don't drive the freeways. And someone I can afford."

"Martha, you're asking for the moon!"

The sting of this rejection awoke me to what I considered reality. Therapists don't waste time on the elderly. We're just not that important. "Okay, so forget it." I'm going to forget it. Bury it six feet deep in my mind. Shouldn't spend money like that on myself anyway.

A few months of sulking passed. Then Linda phoned. "I've found a psychotherapist for you to consider. Her office is three miles from your home. She's a woman in her seventies. I think you two would be compatible. Her name is Miriam Townsend."

Terror and joy vied in my heart. I'd have to relive the tragedies of my life and I'd have to change, a process Freud hadn't believed possible for the elderly. Then I reviewed the many books I'd read about the modern discovery of the plasticity of the brain. Maybe this old dog could learn new tricks.

I shook so hard calling for my first appointment that I couldn't keep the receiver to my ear. Miriam's voice wove in and out. I barely heard her office address but I remembered her saying, "…the Success with Living office is near a video store on Seventeenth Street." I shopped almost daily on Seventeenth. It'd be a cinch to find without an address.

With an appointment secured, buyer's remorse overcame me. Why tell my grief to a complete stranger named Miriam Townsend? Why spend my children's inheritance on my neurosis? My spirit sang its sad refrain, "My husband died. I am all alone. I want to die, too." I dressed carefully for my first appointment hoping to convince my future counselor that I was somebody who really didn't need to talk to her anyway. My hands shook on the steering wheel as I drove up and down Seventeenth, unable to find Success with Living. Miriam had mentioned a video store and finally I entered Blockbuster, though I didn't see any offices nearby.

"Can you tell me where to find Success with Living?" I asked a young clerk lounged behind a cash register. He wore a black T-shirt with a glittering skeleton and his hair stood on end in a Mohawk.

"DVD or video?" he asked indifferently.

"It's an office. A psychological clinic. It's here—near this store somewhere. Are there offices upstairs?"

His eye twitched. "I'm sorry, Madam, but there's no psychological services here."

How embarrassing. As I left hurriedly, I looked back over my shoulder. The clerk winked at me and saluted. Was he making fun of me?

I broke into a trot down Seventeenth, leaving my car behind. This Miriam person might interpret my tardiness as psychological resistance instead of an ordinary old age muddle. As I trotted, my hopes of making a good impression on her drooped like my hair. My shirt came untucked. A button somewhere in my clothing popped. Sweat beaded my face and wet my scalp. Limp locks of hair flopped. I struggled to hold back tears of frustration. "Cry baby, cry. Poke your finger in your eye, and cry, baby, cry," sang my brother Ben's voice from childhood.

Then I spotted a Colonel Sander's Chicken cafe in the cement wilderness. I could buy a cup of coffee while phoning to cancel my appointment. I'd never admit to this Miriam person that I couldn't find her office only three miles from home. Good plan.

I stepped inside and drew a breath of fried chicken and grease. "Cup of black coffee, please." My stomach felt queasy but I trusted in God and caffeine.

A Latina clerk with a thick braid down her back gazed at me with kind eyes. "I'm sorry. Colonel Sanders doesn't sell coffee."

I was thinking, I don't have Miriam's address. I can't sit here and rest unless I order. If I eat, I'll throw up. I'd better go home. I stepped outside. Bright sunlight on the parking lot hit me like a laser beam. I closed my eyes. When I opened them, across the lot I saw a grey building with office doors beside the Atlantic Video store and a woman standing on a balcony.

"There you are," she called in a pleasant voice. "I was waiting for you."

I'd visited the wrong video store on the right block. This wasn't a dream where offices disappeared and boys with Mohawks grinned and winked. This wasn't insanity. It was just one more example of my carelessness and lack of attention to detail. I trotted across the parking lot and up the stairs, fearful of what might lie ahead.

Miriam opened the door to a quiet little room and waved me to a couch. "Would you like a glass of water?"

"Yes, thank you. It's hot today, isn't it?" I felt sweat dripping off my forehead.

"Yes, really it is." I gulped a small glass of cool water, wondering why I was there. The silence in the room felt unbearable. She was in charge; she should speak first. I didn't know what to say. The seconds stretched into minutes. Finally, Miriam opened her arms, held her palms upward and asked, "How may I serve you?"

I pulled a folded square of paper from my purse. "I wrote a note about my goals."

Miriam leaned forward a bit and smiled encouragingly. "I'd love to hear it."

I took a deep breath and dove in. "I want to be contented in my own skin. I'd like to be able to just sit in my patio and feel I'm ok. Those are the goals I wrote down for therapy. But counseling is for the young who have a future, not for the old like me. Maybe I should go home before I make a fool of myself. I'm pushing eighty, too old to change."

"Martha, I think your goals are self-acceptance and peace of mind. It may take a while to reach them, but I believe you could in time. Today we recognize the plasticity of the brain and that we have many opportunities in our older years. Some find these years the best of their lives."

"So you're okay with my age?"

"Martha, I'm coming right behind you. I'm seventy-one."

"I've had a lot of tragedies and my husband Hal—he always helped me through. Now I'm a widow."

"I am a widow, too, and I can understand your feelings of loss." She made an ugly face. "Why don't those guys come back and look after us. We need them."

"Exactly." I felt a tight knotted place in my body slowly untying. "I sure need my husband Hal now. I can't concentrate. His death pops into my mind whatever I'm doing. Then I long to be an old fashioned East Indian woman placed on her husband's funeral pyre so I could die with him." As my fantasy poured into the container of this little room, I had a sense of ease. My hands lay quiet on my lap for the first time that day.

"What a lovely romantic thought," she exclaimed. "I believe this deep yearning to die with the beloved derives from an unconscious belief that if one dies with her partner they will be together for eternity. This is a common belief of people who have been happily married as long as you and Hal were."

Miriam understood the Indian pyre as a romantic comforting idea—not a death wish. What a relief! I leaned forward on the edge of the couch. "Then… then you don't think I'm crazy?"

She responded emphatically, "No, I most certainly don't. It's a common belief, whether or not one is religious, that the spirits of the two lovers will be united when they both die."

"I keep thinking about Hal and talking about him. He died five years ago and even my oldest daughter thinks it's time for me to stop talking about him, but I can't. Memories of Hal's death play in my mind like a movie."

"How fortunate you are to have those memories." She clasped her hands. "My husband died a year and a half ago. I hope I can always keep my memories of him as you have kept Hal's."

"Not all my memories are good. We had a choice to hospitalize Hal or keep him at home with me. I wanted him with me. But maybe he'd have lived longer in the hospital."

She sighed. "Oh, Martha dear, I can say almost unconditionally that you extended his life by keeping him with you. There is much scientific evidence that elders do better at home than in an institution. And just think how important it was for a family man like Hal to see his children and his wife. You must treasure the memories of his last days."

"I don't like the memories. They burst into my life whatever I'm doing. Then I begin to cry and the words 'my husband is dead' beat in my mind like a dirge."

Miriam's voice sounded far away and clear. "Few women have the opportunity to share their husbands' deaths. Why not try setting aside a time in your day for thinking about it? Find a comfortable place. Take three or four deep breaths and remember his death with gratitude for the years you shared with this remarkable man. And then, try to remember how you met him, your wedding, the happy days, and the love you two shared. "

"I'll try, but I don't think it'll do any good."

Returning home after this first counseling session, I leaned back in Hal's blue recliner chair. It was pretty gruesome to deliberately remember his death. Wasn't counseling supposed to pull me away from awful memories, not draw me back? I closed my eyes and the ecstatic state we lived in during our last month's together sprang to life. I appreciated his courage in the face of death and his efforts to lead a normal life and take care of me. Then, instead of remembering a dead face with blue lips, I came face to face with my brilliant, ruddy-cheeked engineer. I remembered how we met and I was with him again. I dashed to my computer to write it down.

A week later, with a sheaf of papers in my hands, I arrived, breathless, at Miriam's office and plopped on her couch, eager to begin our session. "After you told me to remember Hal, I found him in my memories and I wrote a story about how we met."

"That's lovely. I'd like to hear you read it to me in your own voice."

"I don't know if I should." My inner-mother's voice counseled, "Don't push yourself forward."

But Miriam offered me freedom. "This is your time, Martha. You are to do and say whatever you want."

"It seems funny to pay someone to listen to my story."

"Perhaps I can add some insights. But please, decide for yourself. You should do what makes you happy."

My objections melted in the warmth of her smile. "Well, actually, it'd be fun to read it to you. The title is from Camus. It's called, "Love Demands…" And I read aloud.

CHAPTER 3

"Love demands…."

utumn leaves crackled under my heavy shoes. My gray flannel suit, with a masculine flair, weighed heavily on me. In 1944 the Dean of the English Department himself had warned me, "Our English Department has agreed no woman can receive an A, so sign all your papers M. Hunter, and not Martha. Be careful." Three years later, women's rights had definitely not come to Berkeley. I did not mind hiding my womanly curves and pulling my hair in a bun, because I intended to be a spinster and a writer.

When I was eighteen, Captain Johnny Rosenthal had broken my heart and I had resolved no man would do that again. When I was nineteen, I wore my suit, studied for exams all night and avoided the hops, the swing dances of the era. A diet of coffee, Coca Cola, Ritz crackers and cigarettes enabled me to survive. My roomies called me *brain* and offered me discarded boyfriends, but I needed to prove to Chancellor Kerr the intelligence and grit of us women students. In a speech, he had proclaimed, "The University of California is too rigorous for the female temperament." I'd show him.

But now I was twenty and I needed to let down my hair, pull off my heavy shoes, and give my heart away. For the first time, I noticed a sign I passed by every Thursday, "Sock Hop Thursday 4-6. All students welcome." Easing my arm-aching pile of books on a stone planter, I rested near the open door of the Masonic Temple. Glen Miller's "String of Pearls," poured through the open door. I pulled the bobby pins out of my bun and let my hair fly. Maybe, just maybe, I could still cut a rug or two.

Leaving my shoes in a heap by the door, I stepped over the threshold of the temple. A vortex of jitterbugging dancers swept me across the floor. I could jitterbug with the best of them, but who'd choose me for a partner? Bitten down finger nails and a spotted bachelor suit weren't alluring.

Then, just as the Red Sea parted for Moses, a wave of dancers drew back to permit a short man to pass through the waters. He looked dashing in a lieutenant's uniform. I liked his Roman nose and sensuous lips. He stopped in front of me and asked, "May I have this dance? My name is Harold but they call me Hal."

I stepped toward him. "They call me Marty." I waited for him to shake hands or bow as the boys had done in Elisa Ryan's dance class five years earlier. He didn't do either.

"I'm fresh off the boat from Germany where I was stationed. All the way home I dreamed of dancing with an American girl."

"So now you can," I murmured.

He held out his arms. I walked into them. The music switched. Doris Day crooned "Gonna Take a Sentimental Journey" while Hal held me firmly, cheek to cheek. The metal buttons of his jacket cut into my breasts. The wall I had built to keep love away crumbled.

"Are you a Mason?" he asked when we paused for breath.

"No. Absolutely not." I shook my head and my hair frizzed around my face, dandelion style.

Hal grinned. "Neither am I. But I thought the Masonic Hop would be a good place to meet a girl. Why'd you come?"

"I can't exactly say. Something drew me from inside." I tilted my head to look into his face. "I guess I was fated to meet you." My coquettish voice surprised me, for I considered myself superior to the flirtatious co-eds. Yet flirting now flowed as naturally as breathing. I liked this man.

The music stopped. A skinny guy changed the records. Hal mused out loud, "Hmm. I don't believe in fate. I believe in figuring out things scientifically." He squeezed my hand, a touch that sent sparks all the way up my arm.

"So if you don't believe in fate or something like it, what do you believe in?" I asked.

"There is one thing I really love," Hal told me.

"Yes." I frantically batted my lashes. What did he love? Perhaps he believed in love-at-first-sight or loved my dancing or my perfume? It wouldn't be my grey flannel suit. "What is it you love, Hal?" I whispered. My voice had turned strangely husky, making conversation difficult.

"Electronics." He pronounced the word reverently. "I'm an electronics engineer."

"Oh. Electronics." No one in the 40s knew what 'electronics' meant. Did it have something to do with the atomic reactor on campus? Or a strange kind of ruler, a slide stick that those engineers carried in their pockets? I soldiered on with what I hoped was a seductive tone of voice. "What does electronics mean? How is it different from electricity?"

The skinny kid in charge of the music tapped us on our shoulders. "Time to go somewhere else, kiddos. The dance is over." He laughed and switched off the lights. We put on our shoes and lingered awkwardly outside the Masonic Temple. We squeezed hands and whispered good night. I thought I'd lost him forever, but finally, he asked. "Say, Marty, would you give me your phone number?"

"Oh, sure, Walnut 6800."

"Thanks! See you later." He didn't kiss me. He didn't write down my phone number. I'd probably be haunting Masonic hops the rest of the year to find him. I continued my lonely trudge up the hillside.

The next day I hovered near the dorm phone, expecting a call and knowing that never would anyone as wonderful as he phone such a crazy kid as me. When he phoned at five, I jogged down the hill to the Golden Krisp Coffee Kup where he was waiting. He grinned like a kid and I giggled. We were too excited to talk. He took my hand and led me to a booth where we sat and breathed warm waffle air.

I recalled my mother's dating advice, "Never order anything expensive at a restaurant. Your date may not have much money. Always get him to talk about his professional interests."

"I'll just have a plain waffle," I said.

"Oh, what the heck! Don't you want sausage and eggs and stuff?"

"Well, maybe that would be good." More wide smiling and wide silence ensued. Mom's advice! "Oh Hal, last night, at the hop, you were just going to tell me what electronics meant. Then the dance ended. I was so disappointed."

"Electronics is the science of the flow of electrons and how we can use them to create machines." He soared into lengthy and abstruse explanations and, though I still didn't exactly understand what electronics meant, I knew I was in touch with a superior mind. That was a turn-on for me.

He stopped talking when he poured his cream into his coffee. "What's wrong? Is there a bug in your coffee?" I asked.

"I'm trying to see why cream disperses the way it does. Have you ever wondered about it?"

"Never!" I growled.

After waffle grazing, we wended our way hand in hand up Telegraph Hill. When we left the city streets behind, he told me, "I've got some discharge money and I'm going to buy a car. I'll need one if we—" He choked up.

I shivered deliciously. He must be planning a love scene in an auto? "Maybe the car is fated for us, like our meeting."

"Hey, I don't believe in fate. But I'm going to buy a car and then, I'll drive you home. It's a tough march for you to the dorm every morning and night."

"Sounds great." I sighed. How could be think about transportation when I was thinking about sex?

Or, perhaps he was thinking about sex too, for he asked next, "What do you suppose draws people like us together?"

I squeezed his hand a little. "Love, I suppose."

"Chemistry" he announced. "A certain chemical emitted by another person attracts you. Electricity is part of attraction, too. Did you know your brain gives off an electric charge?"

"I've heard that, but..."

He interrupted, "Certain frequencies a person emits draw another person to him like a magnet."

I thought about it. "Hmm. I don't believe that."

He laid his hand on my shoulder, "Don't you feel an electric charge?"

Something deep inside me came alive, but I didn't think it was electricity. "Maybe," I whispered.

"Love," he explained, "is chemical and electrical. You just felt an electric jolt from me."

I sighed. "I believe in love at first sight."

He tossed his head back laughing, "That's silly, but I like you. Well, some psychologists ran an experiment on rats and proved rats choose a mate by proximity. Then they found statistically, humans choose a mate within a mile's radius."

"I hope I'm in the mile limit!"

"I think so. I live in International House." He ran his fingers through my hair and selected one strand. "Your hair's very soft and fine but you should grow it even longer."

"My hair's dandelion fluff. This is as long as it gets."

He grew serious. "I'm an Armenian. All our women brush their hair a lot to make it grow. I'll buy you a brush." He kissed the top of my head, hair and all.

"Thanks." I kissed his hand. No use mentioning that even if I beat my hair to death with this brush, my hair would never be thick, luxurious, Armenian. It would always remain the skinniest part of me.

"So how long have you believed in this 'love at first sight' bunk?" he asked.

"Since this afternoon at four when you asked me to dance."

He kissed me on the cheek. "I don't believe in love."

"I know," I said. "But I'll make you eat those words someday."

We wandered up the hillside, talking and kissing. We turned to watch the sunset light up San Francisco Bay. "Look, Hal, the sky caught fire." He wrapped one arm around my waist. The air smelled of wild lilacs. "Hal, do you know this quote by Camus? 'Love demands the impossible ... the sky on fire, inexhaustible springtime ...'"

"Martha, its autumn, not spring. This is what love demands." He pressed his first penetrating kiss on my lips.

By October, Hal owned a black two-door Chevy and invited me to the Cal Halloween Hop. On Halloween afternoon, I bought a sailor suit at the Salvation Army. On the way home, I recited Shakespeare's Sonnet 29. "When in disgrace with fortune and men's eyes, I all alone beweep my outcast state...." That was how I used to feel. Now that I knew Hal, I could end triumphantly with the poet, "Haply I think on thee, and then ... I scorn to change my state with kings."

When I reached the dorm, I found my roomies asleep. Soki lay draped on our small blond Maplewood desk with her head on a text titled *Economics and World Policy*. Jody looked like a paper doll left on the upper bunk by accident. Gloria lay on the floor, resembling a pile of last night's clothes. I yelled, "Wake up! You've got to help me get my costume ready for the hop."

Gloria, my glamour roomie, proclaimed from her prone position, "Sure thing! We'll spiff you up. I'll do your hair so you don't look like such a..."

Soki lifted her head from the desk "...such a freckle-faced kid."

"Uh, I suppose I need to look more...uh...." I stammered.

My intellectual roomy, Jody, jumped from her bunk and supplied the missing word, "Sexy! If your boyfriend's a genius, it's harder to find the right button to press for action, if you know what I mean."

The sexual innuendo sent us into spasms of laughter. When the spasms tapered off, I managed to croak, "I could press the button all right, if I could ever get his mind off electronics and onto me."

Jody grew serious. "Let's analyze the situation. You see Hal every day but what do you actually do together?"

"Usually, we have really deep life discussions over a cup of coffee. Like, is it better to study electronics or literature? Or how does cream disperse in hot coffee? "The roomies groaned.

Soki warned, "You'll never get him to marry you that way. Don't be such a grind." She swung her slim hips. "Use a little hoo bali bali! Flirt!"

"I know, I know already. I flirted the first night we met. But somehow I can't, now. Growing up with two brothers taught me to act like a pal. That's why I need your help," I admitted. Then added, "I think I'm in love."

"I knew it! Your toes are curled!" Gloria shrieked.

Soki added, "You're always brushing your teeth, too. Sweet breath! O my God!"

Jody dove under the one single bed and pulled out a bottle of Coca Cola and a box of Ritz crackers. We grabbed our toothbrush glasses. "Congratulations! Let's have a toast."

Soki led us, "To Marty. May her Hal—" she broke off, "what's his last name?"

"Sarkissian. He's kind of an American-Armenian prince."

Gloria hooted, "You're in bad shape, girl."

Soki waved the Coca Cola bottle. "Let me finish the toast. To Marty and Hal Sarkissian. May Venus give Mart the power to bewitch?" We all clicked our toothbrush glasses.

Gloria beckoned to me. "To start the enchantment, I'll dabble *My Sin* perfume on the nine important parts of your body. Come here and we'll begin."

I'd always longed for woman- knowledge. My mother, too inhibited and too busy, never mentioned my being female. But now I had my chance to learn. A warm excitement spread through my body from head to toes. "My gosh, tell me, what are the nine places?"

Soki, dabbing my ear lobes with a seductive scent, was too preoccupied to answer. Jody snatched a small drugstore bottle from her desk and began dabbing my hair.

"That smells triple ugh!" I wrinkled my nose.

"Pure peroxide." Jody showed me the bottle. "Wait until your Hal sees the streak."

"But I'm blondish already, aren't I?"

"Dishwater blonde."

"Let me at her hair." Gloria shoved the others roomies aside. She pulled my hair onto the top of my head and fastened it there with a rubber band. She backcombed the streaked locks into a wavy halo. "I'm naming this hairdo the Bikini, after the atom bomb. Kiddo, you'll hit him like a bomb!"

Soki smoothed gardenia lotion on my arms. "Let him smell your armpits or at least your arms. He'll go wild."

Too embarrassed and too excited to bear all this attention, I pulled away. "Is this necessary? I mean, Hal and I are real friends."

"That's okay when you're too old to do it. But he's fresh off the boat and looking for S-E-X. Be the siren luring him to the rocks." Jody stroked an imaginary lute and caroled a loud "Ooooooo." The girls doubled over with laughter. "Now, get your costume on, little one," she added.

"Here it is." I pulled a pair of sailor britches and a middy top off my bunk. "Twenty-five cents each at the Salvation Army."

"Good grief!" Jody snorted, "Why'd you decide to dress like a sailor?"

"I wanted to be a sailor when I was little. This is my chance."

This drew a chorus of boos from my roomies. When they quieted down, Gloria tried to explain my role. "This is your chance to be a wife, not a sailor. Not a pal. Focus on that."

"Dress as a mermaid, a gypsy girl or a princess," Soki suggested.

"Someday my prince will come…." Gloria sang in a tolerable soprano.

I defied them all. "My prince has come. He'll like me in a sailor suit. I don't have to dress up like a gypsy. You'll see."

Jody waved her hookah cigarette lighter for attention. "Listen up, girls. All is not lost. We'll slit the pant leg."

Pandemonium ensued. We lit cigarettes from the hookah lighter and searched under the bunks for lost scissors. Soki slashed the left leg of the trousers. They shortened the middy blouse so when I moved, it exposed exactly one-point four inches of flesh, a fact verified with a ruler. "That gap is our secret weapon. Halfway through the night, he'll find it." Gloria sighed. I tingled with excitement. The hall telephone rang. A girl stuck her head in our room to yell, "Hal's waiting in the reception room."

My roomies, like bridesmaids, helped me walk down the long corridor. A glow enveloped me and my fairy godmother friends. But Jody's advice pierced through my pink fog, "Remember, Marty, don't talk. No discussions. Wet your lips. Then look in his eyes, and say 'Mmmmm, oh' and 'Hal.'"

"I'll try," I promised. They shoved me through the door to the living room where Hal waited. He'd pinned rainbow-colored ribbons on his First Lieutenant's uniform for a festive look. He handed me a gardenia corsage and pinned it on my middy shirt. His hand brushed my breast. My heart leaped. I inhaled the sweet scent of gardenia. I wet my lips. I looked at him and whispered, "Mmmmm….Oh, Hal."

"You've got a blonde stripe in your hair. I never noticed it before." His smile dimpled his cheeks.

I wet my lips, looked into his eyes, and moaned, "Mmmmm….Oh, Hal."

After the dance, we returned to the dorm living room. As we sat on the love seat, at last Hal discovered the slit in my pants and the gap at my midriff.

"It's midnight" The housemother in a flannel bathrobe, jaw outstretched, confronted us. She tugged at Hal's arms and tried to pull him off the couch. Somehow, Hal and I had become glued together. "It's curfew time. Miss Martha, off to your room. And you..." she glared at Hal, "You leave my girl alone. Hal jumped up and answered like the good Armenian boy he was, "Yes, Ma'am."

"No conniving seducer can get his hands on one of my girls. My girls are college women leading the way to a New World." She had the courage of a Carrie Nation smashing bar bottles, and an imposing 6-foot stature to go with it.

"Yes, Ma'am," he agreed and blushed. "Thank you, Ma'am." He backed away. "I'll see you tomorrow, Marty."

"Yes," I said. "You know my phone number."

"Of course. Uh, Marty, I liked your costume. It, er, uh, gave a, er, uh, new aspect to our relationship."

I nodded my head yes and groaned, "Mmmmm....Oh, Hal."

And that is how, thanks to three wonderful roomies, *My Sin* perfume, a slash in trousers, a gap in an outfit, and proper use of 'Mmmmm,' I, the last of the four roomies to get a man, caught her guy.

CHAPTER 4

Our Lady Los Angeles

*M*iriam clapped her hands. "I love it! Oh, Martha, bring me more stories of you and Hal. I'm starting to love him almost as much as you do."

A beautiful process had begun. At home, seated in the recliner, I permitted Hal's and my life together to come alive again. Then I hurried to the computer, poured out my words, and read them to Miriam later.

Soon, however, a sense of uneasiness entered the process. Ethical people just don't read their stories to therapists, do they? "Miriam, am I stealing your therapy time? Shouldn't you be telling me what to do or using behavior modification or something?"

She spoke softly but firmly. "This isn't a doctor's or dentist's office. This is your time and you can do whatever you want."

I scarcely understood such a statement. "That's quite an, er, uh, grand permission. But shouldn't I be trying to get over Hal's death?"

"I think you are. But you're here also to discover yourself. Don't be surprised if you turn out to be a lovely lady in your stories. Writing your memoir can be very therapeutic."

I felt so embarrassed on hearing 'lovely lady' that I wanted to run out of the room that moment. However, I proceeded to use my therapy time the way I wanted and I read my story, "Our Lady Los Angeles" to Miriam in our next session.

Our Lady, Los Angeles

Hal and I fell in love on a hillside in Berkeley. The sky was on fire and spring seemed eternal. Evenings, we stared into each other's eyes over nickel cups of coffee in the White Cabin Cafe. We debated everything, from the use of atom bombs to how cream disperses in coffee. We never tired of listening to each other. In October, when the USC-Berkeley game was scheduled in LA, Hal and I planned to spend the night with my mother. "Be sure and buy a ticket to the game for my little brother Johnny," I told him. He thought I was joking. In his Armenian eyes, I was a wild woman. When the freckle-faced eleven year-old materialized, Hal bought the first and only scalper's ticket of his life and Johnny went everywhere with us that week-end. Mom and Aunt Atty, involved in a marathon bridge game, were scarcely aware of our comings and goings.

Our first night back in Berkeley, Hal and I had the Date Room to ourselves. We settled in the love seat. He handed me a package. I gasped at the sight of a hairbrush. "I want you to grow your hair long, like Armenian women do. If you brush it—it'll grow."

I felt uneasy, as if he'd gifted me a stick of dynamite. But he lovingly brushed my hair with it.

"You see, I want you to be my woman, now. I used to think you were too— er—well…you smoked, peroxided your hair—could you be a wife and mother? When I saw the great way you treated your brother, I knew then, you'd be a perfect mother." He stopped brushing and looked directly in my eyes. "Will you be my wife, Martha?"

I yanked the brush from his hand and huddled in the corner of the couch. Long hair, a good mother, a good wife sounded like a big order for me. "I don't know, Hal." I wanted to marry and yet I saw my dream, a writer in a garret in Paris, growing smaller and smaller.

"Hey, don't cry. It's okay. I'll ask you again tomorrow. I understand women like to be asked three times."

The third time he proposed, I accepted. I brought him home with me to my family in Los Angeles.

❖

I was born in Los Angeles, a city once known as *El Pueblo de Nuestra Senora la Reina de Los Angeles* or the "Town of Our Lady the Queen of Angels". Our gracious lady, Los Angeles, had blue skies so thick you could cut them with a knife. After a rain shower, each vacant lot became an ocean of wild lupine where slippery poppies, like orange fish, darted in and out of the blue. Mondays and Fridays, my friend Polly and I walked home from John Burroughs Junior High together. Whenever the wild flowers covered the empty lot on Wilshire, we dove into the fragrant sea, hid ourselves there and whispered secrets.

Roosevelt declared war on December 8, 1941, the day after Japan bombed Hawaii. The lives of all Americans and the life of our gracious lady Los Angeles changed forever. A childhood friend of mine, Gilbert Kinney, died at Pearl Harbor. Soon the boys, the football players, the dancing-school boys, the mathematicians, the poets, the pigeon raisers—all boys, went to war. My brother Ben, too. I missed them all.

My brother John, just seven, turned himself into a bomber and spent his days spinning in circles, arms outspread until he dropped a load of bombs, "Kaboom!" Mom planted a Victory Garden and became Block Warden. She made certain that all the curtains on our block were closed tight at night. Rumor had it that even a glimmer of light might guide Japanese torpedoes our way. The Japanese students in L.A. High School disappeared; I didn't know where or why. I missed my Japanese girlfriend, Carolyn.

When I was fifteen, I was a pacifist, but now that we were at war, I wanted to be in the war too. Aunt Nancy Anne Welbourne, once a southern belle so beautiful that a Pasha in Turkey proposed to her, laid aside her beautiful gown, donned the dull blue uniform and white stockings of the Red Cross, became an officer in the corps and served loyally for years.

"Martha Albene, you should be a nurse's aide in the county hospital. Almost all of their nurses have gone to war."

Aunt Nancy Anne had always called me by first and middle names, acknowledging me as a person. She never called me Little Sister. So, I followed her advice.

After a two-week training session, the county hospital assigned me to the top floor where one registered nurse, one orderly, and one aide (me) cared for the entire floor. On my four-hour shift, I checked the temperature, pulse and respiration of twenty-one patients and brought them breakfast, lunch, and bedpans. Our floor had an automatic bedpan cleaner, a kind of dishwasher attached to a toilet, an amazing gadget. I still feel gratitude for that dear device.

All my patients seemed a bit creepy but, as far as I knew, sick people were weird. Daily, I comforted Heliotrope, a woman so skinny her ribs stuck out like corset stays and her eyes had sunk into her skull from crying. "They won't bring me my baby. Tell them to bring me my baby."

I always promised, "I will! I will!" But whenever I mentioned Heliotrope to the head nurse, she turned and walked away from me. Perhaps Heliotrope had some terrible contagious disease her baby might catch. I hoped not.

Daily, strange emergencies arose in my ward. I placed a lunch tray on the bed table next to a thin worried looking man alone in his room. I headed for the door when he shouted, "Hey, Nurse, there's worms in this salad."

I returned to his bedside and poked through his salad with a plastic fork. "I don't see any worms, Sir."

He suddenly sat bolt upright and threw the dish of salad in my face. Lettuce and tomatoes bombarded my clean pinafore. I ran from the room, crying. I ran into the nurses' kitchenette to hide and cry. I found a stool and sat down and sobbed. Ed, the skinny black orderly, suddenly appeared.

"What's you fussin' about, girl?" he asked in a kindly way.

"The patient in 1208 threw his salad in my face. He said there were worms in it and there weren't."

He wet a towel and cleaned my face and pinafore. "Girl, don't you understand, these patients are crazy. They don't know what they're doin'. You're in the psychiatric ward."

My tears disappeared. My eyes popped open wide. "I-I didn't know that."

"Tut, tut. It's a pity they don't tell you nothin'. You a good nurse, Girl."

I smiled at him. "Thanks, Ed. I'm ready to go back to work."

One morning, the fearful sound of a siren filled the hospital corridor. Then a loud speaker blared out. "Report to floor 11. Move all floor 11 patients to the basement." The speaker repeated the words over and over. They didn't make sense. Should I go to 11? How could I leave my floor?

Ed zipped down the corridor like a meteor. "Come on, girl, we need you. We gotta move all the floor 11 patients."

I ran behind him shouting, "Is this war? Has a sub landed?"

He stopped a moment and looked at me gently. "No. We gotta move the respiratory patients where they can breathe. The air's turned bad. Come on, run."

For the rest of my shift and an extra two hours we pushed frightened patients, some in oxygen masks, some gasping like fish out of water, into an elevator and down to the basement.

I didn't understand the new catastrophe until I rode home on the top level of the Wilshire Boulevard bus. The vacant lots where Polly and I once whispered secrets in a sea of lupine no longer existed. A dreamy girl, with boys much on my mind, I'd never before noticed the metal skeletons of skyscrapers that arose like giant erector sets on any empty piece of land on Wilshire Boulevard. I heard the grinding of cement mixers, squawking of cranes and the machine gun rattle of drills. And my gaze no longer met the enchanting blue sky Polly and I once knew and loved. The sky of Los Angeles had become sludge gray and did not have enough oxygen for respiratory patients.

GI Joes and sailors jammed the streets of our Gracious Lady now. Once a week my Mom, my Aunt Atty and my brother John ate a $1.00 dinner out, a reward for our hard work. As I sipped my soup, I wondered if the GIs I heard laughing on the streets would soon be dying.

When I turned 18, I moved from our Gracious Lady to the University of California at Berkeley. There I lived in a dorm, believing I was a modern bachelorette and off men forever, but forever lasted just three and a half years. The war ended, and I became clever enough at twenty, with the help of my college roomies, to entrap a former First Lieutenant when he stepped off the boat---my Hal. He told me that he wanted to live and work in Los Angeles, so I transferred to UCLA for my last eight units of study and brought Hal home.

We arrived in post-war LA in his little black Chevy one Sunday afternoon in February 1947. After living in a college dorm or a boarding house for almost four years, my heart leapt with the anticipation of being home once more in 901 S. Longwood, LA. We unloaded suitcases and boxes of books on the Spanish-tiled veranda.

"Holy cow!" Hal breathed reverently as he looked from the brook that flowed below the balcony up to the fourth floor tower room. "How can I take you away from all this?"

"I'm lucky I caught you fresh off the boat. You're a freaking genius and I like the way your hair curls." I tweaked a lock of his hair.

"Hey, I'm just the grocer's son."

"And I'm the lawyer's daughter. A big house can be pretty lonely and I'd rather live with you anywhere than in a freaky mansion."

He pressed his lips on mine. I felt the pounding of his heart through the heavy fabric of his uniform. Mom or Aunt Atty might pop out of the house any minute. Our passion mustn't explode in front of them. I pulled away. When our lips parted, he croaked in a breathless voice, "Man, am I ever the lucky one!" When he got his breath back, he asked, "Why didn't you ever tell me you had such a great house?"

"It wasn't that important to me," I lied.

The Hunter house lived in my unconscious as the magic castle Camelot, with my father King Arthur, and my brother Ben, a prince in his tower room and my little brother John, the page who strung string cobwebs above the reception hall and waded in the brook to capture frogs.

Hal paced around the balcony staring down at the brook in our garden. "Where's the water come from?"

"Artesian wells. The house is built on an arch over the street. Ranchers tried to steal the water in the days when L.A. was a Mexican pueblo. The walls are three feet thick adobe and have gun slits to fight off cattle men."

"Wow! Baby, you surprise me! This house is an engineering feat. But hey! Let's go in and meet your Mom."

"Yeah, let's go." I threw open the heavy carved front door. We plopped our suitcases on the sunset red Spanish tiles. "Exuberant to be, once more, part of the Hunter family, I yelled "Hey, Mom! We're home."

My diminutive mother emerged from the library and trotted to our side, followed by Aunt Atty, slower and paler than I remembered. Mom hugged me. "Oh, I'm so glad you're home, Sister. We've missed you. I'll try to get an appointment for you at the beauty salon tomorrow. "

Aunt Atty had caught up with the action and put forth a weak defense of me. "I think Sister has been studying so hard for finals she forgot to curl her hair."

Mom stopped hugging and stepped back to appraise me. "Yes, she did, and she's been biting her fingernails again."

I took my mom's words as mother noise, to be ignored like frog's croaks and proceeded proudly to pronounce the words I had practiced: "Mom, I want you to meet my fiancé, Hal."

This man adored me, bitten fingernails, flyaway hair, ink smudges, and all, and his brilliant mind would eventually bring new glory to the Hunters.

Mom cocked her head to one side like a yellow bird as she seriously studied Hal. She shook his hand. "Hal, I'm glad to meet you. I'll warn you of one thing about Martha. At first, she likes a boy and then, in no time at all, it's off with their heads. I'm sorry I can't talk longer, but I'm in the middle of a bridge game."

Hal kept his smile in place. "We can talk after your game, Mrs. Hunter."

Mom trotted toward the library, stopped, and looked back to Hal. "Do you play bridge?"

"Yes, Ma'am. We played it a lot in the army."

She sighed. "Well, that's one good thing," and closed the library door behind her.

My brother John, twelve, hurtled down the stairs, "Hey, I didn't know you were home, Sis, I didn't smell cigarette smoke." His wisecrack, butch haircut, and braces made him seem like a guy, not the precocious lad I remembered.

"Meet your new brother, Hal," I told him.

They shook hands. "Say John, can you tell me about this house? I didn't know your sister lived in such a grand place."

"Let's go in the living room and I'll show you the fireplace," John offered. Despite the bridge game, Mom had built a welcoming fire for us.

"Nice fire," Hal commented.

Johnny grinned. "I call Mom a pyromaniac. She's always lighting fires. This fireplace is big enough to roast a goat."

Hal grinned. "If you wanted to roast goat."

Johnny went on, "And the living room ceiling's twenty feet high. I think the writing on the beams is Mayan Indian." We all stared at the thick beams marked with red symbols that held up the roof.

"Hey, let's sit down. We've been driving since dawn."

I plopped on the fuzzy blue couch, and all at once, John and Hal and I were throwing pillows at each other and punching each other and laughing. My love for Hal surged through my body as I realized he knew how to relate to a little guy who had no father. He'd be a good parent too, when the time came. And in a bubble bath of warm good feelings, I forgot my mother's curt greeting.

The following morning, I got up early to talk to Mom before she went to the job she'd had since Dad died five years ago. I found her reading the LA Times and sipping coffee in our breakfast room. Her face looked alert and wary as she studied the front page. I studied the map of the world my mother had hung on the wall during the Second World War. She marked an X on each battleground mentioned in the L.A. Times. X in the Ruhr Valley, X on the Lido Road in Japanese-conquered Burma, X on Sicily, X on the sands of Dover. Surely, she'd appreciate Hal's service record as a First Lieutenant.

She looked up from her paper. "You aren't really going to marry an Armenian, are you?"

"Mom, he's as American as apple pie. Born in Fresno. Graduated from Berkeley University. He was First Lieutenant in the war. How could he be more American?"

She frowned. "Where were his parents born?"

"Armenia. But his Dad got citizenship when he enlisted in the army in the First World War." I slid into a chair near her, poured myself coffee and lit a cigarette. I'd been away from home so long, I'd forgotten my mother's feisty ways.

"Sister, if you insist on marrying that Armenian, I'll offer you a bargain. Elope, and I'll give you the money I'd spend on the wedding. I have to paint and redecorate if you get married here. "

Enraged, I stood up to confront her. "Don't call him *that Armenian*. His name is Hal. You said you bought this house so you could see me walk down the staircase in my wedding dress, and that's exactly what I'm going to do."

Mom stood up too. "You're going to need the money if you marry him," she said.

"You're just ashamed of his being Armenian in front of your friends. And you don't need to redecorate the house. You just want to show off, but it's *my* wedding."

Mom brushed some invisible crumbs off her skirt. "I'm sorry, but I have to leave now or I'll be late for work. I'm darn lucky to have a job in the Geodetic Survey and I don't want to lose it." She gave me a quick hug. "We'll talk later."

"Sure Mom, later, but I'm getting married here in the Longwood house, June 29th."

CHAPTER 5

The Broken Marriage Tie

*M*y therapist gave me a sympathetic look. "How painful it must have been for you to return home from college and have your mother give her priority to her bridge game, instead of to you and your fiancé."

"Not so painful. I was used to being ignored. All my life, bridge got more attention than me. I felt relieved John and Hal and I could enjoy each other without her breathing down my neck. Deep inside me, I always knew it would be hard for her to accept an Armenian in-law."

"What a strong person you are, Martha. I'm glad you stood up to your mom. She couldn't bribe you to elope. You set your goal, and she backed down."

"I guess she did. But I feel more like a quaking leaf than an oak."

"Your experience working as a nurse's aide helped you develop character and a certain type of toughness. You learned a lot about mental illness, too."

"Maybe so." I mentally inspected her words. Were they possibly true? Did I have a strong character? Did I understand mental illness? The barrage of praise confused me. "I was fighting for my life. That old house never knew peace and calm. It had mysteries and whispering voices and bursts of anger. I needed to escape it, yet Hal and I stayed there five months before our wedding to save money for the deposit on an apartment."

"And how did that work out?"

"I have a story about it."

❧

A frenzy of activities followed my defiant words. Mom planned the wedding while working eight hours or more a day. She brought home samples of hand-blocked material for drapes she discovered on her lunch hour. I registered for an independent study course at UCLA to complete requirements for my U. C. Berkeley degree in English. Hal hunted work. "If I don't get a job, the wedding's off," he told me. With a crew of painters already climbing on scaffolds around the house, I couldn't confide Hal's fears to my mom.

Mother and I shared an excitable French temperament. Her anxiety swelled at the thought of "giving Martha" to an Armenian, while my anxiety splattered everywhere: could I learn how to use birth control? Would sex be as good as petting? Would Hal get a job? Would I pass Independent Study at UCLA? I'd been scared to death that when Hal left Berkeley to find a job in L.A., some L.A. gal, cuter and slimmer than I, would grab him. So I convinced the Dean of English to transfer me to UCLA for my last eight units of study, although not sure if I could manage independent study and the fights with my mother at the same time.

We argued constantly about wedding details. She stung me with sharp comments like poisoned needles. "Why in the world do you want to marry an electrician? They're a dime a dozen."

"How can you be so ignorant, Mom? Hal's not an electrician, he's an *electronics engineer,* a person who studies electrons and invents ways to work with them."

Mom tuned me out and continued her thought. "I suppose if you marry him he could rewire this old mansion someday."

After dinner clean-up didn't provide much relief. Aunt Atty plunged her manicured purple-veined hands into scalding wash water, slimy with the new Palmolive soap. "It'll take both of you to keep up with my dishwashing," she claimed. Her sharpshooter's eye targeted missing items. "Martha, run see if someone left a crystal glass in the living room." Mom, Aunt Atty and I didn't whistle while we worked. We bickered.

Our personal Emily Post, Aunt Atty, warned, "Don't put the china plates away without putting a pad between them." Her mind was as organized as the cubbyholes in her antique desk. Mom and I winged it. I yelled above the boom and screech of slammed cupboards and drawers as I searched for pads. "Moth-er! He's a scientist, not a repair man. You can't expect him to rewire."

Hal, waiting in the pantry for me, couldn't stand the squabbling any longer. He stepped in the kitchen. "Actually, I don't know how to rewire the house. I'm a scientist."

Unabashed, Mom continued, "I've always told you, Martha, it's as easy to fall in love with a rich man as a poor one. At least you could marry someone useful, a plumber or a butcher."

Hal chuckled. "Bingo! My Dad was a grocer, and I can do a little butchering between building circuits. The good news is--starting next Monday, I have a job teaching electronics at a private technical school. So—we're ready to roll!" we're all set to go."

I snapped my tea towel and shouted with joy. "The wedding's on!" We ran out of the kitchen to cuddle and pet.

The quarrels continued. At Bullock's Wilshire, I found a straight A-line dress, simple, clean, except for seed pearls about the neckline.

"I refuse to pay a hundred dollars for a wedding dress. You can wear your grandmother Hunter's gown, honor the Hunters and save a hundred."

"I won't wear it. The gussets make me look fat. You're spending money on the house; you can pay for the dress." The family clothing money had always gone on Ben's back. He was dashing—a star. But I won this battle.

We fought over the number of guests. "I've sold a bond for the wedding. I can pay Maggie to cater for one hundred and fifty guests, so you and I can ask a hundred, and we'll let Hal have fifty."

"We'll divide it even. Hal has tons of friends and relatives, and I don't have many."

Winning battles gave me a new sense of my own self. I gloated. My wedding clothes would include something new, my gown, something blue, my garter, and the something old, Grandmother Hunter's antique veil made by the nuns in Paris. For a freckle-faced California beach girl, a veil wasn't hip. I lost that battle.

By day, I wrote my master's thesis on T.S. Eliot's *Murder in the Cathedral* and by night, bickered with Mother. When she went to bed, I listened to Hal present his lesson for the radio school and then we petted. We were committed to wait until our wedding for the *real thing*.

The night before my wedding, Mom, Aunt Atty, Johnny and I assembled at the grand dinner table. Unlit candles and a formal flower arrangement, created by Aunt Atty, waited for appreciation at tomorrow's reception. We three ladies visited our local beauty parlor and had similar piles of orderly curls topping our heads. Hal and Johnny "had their ears lowered" at a barbershop. Beau Peep, Mom's cocker spaniel, had a bath at the vet's and a pink bow in her hair.

Mom, at her end of the table, passed a cut glass bowl of potato salad down the table with the comment, "We're eating from the deli tonight to keep the kitchen clean for Maggie tomorrow."

"Make sandwiches, if you wish," Aunt Atty added from the other end of the table as she passed a silver platter of corned beef decorated with dill pickles and a wooden tray of rye bread. Hal and I sat together, discreetly holding hands under the table. Johnny, in a collared polo shirt and jeans, sat facing us. As we opened the family linen napkins, Hal whispered in my ear, "Wow. You could make a tent out of one of these." Dishes circulated and cutlery clinked on china.

Johnny said, "Please pass the mustard."

"Martha!" Mother exclaimed.

I straightened up and let go of Hal's hand.

"Do you actually want to go through with this marriage? Just look at Hal. He's too short and he's Armenian. You call off this wedding now!"

A hush, the quiet before an earthquake, fell upon our dinner table. How could she say this in front of Hal at our wedding eve dinner? Aunt Atty's blue eyes, like porcelain cups, filled with tears. Johnny crossed his eyes and wriggled his ears in embarrassment. I bit my lips to keep from crying.

I felt ashamed of Mom. *I'm a lily-livered coward and I want to run and hide. I gotta have guts. I won the fight for a home wedding, for a satin gown and for Hal's guest allotment and now she wants to call it off. Damn!* My voice came out in a loud frog's croak. "Hal Sarkissian will never kill himself with alcohol like your husband— my Daddy. You married for money, but I have the sense to choose a fine man and we're getting married tomorrow." I gulped water from an amber stemmed glass.

"Don't insult your father. He had a sickness but he always provided for us and I loved him."

Words I couldn't push through my lips filled my mind. *If you loved him, why didn't you try to stop him the night he died? I wasn't strong enough. I let him die. If Ben doesn't show up soon, there won't be anyone to give me away. I'll have to walk the aisle alone. I want my Daddy by my side.*

Hal broke the silence, calling my mother by her first name. "Albene, don't you know great things come in little packages, like diamonds and you and me."

She smiled. He'd hit a homerun. He squeezed my hand under the table. "Ignore her," he whispered.

Then she frowned. Her penciled eyebrows flew up in amazement. Hal had outwitted her. That felt as bad as losing a grand slam in bridge, doubled. She unfurled her crumpled napkin with a snap as if to say, *I've only started to fight.*

owH I paced around the table. "Mom, you know darn well we're getting married tomorrow. You planned the whole wedding, including me coming down the circular staircase instead of in the garden. It's the wedding your in-laws, the Hunters, didn't let you have. I love Hal; he loves me. We're getting married tomorrow."

She threatened me with a fierce glare. "You'll be divorced in a year, and I've had to pay for new living room drapes, painting the house, the caterer, your dress, a photographer..."

I stopped pacing and lifted my head proudly. "I didn't ask for any of that, except the dress. They are for your glory, not mine. I'm a Berkeley girl, a free thinker."

"Does that mean you're a Communist?"

I lost it. "Oh, Mom, stop picking on me."

My reflection in the mirror above the sideboard showed me, wild-eyed and furious, and Hal with an improbable smile on his lips. He felt he'd won. Why did I let Mom agitate me like a washing machine? Daddy, over six feet and more than two hundred pounds, used to churn our feelings like butter. Since his death, Mom carried on his tradition in her own Albene style.

Pacing again, I rounded the table by Aunt Atty. She held up her hand like a policeman and spoke to Mom. "See how Martha is all worked up. I've told you over and over, Albene, that the bride and groom must never see each other the night before the wedding. You didn't listen to me. Now look at Sister! Hal must go to his bedroom at once."

I almost stuck out my tongue at Aunt Atty. "You can't boss Hal around and send him to his room as if he was a kid. He was a First Lieutenant! And don't call me 'Sister' any more, either. I'm Mrs. Sarkissian to you all, starting tomorrow."

Determined not to cry in front of them, I rushed from the dining room to the laundry room, my childhood refuge. It smelled of Fels-Naptha soap and starch. I wished the washing machine with its hand-run wringer and the always-open ironing board would cleanse and press my emotions. I was kicking a laundry basket when Hal followed me in.

"Calm down, Martha," he ordered. "I've lived all my life with people who don't relate to Armenians very well. I just tune them out. Your mother doesn't believe what she's saying, anyway. She's given me room and board for the last four months and even done my laundry. She's just repeating some phonograph record in her mind."

Like a flower turning to the sun, I tipped my face up to him. "Oh, Hal, I don't want my family to hurt you. I like the Armenian culture. And being short makes it easier for us to kiss."

He whispered, "Here's a butterfly kiss for you." He fluttered his thick black lashes over my face. "That's how my Mom used to kiss me goodnight."

I shivered. "It's delicious."

He ignored my shiver and continued his defense of the Hunters. "I prefer American families where everyone's independent and they aren't always talking about people dying in the Exodus."

I shrugged my shoulders. "So what? I'm fed up with Mom and her prejudices."

"You need to know, Armenians have prejudices, too. My folks wanted me to be a grocer, like Dad—not an engineer. Cousin Zelda plotted to marry me to an Armenian girl, her daughter. That's just how families are. Thank your Mom for spending her money on your college and wedding and forget the other stuff."

My hidden pain suddenly broke out of its prison. "Mom just doesn't care about me," I sobbed. I felt his arms protecting me.

"Your mom adores you. It isn't actually the Armenian thing that bothers her. She'd find something wrong with any man who came to take her Little Martha away." He patted my back.

My jagged breathing smoothed out. I breathed deeply. "Do you really think so?"

"Mm hmm." He drew me closer.

"Oh Hal, you are a truly noble person. Tell me something nice I can do for you and I'll do it. Ask me for anything."

His face and even his ears turned pink with excitement. "After you do something for me, I'll go to my bedroom. I respect Aunt Atty. She's just trying to make our wedding seem normal."

My breath sliced my chest. Hal longed for some secret embrace and so did I. "Darling, what are you yearning for?"

"I'd like you to press my necktie for the wedding." He opened his hand to reveal a wrinkled navy blue necktie.

"Press a tie? Is *that* all you're yearning for?" I dangled the miserable object from my fingers tips. "No one presses ties. You take them to the cleaners!"

"The cleaners?" He waggled his bushy eyebrows up and down. "Cleaners are expensive, Martha. The ironing board's right here."

oH How cheap. He wouldn't pay the cleaners for one necktie, while my Mom paid for everything else. I exploded, "No one can iron a tie!"

He grabbed his necktie and laid it on the ironing board. "It's easy to do. Cut a piece a cardboard and slide it inside the folds to prevent wrinkles. Then lay a damp cloth over it and iron. My mother always pressed our ties."

"My mother didn't," I snapped. I pictured Mom returning from the cleaners, arms filled with ties on clothes hangers and boxes of starched shirts and bundles of underpants wrapped in paper and tied with twine.

An ugly vision of marriage swam before my eyes. We'd never afford cleaners. I'd be sweating in clouds of steam pressing ties and ironing shirts and manly underpants. Married, I would become a one-woman cleaning shop. Did I even want to be married? At Cal, Berkeley, Hal and I were companions, students with a common culture. Now he wanted *me* to press his tie! Couldn't he pay for cleaning one item?

Hal peered intently in my face and seemed to understand my tie-pressing reluctance. He looked at his watch and grabbed the tie. "If there's a cleaners open anywhere at seven p.m. on a Saturday night in L.A., I'll find it. And to heck with the price!"

"I'll press it!" I snatched the tie. I'd prove I could be a thrifty Armenian wife, like his mother.

"Oh no, you won't." He tugged on his end.

"I'll press it or die, and you can't stop me."

"Think again. I'm stronger than you are." He clamped his large hand over mine and pried my fingers loose.

"You can't control me. I learned to fight from my brother, Ben." I kicked him in the shins. He shook me. My hair-do collapsed, but I hung on to the tie.

"I'm gonna press it," I panted.

"You are not." He took two hands to the tie. "Give it to me." He tugged.

"You think I can't press a tie? I can do anything!" I took two hands to the tie, leaned forward and hurled myself backwards. The necktie ripped in half.

The laundry door opened and Aunt Atty marched in. Hal and I, panting and red-faced, each dropped half a mangled tie on the cement floor.

"I told you, it's bad luck for a bride and groom to see each other the night before the wedding. I hope you've learned your lesson," she scolded. Even with Marcel-waved hair, she looked like a portrait of a stern Victorian woman.

Hal hunched his shoulders and pantomimed great fear. "Sorry. I'll go to my bedroom now, Aunt Atty." He turned and looked at me, "Be a cool kid, Martha," he advised.

My freckle-faced brother Johnny poked his head in and yelled, "Your marriage tie is broken, Hal!"

"Smart aleck!" I yelled back and bolted for my room. I lay across my bed sobbing and kicking my feet. Our pre-wedding dinner drama forced me to think of Hal as an Armenian immigrant's son, instead of a genius engineer. I had come home. I had become my mother's daughter. What happened to the Berkeley students who cared about ideas and loved each other so much?

CHAPTER 6

The Marriage Quilt

*T*he tears I wept that night glued my eyes shut. In the morning, I heard a familiar voice. "Hey Sissy, happy wedding! I flew in last night to give you away." My brother Ben lay cozily in bed alongside me. I tried to pry open my sticky eyelids. I felt confused. "I thought you weren't coming. Chris is sick, isn't he?"

"The poor little guy's quarantined in a hospital ward. I'll fly home right after the wedding. So for gosh sakes, wake up and come watch me shave." We laughed, remembering our childhood ritual. Once, I'd been his main audience, but today thousands listened to him on radio. He'd left his wife, his fans, and his three-year old son, hospitalized with spinal meningitis, to give me away—a wedding gift beyond compare.

I trailed after him into the spacious yellow tiled bathroom. The monster-sized bathtub stood on golden lion paws, reminding me of our glorious bubble bath battles when we bombarded each other with handfuls of foam and snapped wet towels on each other's behinds.

As he lathered his face, I realized Ben, my playmate, my confidant, came next in my heart to Hal. "Oh, Benjie, Hal and I had a fight last night and now I'm afraid he doesn't want to marry me."

Ben scraped at his face with a razor. "When I flew in last night, Hal was still up. We had a great talk. He's crazy about you, Sis. I loaned him an extra tie. The wedding's on." Ben twisted his head and flashed his famous tender smile. "How do I look?"

For old time's sake, I commented, "You missed a spot on your chin."

He grinned at himself in the mirror and took an extra swipe with the razor. "You guys are just nervous about sex. Come on, tell big brother about it." He patted down his face with *Bay Rum* after-shave.

I whispered, "Hal and I took a sex course at Berkeley. We went to lectures by Dr. Van der Veldt on human sexuality. We wanted to be cool kids."

Ben's delighted laughter rolled around the bathroom. "That's a new one, studying sex in a college course."

"It's not funny to me. Let me show you something." He followed me into the bedroom where I yanked a diaphragm from under my pillow. "Please, tell me how to use this danged thing! I got it from a gynecologist and I can't figure it out."

"For God's sake, throw that contraption away, Sissy. Hal and I are spending the morning together. I'll talk to him."

"You're sure the marriage is still on?"

"Of course. Don't pay any attention to Mom and Aunt Atty. You and I and Hal live in a larger world than they. You've picked the right man for you."

I drew a deep breath of relief just before we heard a rap on the door. Ben opened it. There stood Mom, one foot in and one foot out of my room. She handed him a tray with grapefruit, coffee, and two cigarettes, one for me and one for Ben. "I'm in a hurry, can't stay to talk. The ladies from my Las Jardinières garden club are downstairs decorating." She examined me with x-ray eyes. "Stay in your room today and rest. Don't mess up your hair again, Sister. Remember, you are the bride." Off she trotted, trailing clouds of anxiety.

Soon Ben echoed her words. "Rest in your room today, Sissy. I'll take your boyfriend out to breakfast and we'll talk." He headed for the stairway.

I tagged after him. "Don't go Ben. Don't leave me alone."

But off he went, taking the Spanish tiled stairs two at a time. I had fought for this wedding and I'd go through with it. But I couldn't press a tie, or really do anything much but analyze literature. What did I really know about Armenians?

"Daddy, do you like Hal?" I whispered to my father, who'd died six years ago. No one answered.

I crept out of my room and peeked through the wrought iron balustrade to the reception hall beneath. The Las Jardinières ladies had buckets of fresh-cut white roses and ivy. They squealed at the sight of my celebrity brother. He threw them kisses and dragged Hal away by the arm. The oaken door slammed behind them.

"Hello, there." I waved to the ladies who were decorating a white wooden arch and the balustrade. "That looks like fun. I'll help wrap the ivy."

"No, no. The bride must rest," they called back.

Aunt Atty shooed me away. "No one should see the bride before the wedding."

I slammed my bedroom door in protest at their medieval attitudes. My opinions about my wedding didn't count. They treated me like a child! Van der Velde's best-selling textbook---*Ideal Marriage: Its Physiology and Technique*---lay on a shelf. I picked it up and started speed-reading, cramming for an exam, when my mother, like a small tugboat, pushed two large Armenian women into my bedroom. "Some new in-laws--just arrived from Fresno for the wedding. They can't speak English very well." She hurried off. So much for no one seeing the bride.

The newcomers hesitated in the doorway, dabbing lace handkerchiefs at the tears caught in the crevasses of their faces. "Come on in," I murmured. They swooped over and crushed me in a damp embrace.

"I'm Aunt Lucy," the smaller weeper said. "You know me."

"Oh, yes. Aunt Lucy. Thank you for coming."

❀

I'd learned about her from Hal when we drank our nickel coffee at the White Cabin Café, Berkeley. Next to electronics, Hal's favorite topic was Aunt Lucy. "I owe my life to her. She nursed me when my mother's milk dried up."

I'd heard of wet nurses in Victorian novels, but never imagined such a situation in Fresno, California, 1923.

"The only trips I ever took were with Aunt Lucy and Uncle Matt. We drove to Yosemite Valley for Sunday breakfasts. I wish you could see Lucy cooking pancakes and homemade Armenian sausage over a wood fire, her cheeks red as apples, happy as a queen bee to feed us. On the side, she served homemade chorig, a coffee cake stuffed with nuts and raisins."

"Oh, Honey, I want to learn to cook Armenian if Aunt Lucy will teach me."

"She will. Uncle Matt and Aunt Lucy are my second parents. In 1927, when Safeway's Market determined to buy up all the Fresno grocery stores, my dad and mom couldn't cut prices like Safeway did, so they became slaves to their customers. My dad, Leon, climbed out of bed any hour of the night to sell feed to ranchers who pounded on his door after closing hours. As the Depression deepened, he carried them on his books. 'We all go hungry if the farmers die,' he warned me.

"My Mom, Abruhi, pressed our ties, darned our socks, sewed patchwork quilts for our beds, while clerking and running a small café in the market. She recycled the day's unsold products into a twenty-five cent dinner of stuffed grape leaves, pilaf, salad, and cheese-filled pastries. Customers from the cannery across the street crowded in to buy her dinners."

"Gosh! Even if I learn to cook, I'll never live up to your mother. Mine drove off daily in the Packard to play golf or bridge and left me with the maid. Hal, you had a hard life." Bittersweet feelings for my boyfriend filled my heart. We ordered more nickel coffee.

He covered my hand with his. "Don't feel sorry for me. I was luckier than my friends because we always had enough to eat. Dad built up the store from a pushcart. I was proud of what he'd done, even though I had to be a clerk when I was eight. I added up customers' bills by hand and got cussed out if I made a mistake. They had me delivering groceries when I was twelve, a service Safeway didn't provide. I stood up in the truck to reach the pedals, but I felt like a man."

"Wasn't that against the law?"

"Sure, but my parents didn't know the law. Uncle Matt did the butchering for the market, and his wife, Aunt Lucy, kept me and my folks and the assembly line at the fruit packing factory laughing at her earthy Old Country stories and her fantastic Armenian swear words."

"Oh, tell me some of her stories," I begged.

"I don't remember Armenian now. Her stories were pretty dirty, anyway. But wherever Lucy went, everyone around her felt better."

"Oh, I can't wait to meet her," I declared, sipping my mug of coffee and dreaming of a jolly apple of a woman.

❧

Now, four months after our Log Cabin chats, it barely seemed possible that this almost mythological person stood in my bedroom on my wedding day, pointing to her large weeping companion. "She no speak English. She cousin Zelda. She want Hal marry daughter, Queenie. I tell her 'Stop crying!' She no stop."

Aunt Lucy smiled, displaying one gold tooth. Her heart's oven, permanently turned on high, warmed and comforted me as she proclaimed her beliefs. "I like Armenians. I like Americans. And I like everybody." She spread her arms wide to include the entire world. Then she plopped on the edge of my four-poster bed and dangled her legs. Her feet didn't reach the floor.

I held out my hand to cousin Zelda. "How do you do, Zelda."

She pulled her handkerchief from her eyes and sniffed. "*Odar.*" Hal had explained *odar* meant non-Armenian or foreigner, and wasn't derogatory. But it was to me, when spoken with a sniff by Zelda.

Aunt Lucy patted a place for me on the bed and cuddled me in her strong arms. A musky scent softened by Johnson's Baby Powder emanated from her body. "We talk," she suggested.

It would be rude to sit while Cousin Zelda, a weeping statue, remained standing. I stammered "But Cousin Zelda…"

Aunt Lucy shrugged her shoulders and dismissed Zelda with her hands. "She stubborn."

"But," I began.

"We talk about you. You marry Hal today." She held up a callused thumb. "Number one. Remember this, when you are a wife. If you want chicken for dinner—don't ask husband to kill chicken." Her voice shifted to a higher childish range. "Oh, Husband, I'm afraid to kill a chicken." Back to a low emphatic voice, "'No! *You* kill a chicken. You—strong woman."

She let go of me, pushed up her puffed sleeves, and flexed her arms. I giggled and squeezed her bulging muscles. "You're sure strong, Aunt Lucy. I'll try to be strong and independent, too."

Nodding happily, she held up two fingers. "Don't think too much. You go to college. Good! But you think too much. Don't put too much pepper in the soup. Don't put too much college in the marriage." Aunt Lucy saw inside my Berkeley student mask and found a frightened girl inside.

I leaned for warmth against her sturdy body. "You're right, Aunt Lucy. Shakespeare said, 'There's nothing good or bad but thinking makes it so.' I'll try not to be so anxious."

"Thinking makes things good or bad," she paraphrased and then held up three fingers. "One more thing. When you want something, maybe a diamond ring, tell your husband no sex till he gives you the ring. That way, you can get what you want." She clapped her hands joyfully and little dimples popped up on her chin and cheeks. "It's simple."

I had read Aristophanes' *Lysistrata,* where the Greek women denied their men sexual favors to end a war. I thought Aunt Lucy clever to have such a strategy in a male-dominated culture. I loved her for talking woman-to-woman with me, but I, Martha Albene Hunter, would never barter sex for a favor, not even from my husband.

Cousin Zelda's sobs grew louder. Lucy jumped from the bed to Zelda's side where she patted her cousin and spoke soothingly in Armenian. I listened intently and repeated words to myself, believing that by listening, I could absorb the language into my soul. I didn't know that Hal no longer knew Armenian.

Other female Armenian relatives crowded into my bedroom and raised the volume on the Armenian language. My bridesmaids arrived and clustered by my four-poster bed, chirping like birds. I couldn't decode their chatter. Mom and Aunt Atty arrived next and pulled my wedding gown over my head. It slithered down my body. "Hold still," Mom instructed as Aunt Atty fastened the Hunter family heirloom veil on my head. A photographer and a minister waded through the wave of women.

"Stand over here by the dresser," the photographer instructed. At that moment, I realized I was leaving my bureau forever. How delicate and quaint my grandmother's silver-backed brush and comb set looked lying on a delicate lace doily. A china dog from my childhood sat next to an enormous photograph of my father and a dainty tin of Johnson's baby powder. I couldn't bear to leave these precious objects, but would there be room for them in Hal's and my apartment, really just a converted one-car garage in Mrs. Mooseberger's back yard? Did I really want to leave the Longwood House?

The minister broke into my ruminations with, "We'll just run through the ceremony here so you remember what to do."

A giant wave of voices, Armenians, bridesmaids, Mother, Aunt, minister, and photographers assaulted me. I cried out, "Everybody, leave me alone." At that moment, the photographer snapped a photo with a sad angry expression on my face and an arm raised in protest. This photo hangs on my wall today.

The room grew quiet. The minister ushered out my new relatives and ushered in my brother. Ben and I were alone. How solemn and handsome he appeared in a pinstriped suit. "Come on, Sissy." he said. "It's time."

"Not yet! It can't be time," I cried. "I'm not ready. I have to pack my books," I glanced around the room, "and my china dog."

He took my arm. "Come on, Sissy, don't you hear the piano music?"

We promenaded around the circular hall above the circular staircase. I was shaking so hard I heard the rattling of my floral bouquet against my satin dress. Ben's arm felt warm and strong. I loved his smell, a combination of bay run and cigarette smoke. Smoke? I glanced at his face to reassure myself. A lit and unnoticed cigarette clung to his lips.

"B-Ben--" I whispered.

"Hush, Sissy, it'll be all right. You're just a little scared about sex. Come on now. Step, step. Listen to the piano and step in time."

"B-B-Ben." My throat closed tight. I fought to spit out the words, "Your cigarette!"

"Oh, my god." He pulled the cigarette from his mouth and snubbed it out on a windowsill. I clutched his arm tighter. We were on our way. My life as a Hunter girl was over. After today, I'd be someone different. I'd be Mrs. Sarkissian An *odar,* foreigner.

Throughout the ceremony, Hal grinned and I trembled. My teeth chattered. Satin rattled. Rose petals fell from my bouquet. I knelt on a velvet cushion beneath the rose and ivy decked arch. My knees hurt. Hal's arm gently, insistently, pulled me to my feet. "Watch your train," he whispered.

I mumbled through the vows that we'd rewritten to leave out the word "obey." At last, I heard the words, "I now pronounce you husband and wife. You may kiss the bride." His deep kiss permeated my body and awakened me to life.

A pianist thumped out the chords of Mendelssohn's Wedding March as we walked down an aisle formed in the living room by my brother John and his Cub Scouts, who held back the crowd with satin ribbons. Hal became increasingly animated. He called out to friends home from the war, "You son of a gun, when did they let you out of Iwo Jima?"

"Hey, I thought you'd settled for life in Italy."

"What's buzzin', Cousin?"

He ignored the satin ribbon boundary when he spotted Fresno's millionaire. "Hey, Wife, Almond King is here." The King, in high black boots and a splendid satin dinner jacket, six foot tall and with a rancher's muscles, grabbed Hal and lifted him into the air with a giant hug. "Cousin!"

That broke up our triumphant wedding march. My spirits suddenly plunged. Hal cared more about this small-town rancher who'd made a million from almonds, than he did about me. Swarthy Armenian men encircled Hal, thumping him on the back or hugging him. "Isn't this great, Martha? My high school pals home from the war."

"Sorry, Sis, I have to leave now and see how Chris is doing." Ben hugged me, waved goodbye and disappeared in the crowd.

Even on my wedding day, I wasn't the center of attention. Ben deserted me. Mom kept rushing from the kitchen to the dining room without a word to me. I yelled at her, "Where's Johnny?"

"Oh, he and the Cub Scouts are running around the garden somewhere."

"Where are my bridesmaids?" She didn't hear me.

Hal's popularity had drawn me to him, but he *should* put his wife ahead of old high school buddies. He ought to be circling the room with me fastened to his arm like a limpet on a rock. I broke into his gang of slim, dark-eyed, exuberant males. "Please, let's walk around the table together," I pleaded.

"Ok, Honey." He tucked my arm under his. We passed Aunt Atty's centerpiece of white roses in her ornate Victorian pitcher and rounded the table, past the champagne punch, which rested in a rented-silver party bowl.

"You have so many cousins, Husband!"

"Not really. Every Armenian calls another Armenian 'cousin.'" He hooked one of Maggie's Scotch scones from the buffet as we circled. Then he stopped. "Hey, wait here a second. I've gotta liven up this party."

He dashed through the reception hall to the living room and tuned our Philips radio, with its magic green eye, to Glen Miller. I wanted to run after him, but my dress would trip me. Maybe wedding dresses had long trains so brides couldn't run.

"Hey, everybody, here's music to dance by," Hal shouted.

Hal and I were a great jitterbugging couple, but before I could stumble down the three steps to the living room, he vanished into the kitchen. I followed in time to hear him tell the cook, "Maggie, your shortbread tastes like my Aunt Lucy's cookies."

Then he continued his explorations in the reception hall where five irises arose regally from a hammered-copper bowl. He asked Aunt Atty, "Why did you use five flowers? Is that symbolic?"

She looked offended. "It's a Japanese arrangement, you know. Our teacher Harumi...."

Why was he talking to Aunt Atty, instead of me! I was sick of trailing him. I'd go see who I could find to talk to. Someone slopped champagne on my train. It picked up crumbs as it swept the Spanish tiled floor. Hal should be protecting me. My high school teacher, Miss Johnson, waved from a distance, probably disappointed that I had married and couldn't be a writer like her, published in *The Atlantic Monthly*.

Hal showed up at the buffet. "Best food I ever tasted!" he called, munching brandy balls and shaking hands with more cousins. How could he stand around discussing the grape harvest in Fresno and eat brandy balls when tonight would be our first real sexual fling? Was he still mad at me, or did I do something else wrong?

After hours of Hal's gregariousness and my sulkiness, Mom stopped running back and forth from kitchen to buffet, and buffet to kitchen. She grabbed my arm with her talons digging into my skin and whispered, "Sister, you and Hal must leave on your honeymoon now. I have a lot of friends who need to go home, but of course they can't leave before the bride and groom."

I felt a blush of shame on my cheeks. The groom didn't want to leave. Maybe the guests thought he didn't want to have sex with me! I pulled Hal out of the crowd and into my father's library. "Hal, mother says it's time for us to leave on the honeymoon. We've got to go."

"What do you mean?" He sounded outraged.

"The guests want to go home, but the bride and groom are supposed to leave first."

"My gosh, Armenian weddings last at least all night, and some two or three days. The fun's only getting started," he protested.

"It's an American custom. No one can leave before the bride and groom. Mother's garden club ladies are exhausted. It's only polite to leave."

"These guys here drove clear from Fresno to see me. We haven't seen each other since I was sent to Germany. And look at the great presents they brought." He pointed to a card table displaying the wedding gifts. "Revere Ware cooking pans and a silver gravy boat. That stuff costs a mint, and you want to stop the party?"

"My mother says..."

"Forget what she says. It's my wedding, too, and I'm not leaving yet. I haven't even spoken to everyone, for gosh sakes." He stalked out of the library and, as usual, I followed him. He intended to chat with every person who gave him a present. That wasn't necessary. I'd write thank you notes.

Finally, an hour or so later, mother and I persuaded Hal the party was over. Most of the guests had left by the time we changed into travel clothes and headed for the car.

At the last moment, Mom pressed an envelope with a hundred dollars into my hand, "This is so you have some money of your own."

What an electric jolt! Mom wouldn't be supporting me anymore. Maybe I'd better save it to take neckties to the cleaners.

Aunt Atty handed me the top tier of our wedding cake. "Put it under your pillow and your dreams will come true."

My little brother and young Armenian nephews finished printing *Just Married* in soap on the windows and tied one last can on the string of cans. Hal yelled, "Hey, leave my car alone!" A few bedraggled Las Jardinières ladies, Cub Scouts and Maggie, the cook, still pert, threw handfuls of rice. Aunt Lucy and Uncle Matt hugged me while Cousin Zelda watched from a distance. Hal held open the door of his used two-door Ford V8 for me. I waved out the window, relieved to finally get away.

As we drove through the night, I lay my head back and closed my eyes. I felt Hal's hand on my thigh. I patted his leg. We drove in silence toward Laguna Beach for our honeymoon. How strange the last day and a half had been. I wanted to escape from my family to the Armenian emotionalism and *chorig",* home made coffee cake, yet I didn't want to press ties. Hal loved everything American, sliced bread, independence and hamburgers, yet his thrift and table manners were strictly Armenian.

By the time we reached the Pacific Coast Highway, I sat up and asked, "Hal, do you think this is going to work for us? You're being Armenian and me being American—can we get along okay?"

"Wife, this is 1947! We're going to forget our families' old-fashioned ways. We'll combine our two cultures and create something new and wonderful! Baby, we're on our way to new lives!" He suddenly swerved off the highway into a beach parking lot. It was night. A thick fog covered the beach. "Let's rest a little and eat our wedding cake."

"Aunt Atty said we should put the cake under our pillow for dreaming."

He reached in the back for the cake box, and tore off pieces of cake with his fingers. He stuffed one in my mouth. "Kiddo, we're already living our dreams, and this is only the beginning."

We fed each other. We kissed. Our lips stuck together with frosting. We stopped talking. The fog wrapped us in a magical blanket.

CHAPTER 7

Waffle Irony

*M*iriam listened with heart and mind as I told my wedding tale. "Well written, Martha! I love stories of you and Hal." She leaned forward and spoke more softly. "It's interesting to me how you drew out the problems arising from different cultures."

"Until I wrote this, I'd forgotten how conflicts do pop up in an intercultural marriage. Over the years, my husband became my best friend, my anchor to windward, my counselor, my only sexual partner. For fifty-three years, I lived for Hal."

Miriam nodded agreement. "You've certainly had a therapeutic marriage." She paused, drew a deep breath, and spoke emphatically. "I hope you understand that you were his equal."

I shook my head no. "I don't think so. He was a genius."

"Think about it. You chose him over family opposition. You said he was extremely intelligent and understood people. Wouldn't such a person pick an outstanding woman?"

"Ummm…maybe he tried to. He told me he and stepbrother, Mike, ten years older, both planned to marry blue-eyed blondes. They both did. But Mike swore he would marry the dumbest woman he could find and train her to be his wife. I remember Hal's words exactly. He said 'I'm going to marry the most intelligent woman I can find and help her to be independent'."

"And they both did as they planned?" Miriam asked.

"They both believed they did."

"Please hold in your mind the thought that your husband found you intelligent and wanted you to be independent."

"I follow your logic but…." My voice trailed off. Since childhood I'd lived with a sense of worthlessness and guilt, and I wasn't about to give them up. They were the comfortable old clothes I wouldn't trade for a designer gown.

"I hope you *do really* follow my logic, Martha." Miriam smiled. I smiled back. She started afresh, "Please tell me, will you bring another story about you and Hal next week?"

"If you'd read it aloud to me. I'd love to hear it in your voice."

"I will."

I left her office with a springy step. Though I now saw how many of our marriage conflicts stemmed from our different cultures, I felt delighted to return to the early days of marriage when Hal was a brilliant engineer and I was a naive bride. The following week she read aloud *Waffle Irony.*

Waffle Irony

At night, on our three-day honeymoon in Laguna Beach, Hal and I became intrepid explorers of the new continent of sexual love. In the daytime, we opened our eyes to a fresh world. We wandered together on golden sand beside a snapping blue sea. A sense of the wonder of being alive filled me. We pulled off our shoes, Hal rolled up his trousers, I pulled up my skirt and we let the icy salt water dash against our calves. Hal found a glittering piece of quartz and displayed it on his palm. A tiny light glowed inside the pebble and I thanked Hal with a kiss. His lips tasted of the sea. I pulled a delicate periwinkle shell with a pink ruffled edge from a pile of amber kelp and displayed it in my palm and he kissed me. We breathed deeply of salty breezes. For three whole days, we explored life and sex with new sensory awareness.

And then, we drove back to our garage apartment behind Mrs. Mooseberger's house. I crawled into bed where I slept the exhausted slumber of a bride giving and receiving love for three days.

The next morning, my husband nudged me with a shove of his bare feet. I heard his words, "Wake up, Wife. I'd like a waffle for breakfast this morning," and my exalted sense of being truly alive in a new world shriveled.

"Husband," I murmured, tasting this delicious word in my mouth. "I don't know how to make waffles." I stretched luxuriously in bed admiring Hal's body, so perfect for me, and his mind, brilliant as a shooting star, and his sensitivity, like a mimosa leaf, responsive to a touch. How had I, such an undeserving person, been so lucky?

"Wife, do you remember I have a job? I have to leave in an hour." He sat up without the lingering caresses of our three-day honeymoon. "I'd like waffles this morning."

Our marriage, a miracle in itself, meant other miracles could happen—even waffles. But I answered slowly, "Husband, I don't have a waffle iron. So how can I make waffles?"

Never before had I heard his voice with this sharp edge of annoyance. "Don't you even remember our wedding presents? Your brother Ben gave us a waffle iron. You'll find it in the cupboard on the left side of the stove."

He'd given up modesty, too, and headed for the shower exposing a bare behind. Didn't gents usually wear Pendleton bathrobes?

I slipped into my negligee, an imitation of Myrna's Loy's 1940 nightgown worn in *The Thin Man*. I imagined myself a wisecracking glamorous wife, like Nora. There was a bit of Cary Grant about Hal, and also a bit of Charles Boyer. I unpacked the waffle iron and threw the directions in the trash. Who needed them? Didn't I already know practically everything of importance? Whee! With abandon, I dumped together flour, baking powder, eggs and salt, giggling as a cloud of flour dust powdered me and the floor like talcum.

When we sat down for breakfast, the waffle iron steamed happily in the center of our tiny table. Totally infatuated with our mates, we grinned at each other. In his new wool business suit, white shirt and cuff links, Hal looked truly important. My bare feet and curvy contours visible through my nightgown made an exciting contrast. He eyed my bosom through the negligee. I sighed. How glorious to be a wife and be admired for one's breasts and arms and legs, which a week ago seemed ordinary. His touch made my body miraculous. I basked in the knowledge I brought him joy. Pure as an angel and sweet as love. The steaming stopped, which meant, the waffle was ready. I pulled on the iron's two handles to open it. The waffle split in half. Hal glared. "You're supposed to wait until the steam stops before you open it."

"I did." With a fork, I pried waffle bits out of the open iron. "But I'll try again, Hal. Maybe you're right. Maybe I opened the iron too soon." I'd dropped the 'husband' label for a minute.

"Okay, but hurry it up, Martha. I can't be late to work." He didn't call me Wife, either. When the next waffle clung desperately to the iron, we dropped the labels Hal and Martha. "For God's sakes, woman, can't you even cook a waffle?"

"Shut up, damn it. I'm doing my best." I drew a few furious puffs on my cigarette to nerve myself for waffle number three. When it split into fragments, he swallowed them with a few rapid gulps. "So long. See you tonight."

Tears ran down my cheeks, I threw myself upon him. "I wanted to fix waffles for you, Darling. I'm sorry I didn't know how." Of what possible use is a wife who can't even prepare breakfast?

"Hey, cut it out. This isn't a tragedy. It's a minor irritation." He gave me a couple of tweaks in certain spots and ran from the house.

I sat in a chair and brooded. When I was a child, if a spoonful of soup leaped from my spoon to my dress or a glass slid mysteriously from my childish grasp, my mother stared at me with rejecting eyes. Now I'd irritated my dreamboat husband too, and he'd left without breakfast. But I'd learn to make waffles if it killed me.

In desperation, I dug through the trash, mostly wrapping paper, eggs shells, banana peels and coffee grounds. Gunk under my fingernails might kill me, after all, but I found the directions on a soggy piece of cardboard. "Before using the waffle iron, season it with oil…." Like a scientist discovering an atom, I found the secret—season with oil. Halleluiah! I brushed olive oil on the iron with a toothbrush and stirred up a new bowl of batter. "Voila!" Even after three days of marriage, I still remembered French and I had learned how to make waffles. Not bad! I was hungry, too, and ate one, or two, or maybe three waffles. I could hardly wait until Hal would come home and taste what fine golden-brown latticework pastries awaited him.

To recover from the emotionally draining events of the morning, I plopped into bed for a nap. I awakened to the sound of a knock, threw a wooly bathrobe over my negligee and opened the door a crack. Randy, our landlady's freckle-faced fifteen-year-old son, called through our screen door, "I smell waffles."

I threw open the door and unlocked the screen. "Come on in. You're in luck. I just learned how to make a perfect waffle!" My heart danced a happy jig at the sight of this skinny kid with sandy hair who reminded me of my little brother. I was lonely. And, like my mother, if someone was hungry, I wanted to feed him. Randy and I giggled over golden waffles topped with pats of butter and floating in pools of genuine Vermont Maple syrup, a wedding gift from a college friend. He was saying, "I'm trying to decide if I should keep my part-time job next fall or try out for football...." when the screen door banged and my husband stomped into the room.

"Sit down, Darling. It took me all day to learn how to make waffles but I've figured it out." I pointed to the kid. "This is our neighbor, Mrs. Mooseberger's son."

Randy's face blanched white. His freckles jumped out an inch or two from his skin. He backed away toward the door. "Thank-you-very-much-for-the-waffles." The screen door slammed.

I faced my husband. Never before had I seen him in a rage. He sputtered like a steam engine, "You might have been raped letting a strange man in the house when you're in your nightgown."

"Nightgown *and* bathrobe, and Randy isn't a man, he's just a little kid like my brother. He dropped in..."

In a gesture of complete dismay, Hal whacked the side of his head with his hands. "Martha, never let anybody in the house when you're in your nightgown. You're as provocative as hell! I was out working at a stupid job to earn money for you. You didn't even bother to market for dinner with the money I gave you, did you?"

I started to snivel and grabbed a mop to wipe the flour from the floor. "I thought you'd like waffles for dinner." Tears splashed on my negligee and left a permanent stain.

He sighed deeply. The big vein in his neck stopped pulsing so visibly "I guess I've got a child-bride, even if she's twenty-one and a Berkeley grad. Well, I don't eat waffles for dinner. I'm a man. What can you fix for us to eat?"

Ideas flashed through my mind. Take him out to dinner with my mother's wedding gift, a hundred bucks? No! Scramble eggs, waffle on the side? No! Dinner waffles made him mad. Peanut butter and jelly? Yes—everyone likes peanut butter and jelly. I dropped the mop and grabbed a loaf of Wonder bread. I slathered it with Aunt Lucy's wedding gift, homemade strawberry jam, and a never-before opened jar of peanut butter. The spongy bread absorbed my tears.

Hal stared into space as if calculating the answer to some unfathomable question. "Are you making sandwiches for dinner?" he asked.

"Yes," I sniffed, feeling very much a failure as a wife despite my success as his sexual partner.

Silently, like a couple of cows, we chewed our cuds. Maybe I spread the peanut butter too thick so neither of us could open our mouths.

Finally, he swallowed the last bit of crust and the words flew. "Promise me, you'll never let a strange man in the house again," he roared.

"I promise. I promise," I stammered like a scared kid. Then I added in my defense, "Randy isn't a stranger. We met him when we rented this apartment."

Was a smile curling his lips? "I'll have another sandwich, Wife," he said.

I tried for a cheerful tone. "Peanut butter, coming up!"

"Wait!" he implored. "Peanut butter kind of sticks in your mouth, doesn't it? I guess I'd rather—why don't we go to bed."

A glorious reconciliation occurred in our double bed. Then Hal began to laugh. He said, "Let's just call this a case of waffle irony."

"Waffle irony. I'll irony you." I hit him over the head with a pillow. We pounded each other with pillows until feathers flew in the air. We kicked and punched each other. At last, exhaustion overcame us and we slumped. My husband's waffle irony had saved the day—and night.

Miriam and I laughed together when she finished reading. "I suppose you understand that this quarrel, like the tie incident, was linked to cultural differences."

"I never thought of it before, but I'm sure that's true. I was a free spirit, ran around with my brother, never felt afraid of men attacking me. But his family worried about sex a lot."

"Yes, but I wonder why you chose that incident to write about? And why did a free spirit have a sense of guilt about waffle preparation? And why did you invite the boy in to eat?"

I shrugged my shoulders. "I don't know."

Suddenly, she smiled. "Perhaps you were immature, more a teen than a young woman."

Her benign assessment relieved me. "Yeah, sure, I was an immature kid and I needed Hal to help me keep my balance. But as it turned out, he often left me for business reasons, usually during some family crisis or other. And now he's died and left me forever on my own."

"Would you like to tell me more of your feelings about Hal leaving?"

"Yes. His first big business trip came when I was twenty-five."

"And how did you feel when he left?"

"I'll write a story about that too." I left her office light hearted, leaving there my sense of shame at inviting Randy into the apartment. Emotionally, on the day after our honeymoon, I was still a kid, and liked hanging out all afternoon and eating waffles with Randy. It never was a seduction scene. But cultural differences had tripped us up. I could laugh at it now and proceed to Miriam's next assignment, exploring my feelings about Hal's business trips.

CHAPTER 8

Artificial Brains Develop: 1951

Two years after our wedding, Hal and I rented a two-bedroom cottage in rural El Segundo, where a mysterious underground tank handled only toilet sewage and a drainage trench in the yard handled bathtub and sink water. This meant I had to bury the garbage every night in the back yard. To conceal the bath water, I planted pink Naked Lady bulbs in the ditch and surrounded it with string beans, peas, squash, and bell peppers. Daily, I measured my vegetables. One morning with the aid of a measuring stick, I determined our string beans grew at the rate of an inch a day. Pregnant, I grew outward almost as rapidly. Busy and preoccupied as any female hummingbird building a nest, I painted the interior of our house. Proud that the wild and gloomy scholar of Berkeley had accumulated, in her twenty-three years, a house, a garden, an electronics engineer for a husband and, on November 1, 1949 a perfect, healthy baby girl, Julie, I shot off on the Earth Mother trajectory.

Hal located a job at Northrop Aircraft, where he joined a group of five scientists and engineers[1] led by Dr. Floyd Steele who were designing a missile that navigated by the stars. In this process, they created an "artificial brain" which performed the necessary math calculations. Soon the "brain" took on a life of its own. Northrop Aircraft wanted only a navigational system, not an artificial brain, so the guys built their thinking machine secretly. Hal shot off on his own trajectory where I could not follow. While he worked night shifts to measure the distance to the stars, Julie and I worked night shifts nursing. One morning at three Hal arrived home, eyes sooty from sleep deprivation, a vein throbbing erratically in his neck, and hot-wired by new concepts. I lay

---

1

in bed, still clad in my satin wedding negligee. "Come lie down, Honey," I murmured drowsily.

"I can't sleep now. We're on the edge of revolutionizing the whole world. Martha, listen to me. You've got to understand binary math."

"I don't want to." I muttered and gazed into Julie's luminous eyes.

"Martha, try to think. You are an intelligent woman. You can learn binary math. Look, in binary math there are only two numbers, zero and one." He held up a yellow legal pad where he had drawn zeroes and ones. "We can use these two symbols to turn a switch off and on." He paused for a comment, but this switch turning ability didn't revolutionize me. I yawned. I wanted sleep— plain ordinary sleep, sleep not nursing a baby, sleep not punctuated with binary math, simple ordinary sleep that "knits up the raveled sleeve of care." I lay Julie over my shoulder and rubbed her back.

His voice took on a frantic edge. "Martha, don't shut your mind. Where's the Berkeley girl I married? Come on, get up. I'll fix us coffee and teach you binary."

"Go eat your dinner. It's in the fridge. I have to finish nursing."

"You aren't really nursing. You're just lying there, letting her chew on you."

"Oh shut up. What do you know? Look at her Cupid's bow mouth. Look how her little bald head has some new fuzz."

He cupped Julie's skull with his large hand. "Hey, that fuzz feels pretty great." Julie looked up at him with an air of adoration. He raised his eyebrows and pursed his lips, an awed expression usually reserved for equipment. "She's a neat kiddo," he added. For a magic moment we three connected. Then a resounding burp sprayed my gown with baby-throw up.

"Whoops!" I said.

"I'll go make the coffee." Hastily, he left the room.

I dipped into our laundry basket and slipped over Julie's head a fresh nightgown that smelled of sunshine. I tied the drawstring at her feet. What a warm, wriggly neat little baby package! I sniffed her fuzzy head, enjoying her special scent. Then I followed Hal to the kitchen and nursed Julie a little bit more, so she'd be quiet while her daddy talked.

"Why are you nursing her again? She's not hungry. She's just chewing for entertainment."

"I'm the Mother. I guess I can decide about nursing without your opinions. Go ahead and explain your binary math." Learning motherhood was tough enough without having to learn a new math. When I peeked at the zeroes and ones marching across his legal pad, my brain ached.

But my words encouraged him and he dug in. "Binary math is the key to our artificial brain. Zero, you see, is 0. One is 01. Two is 010. Three is 0101. Are you with me?"

"Yes, but still don't see why it's so important. Julie's way more important than any stupid 0101. I birthed her, didn't I!"

"You're comparing apples and oranges. Of course, humanity depends on babies. But the concept of a machine that thinks using only two switches, one off, one on, to represent any possible number. This concept will change our world forever. This is like the first discovery of a wheel or how to start fire. There will be robotic factories, robotic medicine—and probably changes in government as multitudes of jobs are lost to robots. We are on the cutting edge of a new world, made possible by binary math."

I thought if his gang of wild engineers and mathematicians ever invents this machine that thinks, we'll all forget what little math we knew and if robots do the work, we'll grow fat and lazy. "Let's go to bed now, Hal. We have to get up at 10 a.m. for the baby."

"Just explain, why do we have to get up at ten?"

"Because Dr. Line told me Julie should sun bathe at 10 a.m., three minutes on her back, and three minutes on her stomach. I'll show you the schedule."

Bewildered, he shook his head. "Female birth hormones have obviously driven you crazy. Please, put your Berkeley brain to work. We can sleep till noon and she can sunbathe then."

I handed Julie to him, and sputtering, gulped down a mug of coffee. "If you ask me, you're the one who's gone nuts over a machine."

"It's not a machine. It's MADDIDA, magnetic drum digital differential analyzer. I saw your eyes glaze over when I was talking. You don't want to think any more. You don't want to be my companion any more. I've lost you to a baby."

"Hal, it's five in the morning. And you're not holding just any baby! She's ours! She's Julie!"

"MADITTA is going to revolutionize the world."

"And so is Julie and she's alive—not a bunch of switches and diodes."

"I don't think you care about me or anything else but that baby. But remember, we'll have a lot of life together after she's grown."

When we stumbled off to bed at seven a.m., we lost ourselves in our separate thoughts. I felt jealous of my rival, though it was only a hunk of metal named MADDIDA, run by electronics. And probably Hal felt jealous of my closeness to baby Julie. The breasts used to be his domain. Why didn't he understand that half of Julie was Hal himself!

At 10 that morning, as I lay Julie in her buggy to sunbathe for three minutes, I thought about Dr. Floyd Steele, the head of Hal's precious group. Floyd claimed in one of his rants, "MADITTA will make humans obsolete." I turned Julie on her stomach. For the next three minutes, I fumed. A baby has infinitely greater power than anything men can invent. A baby is an instance of God's creativity. The future lay in Julie's starfish hands.

I amplified my thinking when Julie and MADDIDA both turned six months old and I became pregnant again. The future would lie in both Julia's and my son Geoffrey's starfish hands.

This was a time of emotional inflation for Dr. Floyd Steele's group of engineers and scientists and their wives. The men dreamed of robots running factories, performing surgeries, writing music and literature. The sky was no longer the limit. Humans could calculate beyond the stars, and put robots on Mars. We wives dreamed of expanding families, owning homes, planting gardens, living in good school districts, and pursuing intellectual pastimes. The guys told us they were leaving Lockheed, taking their patents for MADDIDA with them, and setting up their own corporation. We believed our splendid men's visionary ideas. We never questioned whether they needed more business experience. We'd all experienced the Depression and World War II, and we gals had the smarts to marry geniuses who'd be leaders in a fabulous world based on binary math!

With another child coming and the dream of MADDIDA growing real, Hal and I decided we needed a larger house. Just as we had fallen in love with each other, we fell in love with a Victorian house perched atop a wild grass and wildflower filled acre in Manhattan Beach. Straight out of Dickens, this brown-shingled Victorian house with gables, turrets, and a fireplace with a stew kettle hanging on a wrought iron hook won our hearts. "Your Longwood home was so great! But this is a place where I can put you that has class, too."

We rented it without a thought for the inconveniences an older house might bring, or the isolation it could cause a mother who couldn't drive and had two babies. We were riding a wave of success. "Stick with me, Baby, we're going to the top," Hal predicted.

I loved to entertain, and since I was the youngest of the wives, I won my place in the group with my cooking. We all had babies. Charlotte, wife of the now famous inventor of the CD, Dr. Eric Reed, composed a song with a refrain of "Oh, the diapers they come and the diapers they go," that we sang with parental zeal. J. D., wife of our leader Floyd Steel, worked with me to create a timeline of world history on shelf paper. Researching historic dates with her helped me feel closer to an intellectual world, and reminded me I wasn't completely brain dead.

Nearly every night the men spent from 10 p.m. until 2 a.m. walking the sands of Manhattan Beach, designing the artificial brain and discussing ways to find investors for their new company, Computer Research Corporation.

One evening, Dr. Floyd Steele called a meeting of all the husbands and wives at our house. Floyd and his wife D.J. took command of the evening while their daughter baby-sat our numerous offspring in the sunroom. From the head of the table, D.J banged a spoon against a glass for silence and Floyd announced, "I've called you together to ask you a vital question." The table hushed.

"What should be our Final Goal? Should we endeavor to become a mega-corporation producing computers in a factory in L.A.? Or should our goal be a smaller research organization, living outside L.A., perhaps in Escondido, but earning sufficient income for a home and family?"

His words discharged an electric atmosphere into the room. I circulated the table, offering the stew I'd cooked in a pot hung over an open fire. The scent of rosemary, thyme, cumin and red wine rose in a fragrant steam that stirred the blood. Our guests helped themselves to hearty scoops and ate with relish even while speaking or cheering or booing speakers.

Dick Sprague, an engineer who resembled Tyrone Power, jumped to his feet and read from a yellow legal pad, "This is a summary of Dick Sprague's Final Goals which Includes: Sprague's Start-up Goals, Intermediate Goals, Final Goals and Final Final Goals." Immediately, cheers and boos broke out. Sharp divisions arose between pro-production and pro-research. It became an every-one-talk-and-chew dinner.

D.J. rapped her spoon once more. "Please quiet down. We need to hear from everyone."

Her husband had a different approach. His luminous blue eyes and hypnotic voice turned all heads toward him. "Next Sunday we'll all drive to Escondido and price land. We'd all enjoy raising our families in orange and avocado orchards."

The admiration in Hal's eyes as he gazed at Floyd made me uneasy. I wondered if Floyd was a genius or a charlatan—or both. I had a sudden longing for my father's legal viewpoint.

I raised my voice as loudly as I could. "If you're going to start your own business, you must hire an attorney to protect everyone's rights."

No one responded, not then. Not ever. Privately, I continually begged Hal, "Please, hire a lawyer." My instinct caused me to shrink away from Floyd. His speeches had a hypnotic cultish quality that made me uneasy. He used words with private meanings attached to them. Something was wrong with Floyd, but when I tried to talk to Hal, it drove us apart. I wanted to cry and stamp my feet because I was not heard.

The first of February, Dr. John von Neumann, father of Cybernetics, invited Floyd's group to bring their machine to Princeton's Institute for Advanced Study. Northrop agreed to this, so Floyd's men began to plan the trip by truck and bus from Manhattan Beach, California, to Princeton, New Jersey. Floyd chose Hal to accompany MADDIDA on this trek and be responsible for its safety.

On February 13, at dawn, two weeks after von Neumann's invitation, I doubled up in bed with labor pains. Hal reached for his watch and timed the distance between the pains. I was surprised when at 8 a.m. he insisted, "It's time to go to the hospital."

I objected from a blissful state of altered consciousness. "No, it's not. These pains are light. They're just warming up pains."

"I don't think so. You need to be in a hospital for our baby."

He tried to lift me but couldn't. Reluctantly, I slid my legs out of bed. He wrapped me in a fuzzy bathrobe and helped me to our two-door Ford. He made a return trip to the house while I waited and then settled Julie, smiling and wide-eyed in her bunting, on my knees.

Our hour-long trip from Manhattan Beach to Good Samaritan hospital included a stopover at the Longwood House to leave 15-month-old Julie with Gram. I focused on my breathing while my mind, in a different place, felt disconnected from my body. A strange calm and indifference to the surroundings pervaded me. I came to a bit, as Hal pulled me from the car. Then I was standing in front of a hospital desk and heard the words, "Take her immediately to the delivery room." On a gurney, I continued this breathing while waves of pain rocked me. Hal kissed my forehead as we moved mysteriously down a hall. I came out of my trance. "Do they know the baby and I have Dr. Spock's Rooming-In plan," I gasped.

"It's all set," Hal answered.

This baby would be treated right. I hadn't seen Julie in the delivery room until a stiff nurse handed me my baby, wrapped like a hamburger in tissue paper and scolded me for unwrapping her to count her toes. Words hit me like stones, "Mother, you must not touch her skin. You are not sterile."

Geoff was born two hours after our arrival at the hospital. I watched as they laid him across my chest before I fell asleep. Following Dr. Spock's plan, Geoff lay in a bassinet level with my bed for the traditional three days lying in. Whenever I wanted to nurse him or just plain cuddle him, I swung the bassinet over my bed and scooped him up in my arms. I felt at peace. When Dr. Spock himself visited our ward, I felt proud filling in a questionnaire, "What great joy not to be separated from your baby at his birth." In 1951, Dr. Spock restored the glory of motherhood! Hal also loved Rooming In because dads could scrub up and hold the baby and become partners in parenting. The future *baby boomers* were special from birth on.

Our last night at Good Samaritan Hospital, a nurse served us a steak dinner by candlelight and took care of Geoff while we talked. It was then Hal told me, "The date is set, Babe. I'll be leaving March 8th for New Jersey."

"Oh, no! You can't. Geoffrey will be barely three weeks old!"

"Sorry, Baby. But Floyd chose me to ride with MADDIDA by truck and railroad to the Institute for Advanced Study at Princeton."

"Someone else, who doesn't have a new baby, could ride with it instead."

"Martha, I'm the engineer, the hands-on guy. If the truck or train shakes some parts out of place or some wire gets twisted, Floyd knows I can fix it. The mathematician von Neumann, father of binary math, will watch a demonstration of MADDIDA. It's a real honor for me." Pride and joy filled every nook and cranny of Hal's face. What about Dr. Spock's brave new world and equal parenting? It didn't exist.

The following day we started our life with two babies at home. Hal thought continually of the risks and problems of moving a delicate artificial brain to Princeton while I held to my heart the most encouraging words I heard in Rooming In. I asked a black nurse's aide, "How can I take care of two babies at once?"

"Ain't you got two arms? Can't you hug two babies close with them two arms? Ain't you a mother?"

As Hal packed his suitcase for the trip to Princeton and strode about the house in a new wool overcoat, I gazed in the mirror at myself. I wore a long lace-up back brace ordered by my OB for strained back muscles. My hair looked lank and weary. Black smudges circled my eyes. No wonder Hal wanted to abandon me. I sure looked like a dud of a wife, and I couldn't even look after our monstrous house by myself, let alone two babies. We had no telephone and no neighbors in walking distance and I had never learned to drive. That was my own fault, and now it was too late to do anything about it.

Geoffrey might get sick. In the hospital, he nursed like a tiger but at home, he had to have a teaspoon of green soothing syrup before he ate. Something was wrong with my milk or maybe I didn't hold him right. As I fussed and fumed, I never suspected that Geoffrey might be allergic to my cigarette smoke. I could write an essay about Shakespeare, but I didn't know shit about survival.

Floyd's four-door, brakeless Austin auto rattled up our long driveway. Hal grabbed his suitcase and ran to place rocks against the tires of Floyd's auto to keep it from sliding downhill. We MADDIDAites all drove convalescent cars, lived in falling-down rentals and ate lots of tuna casseroles while dreaming of future riches. But according to Floyd, when the world learned about our artificial brain, we'd all be wealthy.

I ran after Hal with my arms so full of babies I couldn't even hug him. I wanted to scream, "Don't leave us!" but that wasn't in the 50s code. We supported our husbands, no matter what the cost.

Hal's face glowed with enthusiasm. He loved getting away. He loved his MADDIDA. He thought of himself as Odysseus going off to battle. He didn't care what happened to Penelope and her babies. He was abandoning us.

He pressed his lips on the babies' heads. "Bye, little girl Julie; bye, bye little boy Geoff. Take care of your Mommy." His pressed his full lips on my forehead." Keep your pecker up." He chuckled at the UK slang and I chuckled, too.

"I will. Break a leg," I answered. He gave me thumbs up sign and climbed into the small car, which was impossibly stuffed with children. Floyd's two-year-old son, George Steele, sat on his mother's lap at the steering wheel. Floyd removed the rocks. The vehicle glided downhill with Floyd running after it. He swung open the door and climbed in. His wife, D.J., wound down the window and stuck her head out. "I'll come by every day to check on you and the babies," she called. The Austin engine caught hold with a loud clanking sound. They shot down the driveway. They were gone. Truly gone. I was in charge now.

My mother often told me, "Martha, you and I have pioneer blood. We don't need to whine or cry. We can defend ourselves. We're survivors. I had to be a pioneer. I laid the babies in the middle of our double bed. "You watch baby Geoff," I instructed Julie. She smiled proudly and patted his blanket. I dashed to the kitchen, pulled out a huge carving knife and hid it under my pillow. At midnight, I often heard strange cries and howls echoing on our hilltop. If anyone broke in after our babies, I'd kill him. In one hand, I held my fear of abandonment and inadequacy, and in the other hand, the belief that I could do whatever needed to be done because I was a strong, pioneer woman. Later on, I learned the wild screeches came from feral mother cats in childbirth.

"Tell me a story, Mommy, Tell me a story." Julie bounced up and down on the bed.

"I will. But stop bouncing. You'll wake Geoffrey. Well, once upon a time, there was a daddy who had to go far away on a train. The train had a whistle… whoeee…whoeee….The wheels went clickety-clack on the shining black rails."

Julie imitated my sounds. "Whooee, clickety-clack."

"And smoke poured out of the smoke stack."

"Smoke stack," Julie echoed.

"The daddy came home again. He said 'Hi Julie. I'm home. I missed you.'"

"Daddy came. Home. Hi Julie. Miss." Julie said.

"Daddy said, 'Julie, I love you,'" I kissed her baby curls.

Julie said, "Love you." I drew a trembling breath. Hal had MADITTA, but two babies were better than any machine. I would wait at home like Penelope and weave as much of a life as I could.

CHAPTER 9

Tracing the Guilt

How whiny my words sounded, even to me, when I read *Artificial and Biological Brains* to Miriam. During the reading, Miriam changed, too, no longer my *dear lady,* more like an impatient detective as she tapped her fingers on her writing pad. "Why was your sense of abandonment so strong when your husband went on a business trip? Did your parents ever abandon you?" She wanted to get on with this therapy business, but I loved reminiscing.

My neck prickled. "My dad died, but that's not abandonment. I'd rather not discuss it." So far, I'd felt relieved and contented in this little room. Did she want to turn it into a battleground?

"Martha, the more you press down your feelings, the more energy you use," she explained, pressing down an imaginary cloud of sorrow with her hands. "It will cost you less pain and energy to share your feelings than to keep them a secret. Let them rise to the top and sail away." Her arms floated upwards. "Remember, too, whatever you say here is confidential. It goes no further."

"Yes, I know, but I really don't want to talk about Dad in my session... maybe his death was a kind of abandonment....who knows, but I'd rather talk about...other issues."

"How old were you when he died?" Once more—the detective in action!

"Fifteen."

Miriam ripped a scab off my unhealed sore. "It's true that teenagers or even adults feel abandoned when a parent dies."

I wanted to say *Oh, Miriam, shut up. Leave me alone*! Instead I blurted out, "I let my Dad die. I adored him and I tried to save him, but I couldn't. I let him die."

In a matter-of-fact tone she asked, "How old did you say you were?"

"Fifteen," I repeated.

"Do you want to tell me what happened? I do not understand how a fifteen year old could be responsible for her father's death." Her compassionate eyes and voice told me she'd be kind; but if I told her my story, I'd betray my father.

After a silence, she tried again. "Martha, let's let old secrets fly away." She raised her arms again and I pictured crows leaving their tree.

I buried my face in my hands. "I still feel bad. I should have stopped him."

My almost eighty-year-old body shook with the anxiety I once felt as a teenager. I hid my eyes with my hands and entered the old world of the '40s. "My Dad was our King Arthur. Winters we lived in our walled castle and summers we spent in our summer palace, Newport Beach—that is to say, our summer home on Harbor Island." As I recalled the island and our house nestled by the rattling wooden bridge, the words flowed.

❖

It was July 3, 1940, and I woke up early, glad to be awake and on Harbor Isle, away from the stresses of my sophomore year in L.A. High. I pulled on my swimming suit and ran barefooted to the wharf to raise the American flag. The sky looked as gray and sad as an old lady ready to cry. Except for green streaks here and there, the retreating tide had left the sand wrinkled. I dove from the wharf into the cool lavender bay and glided through the water, careful not to splash with my arms or legs. The early morning, with no one around to boss me or tease me gave me a gift of freedom. I absorbed into my being the beauty of the dawn. I swam until I could swim no more. Then I waded to shore and squished through the low tide muck to huddle on the sand and plan our family Fourth of July.

Dad would wear his white linen suit, a straw hat and a red white and blue bow tie for the holiday. Ben and I would recite the Preamble to the Declaration of Independence, and then Dad would set off his twelve-inch brass cannon. We called our father "Yankee Doodle Daddy." My little brother John had already asked me five times, "Will Daddy shoot the cannon tomorrow?" And Ben just as often told me, "You better remember my girlfriend, Eve, is coming to meet the family tomorrow." I'd answered "yes" or "sure" or "okay." I knew what they meant. They meant, "Sis, you keep Dad sober."

Sitting on the seashore, hugging my knees, I shivered. The wind blew harder, yet the air felt warm. Weird weather! Earthquake weather! Grains of sand blowing in the wind stung me. I buried my face in my arms. Heaviness in my chest cut off my breath. Panting, I clawed at my throat. A pain exploded in my head. I rocked back and forth in agony. Lights blinked in my peripheral vision. I fought a wave of nausea that swept over me.

Words appeared in my mind: *Dad is going to die tonight.*

No! Not my beloved Yankee Doodle Daddy, the only man I adored—he couldn't die.

Tears made a path down my sandy face. Where did these dreadful words come from? From the clouds? Did someone speak? From my own mind? Oh, no!

In my pagan youth, the ocean, vast, immortal, omnipotent, served as my symbol of God. I begged the waters of the bay, "Please, please, don't let Dad die."

Mom's voice called me from this fearful place. "Sister! It's time to serve breakfast. We're waiting for you." Paralyzed by fear, I remained shivering on the beach, struggling to understand what had happened.

I'd read about premonitions and prophecies but my family labeled them hooey. We were too rational and scientific to believe in God. If there were some kind of god and he/she/it wanted to send a vision, wouldn't he/she/it send it to someone older and smarter than me, like a boy? Like Ben? Just forget it, I told myself, but terror had me in its teeth and shook me like a dog shaking a rat. *Dad is going to die tonight.* Maybe I was crazy?

Johnny ran with the wind across the beach and skidded to a stop by me. "Come on, Sis, I'm hungry. Everybody's waiting for you." He tugged on my arm. I stood up, a little shaky. If I told Mom what happened, she'd say that I was bonkers and send me to a doctor to fix me. I had to figure this out on my own.

In the house, we obeyed one of Daddy's regulations: no one can come to the dining table in a bathing suit. Johnny pulled on a red and white striped T-shirt over his bare chest and I hid my wet bathing suit inside a middy blouse. I was supposed to wait on the table in the summer because our maid Fanny had extra work with our houseguests, or so Mom told me. I hated this chore. It classified me with "The Help," instead of with "The Family," but I dragged myself into the kitchen anyway.

Fanny, shining black in a white uniform, hands on hips, scolded me. "It's about time you got here, girl. Here's a plate for your brother Ben."

Sniffing the aroma of maple syrup and waffles made me wonder if hunger brought on my vision. Native Indians fast day and night to get a prophecy so maybe swimming on an empty stomach could do it. I slammed Ben's plate in front of him. He winked. Then I remembered his telling me, "Don't get mad that I'm Mom's favorite. You're Dad's favorite. You and I can always talk to each other, we have our special relationship." So I whispered my secret in his ear. "Ben, I had a premonition just now. I was sitting on the beach and a voice or something told me Dad's going to die tonight. What should we do?"

"Aw, cut it out." He swirled on the bench and looked deep into my eyes. Ben, like Clark Gable, had a sweet-guy tough-guy mix. He styled his patent leather hair with pomade to look like him, too.

Ben patted me on the shoulder and whispered, "You think Dad's gonna die because you had a fight with him last week. Kids, especially girls, get weird ideas like that when they're adolescent. Just forget that stuff, Sissy."

His voice, now tender, made me ashamed of my fear. Ben understood the difference between what's real and a teenager's imagination. He knew me as no one else did, so I tried to follow his advice, "Forget that stuff." But when your brain tells you your father will die, it's tough work to get it out of your system.

I think this *Dad is going to die* stuff actually commenced when I was nine. Alone in my room on the second floor of the Longwood house I heard eerie screams coming from Mom's bedroom. A nurse with goat's teeth and a stiff white uniform barred my way into her room. "You can't come in here now. Your mother is busy. Stay out of the way." She slammed the door. I climbed the third floor stairs to my brother Ben's tower room. I pounded on his door. "Benjie, Benjie, what's happening to Mom?"

His door slid open. He pulled me into his room. "She's screaming 'cause she's having a baby and Dad's drunk."

"What do you mean, drunk?" I asked.

He groaned. "For gosh sakes, Sis, you're nine years old. How can you be so out of it! Don't you know Dad's alcoholic? He probably got her pregnant when he was drunk."

Ben's eyes usually spoke of mischief, but tonight they looked soft and gentle and I understood he wanted to help me. I dared to ask, "How did Dad make Mom pregnant?"

"Don't you know anything? Why in Hell hasn't Mom told you?"

"Pl-ease, Benjie, you tell me about making babies," I begged.

He ruffled my hair. "Kid, don't let your blue peepers fog up! I'll try to explain."

While Mom screamed twenty-five stair steps away, I heard the facts of life, which I really couldn't believe, from the lips of my brother.

At midnight, he was still explaining in a tense voice, "Dad is a *binge* drinker. He stays sober when he's trying a case. He's damn smart and he always wins. But when the case is over—wow! He gets as drunk as a skunk. I've gone to a speakeasy with him. He's pretty funny. But he should keep his hands off Mom at his age. I was pretty embarrassed at school when my Big Ten, my pals, found out she was pregnant."

I felt blurry and dizzy, unable to process the details of Ben's rambles, but I got the main idea, and hated it. "Mom never said Dad was alcoholic. She talks about 'Dad's illness.'"

"Aw, she's tries to pretty things up. You gotta know the truth about stuff, though. He's a drunk."

With a crash, the truth landed in my mind. Yes. Dad gets drunk and some-how his drunkenness is my fault. The next morning anxiety filled me even as I rejoiced to hold my newborn brother in my arms. This gnawing sense of some-thing wrong kept growing until on the third of July 1941, it took the form of a premonition as I sat on the beach, shivering, and the baby born that night six years ago called me to breakfast.

After breakfast that day, Mom, Aunt Atty and the maid Fanny cleaned, marketed, baked peach cobblers and sent me to rake the beach and hose down the pier. That afternoon, Ben brought his new girlfriend over. They went wakeboarding. Ben drove the speedboat in wild circles while Evie, a tiny figure, balanced on a long wooden surfboard and hung onto the rope. She looked like a Lucky Strike ad. Johnny, in trunks and T-shirt, amused himself poking crabs with a stick, "for the gruesome joy of it," he confided to me.

Johnny wouldn't go with me that evening when Mom asked me, "Row over to the mainland and pick up Daddy." Ben and Eve had left for a party, so I had to go alone. The slimy algae goop on the ropes to pull the rowboat ashore gave me the creeps, but I tugged away, hand over hand. Finally, I waded out in my tennis shoes, unleashed the boat, and threw myself over the port side. There I hung, half in and half out, until I took a deep breath, scissor-kicked my legs and flopped on the floor of the *Benjie Boo*. The oarlocks screeched as I pulled hard against the incoming tide. The peninsula was a mile and a half from our island.

Fat Ferry tooted a warning as I drew near its route from Balboa Island to the peninsula. I pulled in my oars and let the *Benjie Boo* drift. *Fat Ferry* chugged by within six feet of me. She carried a load of three autos and a bunch of sun burnt kids, lobster red, who saluted me as Captain. Their pup, which could have been an *Our Gang* comedy dog, put two paws on the railing and barked in excitement. *Fat Ferry's* wake rocked the *Benjie Boo* and all the kids laughed.

I drifted backwards while I waited for the ferry and when it passed, I puffed and panted, pulling on oars. I didn't want to be late for Dad. Organ music and the smell of cotton candy from the Fun Zone drifted across the water. We were drawing near the Balboa Pavilion. The distant clang-clang of the electric train filled the air, warning me I'd better not grab a hot dog on the way. Dad would join his commuter pals for a drink in the bar if he didn't see me when the train stopped. I tied up at Marine Gas Station and dashed down the boardwalk, past the Fun Zone with its hot dogs, to the Balboa Pavilion, where I turned right, urging my tired legs past the tourist shop and bakery where Mom bought chocolate éclairs for weenie roasts. I skidded to a stop at the tracks where a crowd welcomed commuters from the miraculous one-hour trip, Main Street LA to Main Street, Balboa. Whew! I'd made it. Men in business suits and straw hats and women in elegant dresses seemed to move in time to the carousel's music.

All at once, I saw my Yankee Doodle Daddy's straw hat above the crowd. "Over here, Dad!" I jumped in the air and waved.

My big Daddy in a white Palm suit headed jauntily for me, his feet dancing a jig. Pinwheels and Sky Rockets peeked from his large market bag. His basso profundo voice rose above the chattering travelers. "Everybody, pay attention!" He pointed to me. "This is my beautiful daughter."

The crowd guffawed because I looked more like a drowned cat than a beauty. "She rowed all the way from Harbor Island to bring her old Daddy home. Ain't that wonderful?" Now the laughter rolled louder. Someone said, "He's sure drunk."

I froze in place, too embarrassed to move. Dad kept coming toward me. "I'm a Yankee Doodle Daddy," he sang, jigging in time. Some of the crowd sang along with him, some waved. One fellow commuter explained, "That's Big Ben!"

I pulled on his elbow. "Come on, Dad, let's go home."

He announced, "I want to wish everyone here a fortuitous Fourth of July."

"Come on. Everyone's waiting for you at home."

He flicked my hands from his arm and continued, "This is a land of law. Our constitution sets us free...."

Somehow, I got him to the rowboat. He was still babbling, "I won the case in court today. Never take a case until it's on appeal. I did damn well, didn't I, Daughter?"

"You did pretty damn good," I answered.

"Don't cuss, Daughter. It's not right coming from a girl."

We reached the Marine Gas Station where I had left our boat. A man in a fake captain's hat with gobs of gold braid stared at us while a kid in a greasy T-shirt filled the *Hawaiian Queen's* gas tank. If that guy complained about us, I'd lose the privilege of tying up here for sure. If only Dad would get in the boat and shut up. "Hey, Dad, give me your fireworks. I'll stow them." I yanked the sack from his hand and hid it in the bow. "Come on, Dad, it's getting late."

He had a funny look in his eyes as if to say, *what's she doing here?* All at once he leaped gracefully, all two-hundred plus pounds of him. I thought Dad would dive into the bay, but instead he made it to the narrow bench in the stern. When he sat down, the *Benjie Boo* nosed bow-upward and steadied. I cast off and jumped in. The guy with the captain's cap glared at us as I shoved the oars in the locks. I forgot about him, turned the skiff around, and counted to myself "str-oke—str-oke" like a boatswain. We took off into the night.

Daddy rambled on. "I'm riding high! Won every bridge hand on the train. Were the boys mad! I promised them a game tonight."

I stopped rowing. Our boat drifted along a silver trail, the reflection of the moon in the bay. A string of lights outlining the turrets, roofs and windows of Balboa Pavilion blinked on, transforming this Victorian gazebo into a fairyland castle. Ben and I used to sneak in there to watch gambling, dance marathons, and jitterbug contests. But Ben was twenty now and not so much fun and counting on me to bring Dad home sober. I'd make Dad stay home tonight, so he'd be okay for the Fourth.

"Dad, would you do something for me?" I asked.

"Sure, little girl. I've a pocket full of dollars here, get what you want." He waved a handful of bills in the air.

"I don't want to buy anything. I want you to stay home tonight with me and Mom and Johnny. We need you. Johnny caught some crabs he wants to show you and Ben."

"I have to go out tonight, Sweetheart. Coming home on the train, we played bridge, a dollar a point. I skunked them." He laughed enjoying the memory and waving the dollars again. One fell in the bottom of the skiff. "So I promised the boys a chance tonight to make up their losses, if they can."

I reached over and patted his knee, rocking the boat and spraying us with phosphorescent drops from the sea. "Daddy, please don't go out tonight. I had a premonition—you'll die if you go out. Stay home with me and Johnny and Mom and Atty."

Then he called me "Tiddlywinkers." When I was five, I'd beat him in a game of Tiddlywinks played on the dining table, dodging crystal glasses and dinner plates and ending with the chips in a coffee cup. Then he gave me the pet name laden with love and used it now. "Tiddlywinkers, Sweetheart, I want to stay home with you but I am a gentleman of honor, and I keep my word. A gentleman cannot leave a game where there's betting and he is the winner."

"I won't let you die. I had a premonition—"

His voice had an ugly edge now. "That's superstitious rubbish. When my time comes, I want to die like a man with my boots on and not hang around the house with the women, anyway."

I fought back the only way I knew how. "If you go out tonight, I'll never speak to you—ever again. Something bad's going to happen. Please Dad, listen to me."

"Gloomy Gus, Gloomy Gus," he sang with a devilish twinkle in his eyes, enjoying my anger. I grabbed the oars again and we sped homeward with the tide.

At dinner, no one noticed my silence and gloom. Johnny and I watched Daddy drink beer after beer. Johnny didn't show Dad his crabs or mention the cannon. We watched our father drift away from us. He didn't give a hoot if I spoke to him or not.

After dinner, he struggled to his feet. "Eight o'clock. I'll be late. How do I look, Daughter?"

I felt the primitive terror a horse experiences when he senses fire. I broke my vow of silence. "Don't go," I begged. I tried to put my arms around him, but he was too fat. I pressed my body to his. I hoped if he knew I was really there, he'd come out of his beery place. "I'm sorry I didn't talk to you tonight. Pl-ease, don't go out." He brushed away a tear on my cheek with a large manicured finger and recited a Joseph Whitcomb Riley poem:

"There, there, little girl, don't cry,
They have broken your doll, I know..
Childish troubles will soon pass by..."

"I'm afraid you'll die tonight."

"I love you too, Tiddlywinkers. See you tomorrow...we'll have the best Fourth of July ever, gentleman's promise. Gotta play tonight...give the men a chance...." He unwrapped my arms, popped on his straw hat, and left, singing, "I'm a Yankee Doodle Daddy."

Over and over again that night, I repeated a line from a poem I had posted in my bunk, "...know despair too frail a figure fashioned by the night, Not to be shattered when the morning hammers it with light,..."

A pagan child of atheist parents, I knew no prayers but I stayed awake reciting my line and hoping until I heard once more his heavy tread on the stairs. He wasn't just Big Ben, the rugged two-fisted attorney, or just my Victorian father, big on Latin and poetry; he was my dearest companion.

That night, his words over the years came back to me. "Someday, Daughter, we'll float down the Mississippi on a raft, like Tom Sawyer and Huck Finn."

"Daughter, I bet you a shiny dime I can eat my peas with a knife." That day, he plunged his knife in the honey jar and then in a bowl of peas. With great delicacy, he licked each pea off his knife while Mom cried, "Daddy, remember the children are watching."

Summer mornings, he knocked on my door at six. "Daughter, wake up. Let's go swimming before the rest of the family gets up." And every day, year in and year out, he shared his books. Together we read *Pinocchio* and *Heidi* and later on Victor Hugo and Dickens. He was my playmate and my father, and I loved him and I could not sleep until he came home. I lay in bed tense and listening. Around 1 or 2 a.m., I heard his steps on the stairs and then the creak of his bed. Dad was home and I could sleep now, too.

Around three o'clock in the morning, Aunt Atty, whose bedroom was underneath mine, stood in my doorway. "Wake up, Sister." She looked strange in a flannel nightgown and bare feet. Her mouth drooped. She'd forgotten to put in her false teeth. Her pink scalp showed through her grey hair. I'd never seen her uncombed before.

"Little Sister, you must come downstairs and sleep in my twin bed," she ordered.

Drugged with sleep, I nodded and followed her down the stairs. This was creepy—Aunt Atty a fraidy cat wanting my protection? Almost immediately, I fell back asleep until my mother shook my shoulder. "Wake up, Martha."

I mumbled, "Is it the Fourth of July? I have to raise the flag. Did I oversleep?"

"Martha, your father is dead. His winnings, dollar bills, were scattered all over the room. He sat up said 'Jesus Christ' and died." Tears streamed down her face.

I heard screams in the distance. "Stop screaming, Martha," my mother said. Were those anguished screams mine?

"You knew he'd had three heart attacks. You knew he was going to die."

Those screams were mine and I couldn't stop them. I had been warned that he'd die if he went out and I didn't stop him and he died.

Mom came to my side and shook me with her strong little hands. "Stop screaming."

I wished she'd hugged me instead. I drew a deep breath. The screaming stopped. "Why didn't you tell me when he had heart attacks?"

"I did tell you, but you didn't pay any attention. Don't you remember when the doctor ordered him to sleep downstairs in the library because of his heart?"

"Mom, I want to see him! Was he smiling when he died?"

"You can't see him. I called the funeral home while you were asleep and the ambulance took him away."

I stared at her face. She'd combed her hair and rouged her cheeks and called the funeral home before she talked to me. Now I knew she hated me because I let him die. She had to let me see him! Maybe he wasn't really dead. Maybe he'd disappeared somewhere. "I have to see him. I want to kiss him good bye."

"You can't. He's already gone." She clicked out of the room on high heels she must have put on for the undertaker. She had cheated me out of my last chance to see the only man I loved.

I felt Aunt Atty at my side. She hugged me close and whispered, "You and I loved him, little Sister."

When I laid my face on her chest, I felt the tiny pearl buttons of her flannel gown cutting my cheeks. I wept. Again, weird screams recommenced, seemingly far away, but coming from my throat. Then my brother Ben wrapped his arms around me. "Stop screaming, Sis. Look, Eve's here. We're going to do the Fourth of July the way Dad wanted. Come on, Sissy."

Those terrible screams stopped. "I'll get Johnny," I said.

Mom and Aunt Atty, Ben and Eve and Johnny and I walked together out on our wharf. We followed our father's protocol for the Fourth. Johnny and I raised the American flag. Ben and I recited the Preamble to the Declaration of

Independence together, "When in the course of human events, it becomes necessary for one people to dissolve the political bands...."

Then Ben fastened Dad's pinwheels to the pier and fit rockets into three legged stands, ready to ignite. He filled the twelve-inch brass cannon with gunpowder.

"Everybody back," he called, and lit the fuse.

The overcharged cannon rose up in the air, exploded and shattered into pieces that fell in the bay. The rockets shot off, trailing fire, until they sank in the water. The spiral pinwheels spun blue, orange and yellow until at last they turned black and lay lifeless in the sand. And where he would have stood with us, laughing and celebrating, there was nothing.

Six months later, December 7, 1941 the Japanese struck Pearl Harbor and the United States entered the Second World War. Brother Ben entered the Air Force. Mother went to work. I was a junior in high school. Dad wasn't King Arthur any more. The days of Camelot had ended.

CHAPTER 10

Taking Care of Daddy

*M*iriam dabbed her eyes with a tissue when I finished reading *Yankee Doodle Daddy*. She wept because I couldn't. She explained, "Because I have come to know you so well, I understood how this experience affected you, and I cried." Her sky cleared quickly and she continued with a bright smile. "Your story seems very well written. As a therapist, I was interested in the line where you mentioned that at the age of nine you learned your father was alcoholic and that from then on, you were afraid he would die."

"I don't remember writing that line."

"Check your manuscript," she suggested.

My voice felt thick and unwieldy as I read aloud my words. "'At the age of nine, I became filled with anxiety that when Dad was drunk, he would die." I groaned. "So that's what made me a nervous wreck."

"I prefer to say, your fear of his dying has caused you great anxiety and compounded your natural grief at the loss of your husband with a sense of guilt."

"Looking back over the long corridor of my life, I see myself---*Sis, Sissy, Martha Albene*--- crouched in a corner under the stairs listening to Dad's mournful song from the second floor balcony, 'I walk along the streets of sorrow,' chewing my fingernails, and pinching my arms saying, *don't die, Daddy, don't die*. Terrified he might die, but unable to tell anyone my fear, when he *did* die, I blamed myself. Why didn't I stop him from going to his bridge game? I filled my backpack with guilt. I've carried it all of my life."

After my confused outburst, Miriam continued with our dialogue. "At fifteen you were immature and still had the type of magical thinking a child has.

You were able to imagine you could control your father. Of course, that was impossible."

"I guess so." I tried to process her words. My mind felt foggy—my premonition, praying to the bay, believing I could save my Dad, magical thoughts. "Miriam, do you think my premonition was real or imaginary? I've always wondered."

Miriam picked her words carefully the way you choose stones to hop across the river. "Martha, I believe that the strong feeling of responsibility you felt for your father, and the powerful fear you experienced for him, caused you to have premonitions of his death. And on the occasion of his death, the premonition was realized. You mentioned your anxiety as a child of nine. I think these feelings started even earlier, before you knew he was alcoholic, perhaps when you were a very small child."

I drew a shuddering breath. "Yes, I was scared to death he'd die. Once Dad fell full length on the floor. Mom screamed; I pulled my little brother into the laundry room. We hid for hours. I didn't want to look at Dad being dead. Somehow, Mom got him up and he wasn't badly hurt—just broken ribs. The doctor taped them."

"How old were you then?"

"Johnny was four. I was thirteen."

"Can you remember when you first had guilt feelings concerning your father?

"Miriam, guilt has been the background music of my life."

"Would you like to reach farther back in your mind and tell me about the first time you can remember taking responsibility for your father?"

I wanted to dam the torrent of emotions rushing through me. "I don't know... it's so long ago. I can't think about it now."

"Martha, you know I love to read your stories and I believe they are very therapeutic. Perhaps you'll bring me a story next week."

"Maybe I will."

The next day, when the torrent of tears had become a manageable stream, I settled down with a feeling of gratitude to the therapist who encouraged me to reflect on and write my earliest recollection of helping Daddy, the ways I tried to save him and help the family too. The scent of night-blooming jasmine drifted through my brain and carried me back to the lawn on the east side of our home, 901 South Longwood, Los Angeles, when I was five.

Taking Care of Daddy

I scrunched up small and hid in the jasmine bush. It felt good to sit in the mud and smell the tiny white flowers. Ben and Kelso could hunt like bloodhounds but they'd never find me, so ha! ha! ha! It's a cinch to double up real small anywhere and hide when you're five. I'd run in free and stick my tongue out at them all.

"Sis-ter, Sis-ter, where are you?" Mom called.

Phooey to you mom! My name's Martha Albene, not Sister. Only my brother Ben can call me *Sister*

"Sis-ter, come home right now!" she called. I didn't want to see her look like a witch. I'd better go. Why didn't she call Ben too Why me? It wasn't dinnertime yet. I crawled out of the jasmine and scuffed my ugly shoes across the dewy grass.

Ben came running. "One, two, three for Sis. You're out."

"Mom wants me. Who cares about Hide 'n Seek?"

I took itsy bitsy steps all the way up the hill to the tiled veranda. Mom was wearing her witch face.

"Don't look at me angry," I cried.

"Did you forget you're going out with Daddy tonight?" She grasped my sweaty hand and hustled me along "Uh uh. I forgot. Do I have to? I'm playing Hide and Seek."

"Daddy needs you to take care of him. Look at you! You're all dirty. I have to clean you up and make you look pretty." She pulled me along. When I dragged my feet, she dug her fingers in my arm and gave a jerk.

"Ouch. That hurts! I don't want to look pretty. Why do I have to?" I whined.

"Little girls need to look pretty to keep their Daddies happy. You'll be meeting Daddy's friends, too."

"I don't want to." I trudged up the stairs and Mom, a stair above me on the circular staircase, administered sharp little tugs to keep me moving. When we reached my bedroom, she ordered, "Sit down on the bed and I'll skin off your bloomers."

After school, Mom let me wear black bloomers over my dress so I could hang by my knees in a tree and stand on my head in the grass. You can't do *anything* in a dress. I wouldn't let her take off my bloomers cause if did I couldn't play Hide 'n Seek. I crawled across Granny's old four-poster bed to get away from Mom. She crawled after me and stretched out her arm like an octopus and yanked off my bloomers.

Now I couldn't be me, Martha Albene Hunter. I had to be a good girl and sing and dance and be Daddy's pal. Yuck!

I wriggled in Mom's arms. "I'm tired of being good."

Mom dropped a silk slip slithery as a snake over my head and then a scratchy cactus dress she called your *organdy gown.* She sang to me "There was a little girl who had a little curl, right in the middle of her forehead. And when she was good, she was very good and when she was bad she was horrid."

"I'm hor-rid. Hor-rid," I sang, loving the new word.

"Stay still. I have to brush your hair. You're squirming like a minnow in a bucket."

Last night she'd wrapped my hair in rags to force it into little sausages. Now she stuffed the sausages into her curling iron. I smelt hair burning. Yuck! "It isn't fair! Ben gets to play Hide 'n Seek. You don't take his pants. You don't burn his hair. Ouch, too hot!" I ended with a scream.

"If you'd hold still it wouldn't hurt. Now be a good girl."

"Don't want be a good girl." I pinched my arm so I wouldn't yell, anyway.

"That's better. Now you're going out to dinner with Daddy tonight. Won't that be fun?"

I stretched my words as long as I could. "I gue-sss sooooo." After Daddy had three drinks, his body stayed where it was but he shut himself up like Aunt Atty closed the living room drapes at night. Weird.

My burning hair smelt awful, but Mom worked her way through my scalp creating Shirley Temple curls "One thing you must remember, Little Sister, after you eat dinner, make Daddy come home early so he won't get sick."

"Make Daddy come home early so he won't get sick," I repeated.

"That's a good girl," she said.

She stood back, cocked her head and frowned. Mom would smile if I looked pretty. You can betcha' life, she looked pretty -- no fat curls, smooth bobbed hair, no icky brown scabs on her knees. She powdered them, made them pretty for Daddy. She pinched her cheeks so they'd look red. She wanted me pretty, too, but I didn't like burning my hair.

"Now promise me," Mother said.

"Promise what?"

"That you'll bring Daddy home early." She sounded cross.

Mommy's hugs were worth promising anything. "I promise." I held up my arms. She gave me one of her wonderful hugs that smelled of rose water and powder and swung me around. Her face looked pink and pretty, a good Mommy. We giggled as we hurried down the stairs together. Daddy waited in the reception hall below.

"Good evening, Mademoiselle." He bowed to me. I curtsied. I'd learned how in Elisa Ryan's dance class. I loved Daddy's smell of Cuban cigars and Bay Rum shaving lotion. I loved it when he swung me high into the air and swung me into the front seat of the old Packard where Ben usually sat, so ha ha ha! to Ben. Daddy patted my head. Maybe I did look pretty after all.

We drove to Charlie's Oyster Bar in downtown Los Angeles. Dad pushed open its Dutch door and I saw a long line of men drinking beer at a counter. Sawdust covered the floor. I gazed in awe at a glass case piled high with cheeses, meats, hard-boiled eggs, and oysters. I stretched out my hand to touch the pile and touched a mirror instead. What a fake. The mirror made it look like tons of food.

Dad explained, "Take whatever you want to eat. Tonight is a free Dutch Lunch with every beer."

Somebody shouted, "Hey, Big Ben's here," "Hello, Little Sister." Everyone waved and spoke to us. They called Daddy "Big Ben" because he was tall, but how did they know my name was Sister?

"Give the gentlemen a curtsey," Dad directed. I spread the edges of my blue organdy gown, squatted as low as I could and suddenly tumbled on my bottom. The men laughed. Daddy laughed, too. I wished they didn't laugh at me.

Daddy helped me up and then lifted me onto a high chair at a little round table. He slid a beer to me. That was a joke, you see, because the beer was really for him. So I giggled. He wandered around slapping people on the back and telling jokes. Everybody loved my Daddy. He was as powerful as a king.

Blue-grey smoke from cigars and cigarettes lay on the floor like a blanket. Then it moved higher, clear up to my table. Would it go up to my neck? Everybody was laughing. They sounded like an ocean wave, then the wave ran out to sea and I could hear them. "Bottoms up!" "Hey Ben, who'd you put in jail today?" "Can you get a judge to fix a ticket for me?" "Bottoms up." "Here's mud in your eye." The words didn't make sense.

Slimy gooey creatures still in their shells looked up at me from a plate that Daddy pushed in front of me. His face looked very large and red, and his teeth looked gigantic. "Watch me," he said. He dug one critter out of its shell, waved it in the air, and dipped it in red stuff and said, "Eat them like this!" He popped one in his mouth and chewed with his big teeth. "Your turn, Little Sister. Go ahead. Eat it."

"Is it dead?"

He looked irritated. "Of course it's dead."

"Is it cooked?"

"You're supposed to eat it raw. Best treat in the world. Go ahead."

"I can't." I closed my mouth and shoved my lower jaw forward.

"You're as stubborn as a billy goat." Dad lost interest in me then. He wandered over to the bar. After a while, he brought hard-boiled eggs, chunks of cheese, and peanuts and dumped them on my table. I gobbled the food while feeling sad to the bottom of my Mary Jane patent leather shoes because I couldn't eat the oysters. I had failed Daddy's test. I wasn't his "Tiddlywinkers" any more.

I rocked back and forth in my chair and told myself a story. *I am a princess and a witch imprisoned me in a tower surrounded by thorns.* I leaned over to stare at the floor. No thorns, but weird sawdust smelling of beer and oysters. "*Rapunzel, Rapunzel, let down your hair,*" chanted the witch. I tugged on my curls, and made my chair rock a little. I waited. And waited. Just as I decided to think of a different fairy tale, Dad lifted me in his arms. My heart sang "Going Home. Going Home."

No, we weren't. Daddy lifted me out of my chair and stood me on our little table. "Come on, Little Sister. I'll sing 'East Side, West Side'—you dance." He sang in a voice as deep as the ocean, "East "—I tapped one, two, three, four, five, "West"—one, two, three, four, five, "All around the town." Now I had to speed up. I was a pony clicking my pony hooves all around the table. No, I was a New York actress tapping all around the table. No, I wasn't an actress. I didn't know who I was as roundabout and roundabout the table I went. The room whirled faster and faster. The Dutch door swung open. Yellow light shone in. Streetlights! It was night. I stopped tapping.

I was supposed to bring Daddy home early. I'd broken my promise! My chest prickled. If Daddy fell down sick, I'd be a bad girl. I whined, "Daddy, I want to go home."

He didn't pay any attention. "All around the town...." The crowd sang along with him.

I tugged on his sleeve. "Daddy, it's late. I want to go home."

"Boys and girls together, London Bridge is falling down," he sang.

Falling down. I could fall down. Plunk. I threw myself down on the table. I felt his strong Daddy arms around me. "I'm sick. I want to go home." I cried a little. That wasn't hard, because I was a bad girl. I'd broken my promise to Mommy to bring Daddy home early, and hard-boiled eggs and peanuts for dinner made my tummy feel funny.

"Hey, Big Ben. Don't leave now."

"Hey, Big Ben, sing another."

"Kid's sick. I have to go." He carried me through the swinging door to our black Packard. I pretended to fall asleep in his arms. No more oysters, eggs and peanuts. No more tap dancing on the table.

When we got home, I heard Mommy say, "What's the matter with Little Sister?"

"She's sick. She fell down at Charlie's." Daddy didn't say I was a bad girl. Daddy didn't say I danced on the table. He lay me down on my bed and patted my hot cheeks before he left.

Mommy bent over me. "What's wrong, Sister?" I opened one blue eye. "I got Daddy home on time."

She whispered in my ear, "You're a good girl, Little Sister. You didn't let your daddy get sick." Mommy gave me a wonderful hug because I brought Daddy home. I was a good girl. I was a smart girl. So, ha ha to Ben.

After recalling this ordeal, I lapsed into a reverie, humming *Eastside, Westside* to myself,

"Were there other occasions when you took responsibility for your father?" Miriam asked.

Did we have to return to reality? I'd rather dance on a table and outsmart my father than chase down his failings. But I wanted to be a good client, so I answered, "Mother often asked me to take care of him when he was drinking."

"You've proven yourself to be a very strong little girl. Would you like to tell me about other occasions?"

I supposed she meant occasions when he was drinking. "No, I wouldn't." I felt a flash of anger. Miriam always asked me would I like to tell her something or other. Hell no, I wouldn't like to. Telling my stories was like vomiting--necessary but unpleasant. As I reflected on my father's addiction, his strong presence and his anger filled the room. I shivered.

"Take three deep breaths and relax." Miriam modeled deep breathing. I copied her. This made it easier for me to continue. "I don't like to think about it, but I suppose I need to. Mother always referred to it as "Daddy's illness.""

"What was Daddy's illness?" Miriam inquired.

"Alcoholism."

I could see him now, the memories of so long ago vivid, my feelings about my beloved Daddy vivid too. I wondered, as I went on talking to Miriam, if I weren't being disloyal to Daddy by talking about his "illness," but it was too late to stop now. The next story explained more about his "illness," as seen through my child eyes.

❧

He never drank when he was on a case, only when the case ended. Mommy liked me to keep him company before dinner while he prepared his brew. He had an important hammer, like Thor, the Norse god of thunder. I watched him fascinated as he pounded a canvas bag full of ice. Then he poured the crushed ice into a cocktail shaker and added a mysterious white liquid and a thick gooey one.

"Orange blossoms, my dear," he said. He shook the shiny shaker above his head, in front of his belly and below his knees in a weird dance. The ice sounded like Mexican maracas. When he drank his orange blossoms, his eyes turned red, just like Thor's.

"Tiddlywinkers, I'll make you your own drink. This is a bottle of grenadine. Smell it." He held a dark red bottle to my nose and I sniffed. "It's made from pomegranates. Now I'll fill your glass with ice and Seltzer water." He pumped fizzy stuff from a sprayer attached to a bottle. "Add grenadine for flavor and a grenadine cherry on top." He handed me a glass, filled his own from the shiny cocktail maker and winked, "Here's looking at you."

That meant we were supposed to take a swallow from our glass. We sat together on the fuzzy couch in the living room, and I watched him slowly change from all-powerful Thor to an ordinary giant who couldn't talk right, who wobbled to and fro when he walked, and who forgot about me.

One night, after a shaker full of his magic drink, he left his cozy seat in the armchair and headed for the front door shouting, "I'm going down in the garden and eat worms." I stumbled after him, unsure what to do.

Mother, wild and staring, suddenly appeared by the open door. She wrung her hands. "Please follow Daddy. If he falls in the brook, he'll hit his head on the rocks and he'll die."

"I don't want to." Our garden, a fairyland in the morning when the sun squeezed through lacy branches, changed into a creepy place at night. Frogs in the pond croaked and the log bridge Dad built creaked mysteriously. You couldn't see the dangerous rocks in the creek that'd kill you if you fell. My legs felt squishy. I couldn't go down in the garden.

Mom glared at me and I hated her angry face. "Do you want your father to die? Go down in the garden and make Daddy come out."

Now I heard him singing in his drum-like voice, "I walk along the street of sorrow, the boulevard of broken dreams."

I felt like a puddle of vanilla pudding, soft, gooey, stuck to the floor.

"If you don't get him out of the garden, something terrible will happen."

I had to go down in the garden at night and save Daddy. My feet in high-top leather shoes sounded thump thump on the steep path. Wet leaves and frogs and peat moss smelled strange at night. I made up a song. "Thump, thump thump goes my shoe. I'm not afraid of spiders. I'm not afraid of rocks. I'm not afraid of Daddy. I'm not afraid of you. Thump thump goes my shoe."

Daddy sang louder, "I walk along the streets of sorrow." I didn't want to listen to him. I drowned out the streets of sorrow with "Thump, thump goes my shoe."

Something dark moved near the bridge! A big black blob! My breath cut me. A robber! A murderer! Couldn't run. I had turned to pudding again. The blob took shape. A six-foot shadow. A big fat stomach. Great big shoes. I knew the shoes. Daddy's shoes. I danced on his shoes when I was little. I had to save Daddy. I ran to him and kissed his big warm hand. I tugged on it with both my hands. "Daddy, come back to the house with me. Daddy, I love you. Please, Daddy, please."

"You still love me, little Daughter?" he asked in a surprised voice.

"Yes Daddy, yes Daddy. I love you." I was like a little tugboat turning a big ship around to drag it into the harbor. I pulled on his arm and slowly, slowly, he turned. I didn't want to hear his sorrow song. We needed a happy song. "Daddy, Daddy, let's sing '*Yes, We Have No Bananas*'."

He chimed right in, "We have no bananas today."

Together we sang, "We've string beans and onions and carrots and scallions, And all kinds of fruits and say…" we'd made it out of the garden and onto the veranda, "You can take home to the womens, nice juicy persimmons…." Mom waited by the porch light and we belted out the last line, "But yes, we have no bananas, we have no bananas today." I saved Daddy from walking along the streets of sorrow. I was a good girl and Mommy loved me.

CHAPTER 11

"Facing the Lion, Being the Lion."
Mark Nepo

*T*wo weeks after humming "Yes, We Have No Bananas," my legs shook so badly I could scarcely drag myself up the stairway to Miriam's office. I longed to run away and hide, but where can you hide from your feelings? Her office accessories, the box of Kleenex, the stone labeled "courage," the dim lights, felt distasteful. When Miriam, looking a trifle worried, hurried in, I wondered if the folder she carried bulged with papers about me. I handed her a check as quickly as I could, wanting to get that part over. Then I sat still and shivered. Where had my *Yes, We Have No Bananas* attitude gone?

She focused intently on me. "Thank you so much. How are you this morning?"

"Well, not so well. I seem to have the jitters today. I started shaking on the way up the stairs and I can't stop. You've been a healing presence to me up till now. But now—I don't understand why—I'm frightened. Even this office scares me."

"Of course you're frightened here. In our last session, you described your father's alcoholism and now, I believe, you are afraid of him. He was a very dominant figure in your life. You may feel you betrayed him, and you would expect retribution. It would help if you told him out loud how he disappointed you." She pointed to the straight back chair in the room. "Pretend he is sitting in that empty chair and tell him of your anger."

"I can't do that. I don't want to destroy my father's image." I couldn't even imagine doing what she asked. She pressed on. "What image of your father are you trying to protect?"

"The image of a literary man! When he was nine, he'd already studied all of Shakespeare and could recite most of it by heart. He never carried his law books into court because he knew them by heart. He could cite page and number from memory. Dad wasn't really a drunk. Drunks don't dress in tailor made suits and appear in the state Supreme Court and win! Dad was a dreamer. He and I planned someday we'd go on a raft down the Mississippi like Huck Finn. I can get mad at my father's illness, but not at him. I love him."

After a long wait, Miriam suggested, "Maybe you just don't do anger."

"It's all so long ago. What's the use in getting worked up about it?"

"It is a long time ago, "Miriam agreed, "but you are shaking with fear now. Perhaps the time has come for you to have the courage to face the Lion."

Once more, I noticed her bowlful of stones, each with a word traced on it in a delicate calligraphy. The pebble labeled "Courage" stood out. I drew three deep breaths. Yes, it was time for me to face the lion.

I spoke to the empty chair. "Dad, I know you loved me, but you let me down when you got drunk. Dead or not, Dad, you still terrify me and you still quench the spirit in my life. I have to sit here and confront you now, because I never dared tell you when I was a child.

"At my junior high graduation party, you embarrassed me in front of my friends. You came out on the balcony to look down where we kids were dancing. You wore only your nightshirt. The kids could see up your body. I felt embarrassed, humiliated, unclean. I was never able, after that experience, to look those kids in the eyes again."

As I spoke, the lion I confronted became me, not my father. My rage leaped to life in the room. "You ruined my life with your vulgar behavior. How could I be friends with the kids after that?

"I caught despair and self-destruction from you. I was there with you, all the time, listening while you sang of streets of sorrow and broken dreams. I was always attempting to save your life. I snubbed out your cigarettes, led you out of dangerous places, I begged you to come home with me, but I couldn't save you. You said you wanted to die with your boots on. Your boots were on my heart. You broke my heart."

The room grew quiet. I wasn't shaking anymore. My eyelashes felt wet, but I wasn't crying. I had separated from my father. I no longer lived in his kingdom.

Then, I wanted to understand this tortured man. "Miriam, why do you suppose he sang "The Boulevard of Broken Dreams" over and over? He had our family, a career and money. Why wasn't that enough?"

"I imagine that he expressed the sorrow and loneliness alcohol caused him and his powerlessness to control it."

"That's really sad," I said, feeling a heaviness in my chest.

"Yes, it is."

During sessions in the following weeks, I still talked about my father and clung to the belief that I could have prevented his death. Finally, Miriam remarked, "Nobody can save an alcoholic but himself."

I sighed. "I think you are right." I felt that I'd pulled one heavy rock out of the overstuffed sack of guilt I carried.

That night I had a strange and lovely dream. I saw myself as a little old woman in blue slacks and a blue jacket, tangled in the limbs of a great oak tree. This tree had a wide bulging trunk with knothole eyes where the branches started, and below a gaping, black mouth-hole. I untangled my legs from the branches. I raised my arms. Slowly, slowly I arose into the sky through a canopy of leaves. I crossed my ankles and held my back very straight. I looked prim and proper like Mary Poppins as I soared into freedom with my arms stretched into the heavens. I awakened from the dream knowing I had escaped my father.

In our next session, Miriam laid down a different thread for me to follow through the labyrinth. "Have you ever wondered why your mother turned her husband's care over to you? Did you ever think she should have been the responsible one, not you?"

She'd asked that question before, and I'd always shrugged. The life children lead from their birth on seems normal to them, whatever it is, and I'd accepted the situation. What else can a child do? But Miriam challenged this and during the months of therapy, I learned to understand the needs of my child self and to wish I'd cared more for the little girl who tried too hard to make her family happy. I pondered Miriam's question. "I guess Mom thought I could help Dad better than she could."

"Did she honestly believe a child of five could control her husband better than an adult? Or did she send you to Charlie's Oyster Bar that afternoon because she wanted to escape the responsibility?"

I wriggled my toes in my shoes. Taking care of Daddy had been heavy, like the rocks of guilt I carried when I failed to help him. "I really don't know, Miriam."

"I believe she protected herself by expecting you to control your father, rather than deal with his addiction herself."

"Yes, but as I recall, I was born with a serious nature. I wanted to look after Dad, though I thought it'd be fun to be light hearted like Mom, too."

"Martha, when you were five years old, how could you have made such a decision? You were trained to take responsibility for your father from an early age. I want you to talk to your mother today like you did with your father. Tell her out loud how you felt about her treatment of you as a child. You've often spoken your of your need for more attention from her. Tell her now."

I whispered, "How can I? After Dad died, she changed. She paid me more attention. She called us the Hunter girls. Later, she turned into Gram, a spunky purple-haired grandmother who drove a golf cart with the flair of an auto racer and I loved her."

Miriam spoke in a tiptoe voice. "I am sure you loved her and took care of her. From your stories, I know she was a remarkable woman. I have admired her along with you. But when you were very small, did she give you the attention then that you needed?"

Tears leaked out of my eyes. I muttered under my breath, "She was always busy with other things. She never held me on her lap." I struggled back in time to visualize my mother. "Often she just stared off into the distance and hardly noticed me at all."

Miriam said softly, "That's probably because she was preoccupied with your father."

I wiped my eyes and tried to remember more. "I've never thought of the pain Mom suffered as the wife of an alcoholic. She never talked about that. She liked to tell funny stories about the family. She said I scooted around the house on my bottom, dragging a book with me and begging, 'Read me, Mamie, read me.' She giggled when she told this story, but I used to wonder why she didn't pick me up and read to me."

"So, tell your mother now how you felt about that," Miriam directed.

"Too hard, too long ago."

"Just pretend she's sitting there, in that chair." She pointed to the same hard-backed chair that had stood in for Dad.

"I feel silly, doing this," I commented.

"That doesn't matter. Just let your words flow. Talk to your mother."

"I'll try." I no longer saw Gram, but my Mom, Albene, a sparkler, charming everybody. I wanted to be her special baby. "Mom, when I said 'read me', why didn't you stop right then and read to me? I don't remember you ever holding me in your lap and rocking me. I only remember Fanny rocking me in her chair. And you took Fanny away from me."

"And who was Fanny and how did your mother take her away?" Miriam asked.

"Mrs. Miller, my first grade teacher, started the trouble. She asked my Mom to some to my classroom for a conference. They sat together at Mrs. Miller's yellow oaken desk, and I sat at mine, three rows away."

It was time to tell Miriam more about my mother and her prejudices.

A Child's World Changes

I dipped my nib into my desk inkwell and drew a butterfly wing on the back of my math paper. Suddenly, my teacher's voice broke into my world. "Mrs. Hunter, I called this conference because your daughter Martha has a Negro accent. She is spending too much time with your maid. You should be speaking to her more."

My teacher, Mrs. Miller, old and dusty as a flourmill, looked like she could grind us first graders into wheat to make her bread. My Mom, pretty as a butterfly in her dress with roses, looked scared just as though she were a first-grader, too. My seat screeched as I wriggled out. I ran to my Mom and tapped her on her knee, "Mommy, what is a Negro? What is an accent? Tell me, Mommy, tell me."

"A Negro is a black person like Fanny and an accent is the way Fanny talks. You need to speak like a Hunter, not Fanny."

I scrunched up my face like a monkey and stamped my feet. "I like Fanny. I like the way I talk."

My Mommy shot me one of her super-frowns. "Martha Albene, be quiet. Behave yourself." She looked at my teacher now.

"Mrs. Miller, I never realized what was happening. I'll see that Martha eats dinner with us at the adult table instead of in the kitchen. And when I'm not home, Aunt Atty can take care of her, instead of Fanny."

She glared at me. "Martha, go sit at your desk while Mrs. Miller and I finish our conference."

My shoes clumped really loud as I scuffed my way back to my desk. Bang went my seat when I pulled it down and slid in. I dipped my pen deep into the ink well until the nib dripped. Then I held it over my paper and shook it and watched black blobs of ink slowly kill my butterfly. Mom and Mrs. Miller were whispering now but I didn't hear them anymore. I only thought about murdering my butterfly and loving Fanny.

No time before Fanny existed for me. She was always there, like my family--Mom and Dad, Aunt Atty, my brother Ben and my dog Snowball. Fanny, plum-black, smelled of butter and flour and honey and laundry soap. She wore a white uniform and slippers with toe holes cut in them to let her corns peek out. "Here, you make yo' a man and I'll bake him with the biscuits. Hold out yo' hand." She poured nine plump raisins into my hand. "Two fo' de eyes, two fo' de nose, and five fo' de mouth. I'll bake him fo' you."

On Mondays, Fanny vacuumed. "Now, Chile, you ride on de Hoover. We gonna pretend it's a train." I sat down on the vacuum cleaner and she called out train stations. "Next stop, San Francisco." Fridays, Fanny and I waxed the Spanish tile floors. We tied rags on our shoes and ice-skated on a layer of wax. "When I go to Heaven, Sugar Plum, I'm gonna wax the floors in Jesus' mansion. Mm Hmm."

Big brother Ben scalped my doll and I ran screaming to the kitchen. "Fanny, Fanny, Ben's playing Indian and he scalped my doll. He's going to burn her at the stake."

"Um, um, Ain't that a shame." Fanny made Ben give me back my doll and sewed a bonnet from a flour sack to cover dolly's bald head. She settled me on her lap in her rocking chair and sang in a molasses voce, "Honey Lamb, we got sorrows. We got sorrows '…so high, we can't get over them. So low, we can't get under them. So wide, we can't go around them. Oh, rock-a my soul.'" I can still hear the squeak of her rocking chair and the slap of her feet as she kept time. I remember the feel of her, soft on top with hard muscles underneath, like chocolate-coated taffy.

Every Thursday and every other Sunday, her days off, Fanny and I rode in a bus to her apartment in downtown L.A. There her friends and relatives admired me, too. "Mm, mm, ain't she wonderful. "Look at them yellow curls."

"Look how she claps," they'd say, when I kept time to their Gospel songs. Ben could beat me in every game, but when I played Shoo Fly at Fanny's house, I always won. "That's my baby," Fanny bragged.

But now I was six, and Mommy said I mustn't go in the kitchen anymore. Banned from Paradise. Banned from the smells of honey and butter. Banned from the love that was once as available as a mother's breast. Fanny's Honey Lamb in the kitchen became a lump of clay in Aunt Atty's hands. She told me, "You're a big girl now, Sister, and you need to learn to speak properly. I've found an articulation class for you."

A southern drawl was my language of love. I told my dolls, "I ain't gonna to ar-tic-u-late none." But I did. I learned to hold a feather in front of my mouth and keep it still, except when I pronounced *wh*. And next, Aunt Atty decided on ballet class. "It will make you a graceful woman one day. Tap dancing is just play." I learned to balance on one leg, wear an itchy-scratchy tutu and walk on my toes, but I knew short plump girls with bowed legs don't become graceful ballerinas. Worst of all, Fanny didn't call me her "Sugar Lamb" anymore. Just "Miss Martha." She grew stiff and proper toward me. I had lost my babyhood forever.

Soon, adult concerns became a part of my life. In the fourth grade, I earned a high score on the official aptitude test, so the Wilshire Crest principal moved me into a special class for gifted children. Taught by Mrs. Treister, this classroom, instead of Fanny's lap, became my Paradise. We studied *Mein Kampf*, and learned how the Germans made scapegoats of the Jews. We read history books and learned how greed and prejudice against Negroes led to slavery and more prejudice. We studied black and white photographs of the dust bowl in Oklahoma and learned that Okie kids were just like us. From then on, I watched the streets of Los Angeles to find battered model-T Fords carrying a family's belongings tied to their roofs. Sometimes a sad-eyed tow-headed girl or boy would lean out of the window and wave and I always waved back.

I cornered Mom one morning in the sun garden where she was clipping cherry tree boughs for an arrangement. I fired questions at her. "Mom, why can't Fanny eat dinner with the family?"

She didn't pause in her clipping. "Don't be ridiculous. Servants don't eat with the family,"

"Why can't Fanny go to the chiropodist for her corns? They're awful."

Mom turned and looked directly at me. "Martha, she wastes her money on keeping her own apartment. She could stay at our house free on her days off. She'd have enough money to fix her feet, if she did."

"Everybody wants a home, Mom. Maybe you could pay her more."

She looked startled. Almost dropped her branches. "Martha, your father mails me a set amount of money from the office every month to run the household. It doesn't include more money for Fanny. Negroes are different. They don't have the same needs we do."

I yelled at her "You're mean," and frightened by the way I was becoming different from my family, I ran away, down the rock steps.

She shouted after me, "That progressive education class is ruining you. We should put you in Marlborough Private School." I heard her, but I didn't answer.

That night, I stood outside my Dad's library door to listen to Dad and Mom talk. Dad's deep voice oozed sarcasm, a weapon he often used in court. "Oh, isn't Sister's school de-light-ful! She writes beautiful thoughts and loves niggers and Jews and doesn't give a tinker's damn about spelling, and handwriting, and arithmetic. Isn't that just lovey-dovey!"

To my surprise, Mom defended my class. "But she never liked to read and now she's reading everything. She even wrote some poems."

"Progressive education is dangerous. Makes Commies of the children," he thundered.

"Sister has good sense. She'll be all right. I don't think she'd like a private school."

The talk grew political. I stopped listening, but I promised myself if they took me away from Mrs. Treister, my special teacher, I'd run away, become a hobo, cook beans over a campfire at night and read whatever I wanted. Probably, hobos would like me. They wouldn't be snooty like the cygnets in my ballet class who thought I looked like a gnome, even in an itchy tutu. But Ben told me girls couldn't be hobos so maybe I had to be a Hunter and hate black people and feel guilty about Fanny's sore toes. Or maybe—it's easier to just die.

❖

Miriam had listened to my ramblings patiently, but now decided to enter into a dialogue. "At a very young age, you thought of death as an escape."

I hid my face in my hands. "Yes, I did. I wished I were dead."

"And this thought became a part of your core beliefs and whenever you were under pressure you thought, 'I wish I were dead.'"

"Ummm, yes." Miriam and I both needed time to think. We sat quietly and reflected.

Miriam broke the silence first this time. "I think your desire for death is more of a mind habit than a deep desire."

As sunlight filters through pine branches to lighten the darkest forest, her simple words *mind habit* trickled into my consciousness. "You mean, when words like *I wish I were dead, I want to die,* pop into my mind they're only a mind habit, not some deep obsession, not an ardent desire, just a bad habit, like picking at cuticles or munching on potato chips?"

"Yes, a mind-habit."

Freed from the idea of obsession, I laughed from relief and joy. "I get it! I do! I walked the streets of sorrow with the dad I adored and I absorbed some of his habits, but they aren't me! I love life—in hard times and good. That's the real me."

Miriam laughed with me and smiled. "I'm so glad that's the real you. And I imagine that by now you also realize that you did not cause your parents' attitudes toward minorities and that whatever Fanny had to endure was not your fault."

"I've always felt to blame. Being a Hunter made me a part of it."

"But deep inside you know it wasn't your fault."

I sighed. "No, it wasn't." I drew a healing breath. Another rock of guilt crumbled in my hand and became dust. I felt proud of the child who wanted Fanny to eat with the family. That child skipped down the stairs from therapy, though her old knees couldn't. Fanny and Miriam only loved, and never judged me. Through the mysterious workings of therapy, I became Fanny's Honey Lamb again.

"So high, I can't get over it.
So low, I can't get under it.
So wide, I can't get around it.
Oh, rock-a me Lord."

CHAPTER 12

Pinching Pain

*A*t the start of our next session, Miriam asked, "Did your parents move you to private school?"

"No, they didn't. That was only a threat. Maybe my parents saw how happy I was in the Opportunity Room, an experimental class based on John Dewey's Learning by Doing. I was in charge of the silk worms because our garden had a mulberry tree. After the butterflies hatched and flew away, we unwound the cocoons at school, made silk thread and tried to weave."

"What an interesting experience for you."

"It was. We wrote a class play about China and produced it on a wooden stage we built. I even had a best friend, Adele Mendelsohn, a half-Jewish girl who played violin in the Youth Philharmonic. She had her own little red chair on stage and I adored her. Mom forbade me to play with her because she was Jewish, but I played with her anyway. Whenever Mom said something mean about Jews, or Fanny, or divorced women, I'd pinch my arm."

Miriam leaned forward, concern in her eyes. "Can you explain how you pinched yourself?"

"Just like this." I pinched my arm. "I did it so hard and so often my arms became black and blue."

"Do you want to tell me about it?" she asked.

"I knew it wasn't right to do it. I blamed myself for hurting myself. But whenever Dad's drunkenness or Mom's prejudices threatened me, I gave my arm a pinch. That sharp little pain focused my thinking on the sore arm, not on the miseries of my life. It was my pain-control method. Every drunken spell of Dad's added a new bruise." Suddenly I remembered kids I had taught who had metal dangling from the ends of their tongues or from their nostrils. "Do you think that why kids today pierce themselves?"

Miriam tightened her lips. "There are many factors affecting today's kids. But we're together today to think of your story."

So I replayed a childhood memory for Miriam.

Pinched

I was eleven, and it was May and the sun splashed in my windows. I pulled on a sundress, forgetting I needed a garment with long sleeves to hide my pinch marks. A serious practitioner of jump rope, I hopped all the way down the circular stairway and landed in our breakfast room with a giant leap.

Mom, as usual, was handing bites of buttered toast and jam to Dad while he studied the L.A. Times. Mom dropped his bite of toast and rushed to my side. "Sister! Your arms!" I was always Sister, never Martha, at home.

"Oh, it's okay. I fell." I didn't like the fear in Mom's eyes.

"It doesn't look like you fell. Has Ben been tormenting you?"

Ben, in beige corduroy trousers and a crisp white shirt, looked up from the comic papers. "She pinches herself," he announced.

"I do not. I fell from the swing. On my arms."

Aunt Atty arrived and came to my side. "Little Sister, I want you to look me in the eyes and tell the truth of what happened to your arms."

"Nothing. I fell." I couldn't look her in the eyes. Everyone believed Ben. I wished I could hide under the bed like Rosalie my cat did when Ben teased her.

Daddy, alternating sips of coffee with puffs of cigarette, looked glum. "We tell the truth in this household," he thundered. I wasn't his Miss Sunshine or Little Sweetheart, today. Clearly, pinching self was bad, like spilling soup and skinning knees. But I couldn't bear the humiliation of confessing it.

Mother admonished me. "Don't frown. You'll have wrinkles when you grow up." I tried to relax my forehead.

Aunt Atty suggested, "Albene, rub Vaseline on her arms. Maybe that will help."

"Leave me alone, all of you." I sobbed. I hated the disapproval that hovered over the breakfast table like cigarette smoke. I tried to hold my head up as I left the room. "I'll get even with you, tattle-tale," I whispered to Ben as I retreated to my bedroom.

"Just change your dress," he hissed my way.

I did, and soon, immersed in the vital world of my classroom, my morning's humiliation drifted away. Walking home, however, I stopped to stare into a large mud puddle in a vacant lot. I wondered if there was another world inside the blue reflection of the sky in the water. Suddenly, I leaped into the puddle, hoping the reflection would lead to another world, as it did for Alice when she jumped into the Looking Glass. Muddy water splattered my clothes but no secret gate opened. Of course, there was no other wonderful world. You had to live in this one, unless you died.

Frustrated, I yanked tall weeds from the vacant lot. They had clods of dirt clinging to their roots and when I hurled them at the house on the next lot, they stuck to the walls. I threw until my arm ached and then sauntered home. Dad and Mom were waiting on the veranda. Why wasn't Daddy at work?

"Why are you late? Did the teacher keep you after school? What happened?" Mother wrung her hands and her wrinkles pulled her face together like a drawstring purse.

I shrugged. "Nothing happened. Don't know why I'm late."

"And your shoes! They're muddy. And your dress, too. Quick, go change. We're late."

"For what?" I asked.

I looked at Dad, my supreme judge leaning over the balcony railing, smoking and staring into the garden. He noticed my glance. "We leave in fifteen minutes." He pulled his gold watch out of its tiny pocket. "And when I say leave, I mean the wheels will be turning in fifteen minutes. Get ready."

How could I dress in fifteen minutes when I couldn't even undo the double knots on my shoestrings? I wriggled my feet free without untying, and forced them into my Mary Joseph, my only other shoes. I changed my mud-spattered dress. No time to wash. Slid down the banisters. Ran for the garage. Dad at the wheel, Mom waiting. The motor running. The wheels hadn't turned yet. I'd made it in time—for what?

Dad backed the car out. Together, Mom and I pushed down on the garage door. It slammed shut. Mom climbed in the front seat. I climbed in back. I decided to sleep. If someone drags you off somewhere and you don't know where or why, the best thing to do is curl up and sleep. I shut my eyes. My body told me we were driving downtown.

I heard Mom's voice. "We're taking you to Dr. Pyna." Oh—just to a doctor, not to an execution. Maybe to get a shot. I didn't mind. Dr. Pyna was on my side. I'd be like her when I grew up, a spinster, in a black serge suit, healing people. I dozed until we reached the cottage where Dr. Pyna lived and practiced medicine. Dad led us into a sitting room filled with waiting patients. A nurse ushered us past the crowd and into the examining room.

I delighted in this room. A full skeleton dangled from the ceiling. Flasks filled with various colored potions and a mortar and pestle for grinding medicines waited on a marble counter. A huge leather table was waiting for a patient to climb up a three-step ladder and lie down. Dr. Pyna, with a *pince nez* and wearing a white coat over her suit, strode in and sat down. She gestured to four folding chairs set up in a corner. "Sit down, sit down, family. How are you today, Martha?" she asked kindly. She always called me by my name instead of Sister. She once told me she thought it important to use names, not relationships, when talking.

"Fine thank you, Dr. Pyna." I answered as politely as I could. "I'm not sick," I added.

"I'm sure you're not." She smiled.

"So what seems to be the problem?" She directed the question to my mother.

"I'm just worried about Sister. Show Doctor your arms," she directed.

I flushed with embarrassment but nevertheless pushed back my sleeves and held out my arms.

Dr. Pyna studied my bruises through her *pince nez*. "No rash, no disease. She's a healthy young woman." She paused and added, "Perhaps she's been in a fight."

Dad and Mother stared at each other until Dad finally announced, "She's been pinching herself."

Mother added, "She always has her nose in a book. She hides. She's too nervous."

Now I wanted to die. Jumping in a mud puddle wasn't enough. I should dive in the ocean and drown. Mother had burned "too nervous" on my forehead like branding a calf. I was unacceptable and I knew it.

"Well, well." Dr. Pyna drew a deep breath. "Please, Parents, look at you. "With a mother like you, Albene, and a father like Ben, there's very little chance of your raising a calm child. I think she copes very well. There's nothing wrong with escaping in books. Martha, will you promise not to pinch your arms again?"

"I'll try," I said, not wanting to give up my pain management system.

"If there's nothing else you need right now, I have some very sick babies waiting for me." We all stood up. She spoke directly to my father, "If you want a calmer Martha, make the home calmer." She strode from the room.

Dad stormed all the way home and headed to the kitchen for his cocktail shaker. Mom and I pulled down the garage door and she chased after Dad.

"Mom, wait," I yelled. I wanted her to tell me it was okay if I was too nervous, but she didn't stop running. Dad shouted, "Dr. Pyna is a quack! Never trust a female doc, I say."

Mom shouted back, "You can't talk that way about her. Remember how she helped us with my miscarriages. Four miscarriages. Why, we wouldn't even have Martha if it weren't for Dr. Pyna. She…"

It was my fault they were fighting. Dad would drink a lot tonight because I pinched my arms. I ran to my bedroom as fast as I could and pulled a quilt over my head. I wished I were dead.

My long hidden fountain of anger shook Miriam's office and gave me the courage to speak. I spoke to Mother in her empty chair. "Mom, if you're listening, I wanted your attention, not a doctor's. You treated me like a broken machine that needed repairs. But it was my heart that was broken. I didn't understand that I couldn't change alcoholic behavior. I felt so guilty when Dad got drunk. And all you said was, 'Sister is too nervous.' Why didn't you protect me from Dad?"

I stood up. I wanted to get the heck out of the office and go far away from that stuff. Miriam held up her hand to stop me. "Wait, Martha. Concentrate on the words 'Dr. Pyna said.' She told your father the truth, despite the risk of alienating a wealthy customer during the Depression. She wanted you to take those words to heart. She said you coped very well under the circumstances and I agree. You did. And you've grown up to be a lovely, charming woman," she added.

"Thank you, Miriam," I said aloud, as you should when complimented. But inside I thought, *she's paid to say nice things to me. She doesn't really believe them.*

And yet, maybe I did cope pretty well as a kid. I'd never had that perspective on my life before. And perhaps—just perhaps—I had moments of charm. "Thanks," I repeated, and practically ran from the office. Good stuff is often harder to hear than bad. The therapist officially declared me to be a charming lady. I'd better buy a latte and celebrate freedom from hurtful childhood memories.

PART II

Jennifer's Story

CHAPTER 13

A Scream Hung Over the Canyon

A scream hung over the canyon where coyotes and snakes had not yet crept out of their dens and into the morning light. The English-style cottage, surrounded by dichondra lawns dotted with Johnny-Jump-ups and orange and avocado trees, appeared tranquil. Did the children living there and the father, Hal, the entrepreneurial engineer, and his wife Martha, the devoted mother, remember how, at midnight the week before, a coyote climbed the wire enclosure to the pets' area and broke the neck of the duck who usually ate the garden snails? Hal buried the duck in the dark of night, for why should he worry Joseph, four, Geoff, nine, and Julie, eleven years old, and the baby? Even the youngest, Jennifer, with her blue eyes and pixie ears, who followed conversations with interest, might feel the death of the duck. Who knows?

Hal joked, "I feel like the family undertaker. I buried a baby rabbit last week, too."

"Just so we don't worry the children." I murmured as he shoveled soil on the plastic-wrapped body of the duck. Society or a clever journalist had labeled the sixties children "baby boomers" and we knew they needed to be reared with optimism and a sense of adventure. These children, our children, would save the world; they were clever and bright and charming.

A month ago, at dawn, a rattlesnake slithered out of the canyon and lay on the cement floor of our patio. Probably looking for water, poor thing. The children lay safe in their beds, so I wasn't frightened. I gathered stones and leaning over the cold iron banister, pegged them at the serpent from the stairs leading downward. It slithered away. Perhaps he only wanted to lie in the patch of early dawn sunlight while the canyon still lay in the dark. I would warn Julie and Geoff never to go in the canyon without boots, in case they might step on a snake, but I didn't want to frighten them. They had to grow up courageous and optimistic.

But did the children hear the scream rising over the canyon and catching in the tangled chaparral that smelled of sage and pine and wild lilac? The scream spread out over our town, Pacific Palisades, and west to the ocean. It lay in the swell of gray breakers and in the swirl of the fog. I placed my hands around my throat. It vibrated. From the crib, I lifted the tiny bundle of my baby, larger than the baby rabbit, smaller than the duck, laid her next to my breast. Jennifer did not move. The scream that rose over the canyon was mine.

I pulled the pink knit blanket from Jennifer's face. Miniature blue eyelids covered the sparkling elfin eyes. Milk trickled down my chest. Jennifer didn't move. The screaming that hung the canyon grew louder. Joseph, three, sat up in his bed, looking frightened. "Baby," he said.

I held her against my breast with my right arm. I did not feel her breathing. Dr. Russell will save her, I thought. My car waited on the long curved driveway. I slammed the transmission into reverse; rammed the car into wooden front gate. Drove forward.

"Goodbye, Mom, goodbye Mom," called the children. Julie, Geoff, and Joseph, all in pajamas, stood on the dichondra lawn, waving. I sped through the sleeping town, steering with my left hand, clutched Jennifer to my breast with my right hand.

The Chautauqua Canyon screams followed me into Dr. Russell's office and filled the waiting room. The doctor and nurse ran toward me. I hugged my baby to my breast with both arms.

Doctor Russell commanded, "Give me the baby, Martha." With strong physician's hands, he pried my fingers loose and wrenched my little girl from my arms. "Find Martha something to wear and take care of her," he instructed the nurse.

She pushed my arms into a hospital gown. "Hush, hush, stop screaming," she crooned. Was the scream I heard for all living things in Chautauqua Canyon really my own voice? I traced a finger down a trail of milk tears on my body. The straps on my pale blue negligee had broken and my breasts kept gushing milk. Weird. The nurse buttoned up the gown and led me to a cubicle designed for children.

A rag doll with blue eyes and pixie hair lay on the examining table. She wasn't Jennifer. The TV screen of my mind unplugged, the screaming faded. A warmed blanket cradled my body. Dr. Russell's face hovered over me like a pinkish balloon. "Mother, you should have called an ambulance, not driven here."

My lips felt stiff. My throat ached. I forced words from my mouth. "Did she die while I was driving here?"

"She died around 12:30 a.m., so this time it didn't make any difference. But another time."

How could there be another time when Jennifer was dead?

"The police will be talking to you. This type of death is known as a crib death. I have told the police you are a conscientious mother, but they need to investigate anyway."

I nodded my head. Of course, investigate. When a baby dies, it's the mother's fault. Jennifer was dead and I was dead too. Yet milk flowed from my body. That proved technically I was alive. Only my spirit had died.

"With your consent, we can hold an autopsy, and perhaps find the cause of her death."

I nodded agreement again.

"Where is your husband?"

"On a business trip." Cold was spreading through my whole body. My lips were frozen shut. Warmed by the blanket, I fell into a trance. If I pinched myself, it wouldn't be to control pain. It would be to make certain that I was a loving mom who lived with her engineer husband, four charming children, Julie, Geoff, Joseph and Jennifer. For an instant, Joseph's tortured eyes and baby voice whispering "Baby" appeared on my mental screen and then disappeared.

❦

Our charming children didn't live in a shoe. They lived with Hal and me in an English style cottage equipped with half-hip roofs and a chimney large enough for Santa Claus. Pet ducks, rabbits, and cats lived there too. And in the canyon lived coyotes and opossums and snakes and wild rabbits that sometimes came to the garden at night. You could see their eyes gleam and hear wild cries. But in the daylight, children flocked to the acre of land fertile with fruit trees, roses and rhubarb. They chased and they laughed and they hung by their knees in the trees. The peeked at my baby and patted my cats. My duck quacked.

Welcome to the neighborhood children. Welcome to all the neighborhood moms and dads who filled the patio that hung on the cliff over the valley. Friends and neighbors gathered to eat Hal's favorite dish, Armenian shish kabob. They laughed and sang and told each other jokes. Hal and I felt inflated: lucky, successful, popular. But a scream waited above the canyon.

"...and we make good children," Hal said. "Honey, I'd like to have enough children to form our own baseball team."

"I'd love a big family, too. But listen here, Hal. I'm not going to produce another Sarkissian heir unless you help take care of it! I don't want so many kids I can't be a good mother"

He stuck out his hand. "I promise, if you have another baby, I'll help take care of it. Shake." Solemnly, we shook hands. We never doubted our ability to conceive. A month later, I was pregnant with our third child and Hal bragged, "I only have to walk through the room and a baby's on the way."

Dr. Linee, our gynecologist, announced, "I'll induce the baby December 30[t.h] so you get a tax deduction." This seemed modern and hip.

After nine months of pregnancy, I walked into the hospital, lay down on a table and a nurse stuck a needle in my arm. I lay there calmly waiting for the miracle baby when wham! No warming-up pains. No bones loosening. Just wham slam! An onslaught of agony. A few whiffs of ether. And then a beautiful baby boy, Joseph Hunter Sarkissian, long lashes and red curly hair, lay on my stomach, December 30, 1957. Hal kept his promise to help and developed a knack of easing colic pains by rubbing Joseph's back. Nearly every evening, Joseph lay across Hal's lap while he watched sports on TV and Joseph's body relaxed.

Hal and I easily decided that since Julie and Geoff were a pair, Joseph and a new baby would make another pair. Jennifer's birth two years later in 1959 completed our happiness—we had our family. Julie and Geoff shared a room down stairs divided by bookcases. We would separate them by sex when they were older. Joseph loved his baby sister, and enjoyed peeking through the crib rails at her, especially after she learned to smile at him.

Hal and I slept upstairs in the master bedroom. Hal had extra sensitive hearing and nudged me awake whenever he heard the kids. Julie, an extremely responsible child, always called us when we were needed.

October 30, 1959, seemed like any other evening, except that Hal was out of town on a business trip. I kept Jennifer with me after the other children went to bed. I wanted her all to myself, with no siblings claiming her giggles. I put the squirming baby to my breast. She pursed her rosebud lips and made a smacking sound. Her starfish fingers touched my breast. Her eyes adored me. Jennifer was one more example of what Hal and I considered our success in life.

I let her sleep on my breast until 11:30. Then I slipped her into the crib in the room she shared with Joseph and watched her until she fell asleep.

A pat on my hand from Dr. Russell brought me out of my trance. I saw a pinkish balloon of a face and heard his voice. "I asked the nurse to call your friend, Gloria to help you out. She's here and has brought you clothes, and she'll drive you home."

Gloria's balloon face with bright blue eyes floated in front of me. "Don't worry about Julie, Geoff, and Joseph. They are safe and sound with my husband, Clovis. Julie came and got me this morning. Your daughter uses her head."

I stared numbly at the balloon face.

"Come on, Chicken, stand up and let me slip this robe on you."

The doctor whispered, "She's in shock."

Gloria chattered as if silence would intensify my grief. "Your children are eating pancakes with Clovis and the kids. I phoned Hal. Clovis will pick him up at the airport this evening. I called your mother. She's on her way to get the children." Of course, my mother would take care of them because I had proven myself a bad mother. But oh, how I needed to feel the warmth of their childish bodies next to mine.

"Come on, Chicken." Gloria tugged on my frozen body. I moved it for her. Step. Step. Step. I'd have to move a frozen body from now on. Gloria gave me a big hug before she helped me in her car but I couldn't respond to her love. "Wait till Hal gets home. You'll feel better then," Gloria promised.

I roused from my stupor when she drove me to her beauty parlor for a hair styling.

"I don't give a damn how I look, "I muttered. But Gloria rambled on "Hal is coming home tonight. You need to be beautiful for him." I sat and baked under the hair dryer. The heat didn't warm me.

"Look in the mirror. Now, don't you like the way I've fixed it?" I stayed silent. They style hair and rouge your lips to put you in a coffin, too. I was spirit-dead.

At home, Gloria clothed me in my most elegant dress, green velvet and lace cuffs, and planted me on our white vinyl living room couch. I interrupted Gloria's quiet weeping. "Why did you dress me up, Gloria?"

"Hal will be here soon. You want to look lovely for him. And your mother and Ben are coming tonight. Others will probably drop in, too. Don't you want to look pretty for them?"

I shook my head and my new hair-do tumbled over my face. "Hell no. Don't you get it? This isn't a party. Jennifer died."

"I know, Chicken, I know." She massaged my back and between firm strokes of her hands got out the words, "Everyone's bringing food and love. You'll be glad to see them. Just close your eyes and wait."

I closed my eyes. Time had no meaning for me. Like a manikin, coiffed, encased in velvet, I posed motionless on the slippery sofa. My fingers wanted to tear out my hair and rip my skin but they were frozen.

Finally, I felt a familiar hand on my shoulder and smelled Old Spice after-shave lotion blended with a tang of copper wire. Hal had come home.

He sat down beside me and gently drew me toward him. "I'm sorry I wasn't here with you. Now I'm scared to touch you. I'm afraid you'll break."

I reached my hand toward him. He held it and kissed it. We both broke into sobs. How long we held hands and wept together I do not know. Then tired beyond anything I'd ever experienced, I closed my eyes again.

When I opened them, I didn't see a vista of the living room, but scraps of its green wall shimmered in a mosaic with fragments of people, an eye, a hand, a leg. When I shook my head, the kaleidoscope changed. Lights flashed in my peripheral vision and patches of wall glowed. People had fuzzy luminous outlines. I reached out my hand to feel Hal, but he wasn't beside me. I shook my head again. The kaleidoscope became a dark blackboard. I listened. Sounds of the front door opening and closing. Chatter like a flock of birds. Footsteps fast and slow. Talking balloons floated over to the couch. One balloon had slick black hair on top—the T.V. personage Ben Hunter, my brother, who saved my wedding night. Ben, Ben, rescue me now.

He handed me a shot glass of Scotch. My numb hand held it steady. "Sis, this is tough. Sometimes life reaches out and bashes you, bam! Right in the solar plexus. When my son Chris went deaf—bam! There's only one thing to do. Take a drink. It helps, Sissy." I had turned to him for living water, but my beloved brother had only a dry well. There was nothing there.

"I can't drink it, Ben," I said.

He sat down beside me and wrapped his arm around me. The warmth and feel of him was comforting "Come on, Sissy, take a little sip. You have to live."

"But I don't want to live, Ben."

"I know, Sissy, I know. But try a sip…."

The doorbell chimed. More balloons bobbed in bearing gifts of food and unwanted advice. Virginia, my childhood friend and wife of James Arness of *Gunsmoke,* floated above me.

"Why did you want another child anyway? Three is more than enough." Her words smashed our childhood friendship. I doubled over with pain and closed my eyes. All things end. I longed to be in a dark and silent place. Should I go to bed or to a grave?

A mellow voice broke into my silence. "The Lord giveth and the Lord taketh away" I opened my eyes. A licorice black balloon face bobbed in front of me. Dark eyes in circles outlined in red, stared at me.

"You're right. Your God sure taketh away." Ida, my cleaning woman, gathered my cold body in her arms. For a moment, I thought about her instead of myself. "I bet Him taketh a lot away from you."

"I got love left," Ida said. I nestled my head on her shoulder and patted her on the back. Our tears mingled.

Then Gram's face appeared as a wrinkled balloon losing air. "I'm taking the children home with me for a week Try to remember Hal needs you. Your children need you. Do you hear me, Martha?"

I made an effort to answer "Yes. Okay. Mom."

She's taking the children away because she thinks I can't take care of them—but I can. I will. I shook my head to change the kaleidoscope. Everyone disappeared. The house grew silent. Dust settled on the philodendron. I hadn't taken good care of it. Soon it would die, too. Like Jennifer.

❧

When I finished my story, Miriam spoke softly. "Are you saying you blame yourself for her death?"

I gouged the cuticles of my fingernails. "Of course I do. Instead of flowers for Jennifer's memorial, we requested money for research on crib deaths. We learned that smoking mothers have a higher incidence of crib deaths than nonsmokers. I smoked a lot."

Miriam raised her arms in a helpless gesture. "We all smoked then. We didn't know any better. It frightens me to remember. However, that connection has not been fully proven, Martha."

"I know. They've discovered that crib deaths are connected to heart problems in a baby and that infants should be placed on their backs to sleep. I laid Jennifer on her stomach. She had a little cold too. The coroner said she might have had a fast-acting virus. Maybe if we'd seen the doctor, maybe if I hadn't slept so soundly, I could have saved her. Oh, Miriam, one way or another, I caused her death."

"I hope you understand by now that that you have a type of compounded guilt. Your emotions around the death of your father have made you vulnerable to guilt feelings. Losing a baby is a major trauma for any woman, and sometimes others do not recognize that. Did you receive any medication for depression?"

"No. People didn't think of medications for depression then."

"Did anyone give you emotional support?"

"None of my family or friends did. This was the first time Hal didn't have the strength himself to rescue me."

"Do you still blame yourself?" she asked.

"I think I always will."

"We'll see. We're not finished yet."

Her optimism seeped into me. "There's a lot more I want to tell you about her death." I traveled at the speed of light to the far country of the past. Or had I had never really left it?

CHAPTER 14

God in the Rose Trellis

I was seated between Ben and Hal, the only mourners at a funeral chapel in Santa Monica. Light filtered through a stained glass window and lit up a tiny casket covered with a blanket of Cecile Brunner roses. I sobbed uncontrollably. Ben took nips from a hip flask to steady himself. Hal whispered in my ear, "Don't lean too hard on me, Martha, because I'm leaning on you."

I sunk into feelings of abandonment. If I couldn't lean on Hal, who would support me? Not Gram, who was "keeping the children," and not my brother John, who never contacted me after Jennifer's death. I'd have welcomed Aunt Lucy with her plentiful tears, but the drive from Fresno had become too hard for my relatives. Aunt Atty had become unreachable by phone. Gloria needed special permission from a priest to attend a Protestant service. She didn't show up.

Almost everyone abandoned me. Maybe they hated me for letting Jennifer die, or maybe they hated church stuff. But Hal came, and Ben, too, though they didn't believe in "empty rituals." Or perhaps Mom, Aunt Atty, and John plain didn't love me. But Ben did, and I didn't mind that he took nips of whiskey during the service. His arm steadied me.

A Lutheran lady, her hair tucked in a bun, struck a chord on a small organ on the left side of the room. Pastor Schweiss, in a blue serge suit and bow tie, walked in and stood beside the rose covered casket. I saw tears falling as he read aloud a note. "This blanket of Cecile Brunner roses is from the children of the Methodist Cooperative Pre-School. We respect your 'no flowers' request, but the children wanted to send them for Joseph's baby sister."

Each tiny rose was as perfect as my Jennifer. I breathed in their perfume and their promise of hope. The only other words I remember were from a verse

Jacque Schweiss read, "But women will be saved through childbearing..." from I Timothy 3:8.

I was sleeping when Jennifer was dying and that condemned me. But this thin muscular man in a blue serge suit proclaimed that since I'd borne five children, I'd be saved. Saved from what? From the crushing rocks of guilt I carried?

Hal thanked Pastor Schweiss and offered him an envelope of money. Jacque passed it back. "I don't take money for conducting a memorial service."

The next day, Hal and I took our three children to a resort on Catalina Island. When we returned home, life was supposed to "go back to normal," but I felt my mourning would never end.

Two weeks later, I awoke at midnight, curiously alert and energetic. Some inner prompting urged me to go to the garden. Perhaps a coyote had breached the fence where the rabbits and duck slept. Perhaps I'd left a hose running. Hal, ordinarily the family insomniac, slept quietly beside me. Careful not to awaken him, I slipped out of the bed covers and tiptoed down the stairs. I peered into the children's bedrooms. Healthy children, sleeping sweetly. I turned the knob on our heavy front door, careful to prevent its squeaking.

I came to the garden alone. It slept peacefully in the moonlight. A fragrance stronger than the night blooming jasmine or the orange blossoms hung in the air. Cecile Brunner roses had covered Jennifer's casket, but they didn't grow in my garden, and my six ordinary rose bushes near the gate weren't in bloom. It was November. And yet...and yet the tender scent of the Cecile Brunner rose engulfed the garden.

Could the straggly climbing rose on a trellis against the neighbor's fence be blooming now with a rare perfume? I breathed deeply of the scent. I'd look at the trellis anyway.

I walked barefooted across the dichondra lawn to the trellis. Two ragged white roses bloomed there, defying winter. The branches of the orange trees cried and their leaves whispered of the evening mist.

I fell to my knees overcome by the awesome mystery of nature. I didn't know how to believe or how to pray. But from an instinct long buried in my unconscious, words flowed into the night. "God, if there is a God, let me see you. I am a dead person already and I want to die. But God, if there is a God,

give me life so I can take care of my husband and my children and our little creatures, our rabbits, our ducks, the cats." All at once, I recalled the words from
the memorial, "God, if there is a God, I want to be *saved.*"

I raised my eyes to the trellis with its spare winter blossoms. A fluorescent
figure appeared in the midst of the rose branches. A Holy Being held out arms
toward me, the Holy Being shared my grief. The rose perfume became a sacred
incense.

A hand touched me and the warmth of the touch spread through my body.
Leaves from the orange tree loosened their hold on the branches and fluttered
to the ground. I clutched them to my heart. They proved the night was real.
Mud oozed through my toes and I rejoiced in the earth.

Transfixed, I knelt there until the light of dawn pierced me and I awoke
from my trance. I ran to the house. Inside, the children slept soundly. My
husband roused as I crept into the bedroom. "Martha, what've you been
doing?"

I had to protect my vision—a few words from Hal would rip it to pieces—
so I hid it in a deep place in my mind. "I've been walking in the garden."

He opened a reluctant eye. "For gosh sakes, Martha, you're cold and muddy.
Wash up and come to bed." Annoyed with the righteous anger of an awakened
insomniac, he turned away from me and buried his head in a pillow.

I wanted to kiss him. I wanted to wake up the children and have a party. I'd
say, "I saw God tonight. He was in the rose trellis. He grieved for our loss." And
they'd say, "Mom, you're crazy." Maybe I was. So I washed my feet and went to
bed. I'd tell the family in the morning.

When the sun catapulted us into Monday, the day's momentum carried me
away from my vision. Hal, in a white shirt with gold slide-rule cuff links, deftly
dodged my sticky waffle embrace and ruffled my hair. "Clean shirt, Kiddo. I'm
meeting with the president of National Cash Register this morning."

I ran to the bathroom and peered in the mirror. Syrup and cocoa and tears
smeared my face. Coffee stains degraded my velvet bathrobe. No wonder he
didn't want my goodbye hug.

Julie and Geoff grabbed their sack lunches and slammed the front door in
a way that said, "Out of here! Whew! School's better than watching Mom cry."

Good! That meant they were survivors. Even Joseph giggled with joy when
I carried him out to the carpool for preschool. I kissed his reddish-brown curls
and tucked him in the back seat next to his best friend, Stephan. Joseph raised
his arm to wave goodbye. As the car backed down the drive, his small arm in
a rust-brown T-shirt moved to and fro, to and fro. Goodbye, Joseph, goodbye.

A house accustomed to children, feels very empty when they have gone to
school or died. I sat alone at the kidney-shaped table my husband designed for
a family of six. I sipped tepid coffee, lit a cigarette and stared at a saucer grimy
with wet cigarette butts. The waves of the nearby Pacific sounded a death knell.
Trees in the canyon moaned. Can a house weep?

Images collided in my mind and shattered. Jennifer's giggle, her hold on my
finger, her smile, I had lost them. But even harder to bear, I'd lost her future;
her first painting of a rainbow, her first poem printed in crayon letters. And
still worse, I'd lost the babies she would never bear. I must live forever without
Jennifer.

Did I want to live? Solitude gave me permission to kill myself. Nobody said,
"Kiddo, hang on." Nobody said, "Mommy, we love you." Instead, voices inside
my head accused me of letting Jennifer die. Her death, like an earthquake,
opened a fissure in my world. I was tumbling down inside it. Solitude terrified me. I stubbed out one cigarette in the saucer and lit another. Could my
vision stop this downward spiral? Either I was crazy or it was real. I had to talk
to somebody, but who? Anybody at all would be better than nobody. Time for
another smoke. I jammed my hand in my purse for a smoke, but it closed on a
sketch of a church, an address, and the Reverend Jacque Schweiss' phone number. The kids liked his Vacation Bible School, and I liked his words when he told
me, "Whether or not you believe in God, you need a special place and time to
honor Jennifer's life." He'd refused money for her memorial. I could trust him.
He'd tell me the truth about my vision. I reached for the phone.

Fifteen minutes later, our doorbell chimed. Reverend Jacque Schweiss, blue
eyes, wheat hair and gold-rimmed glasses, stood on my doorstep. "My wife
couldn't come with me today, but she wants me to give you this loaf." He handed
me an unwrapped loaf of bread, warm and comforting in my hands.

"Thank you," I muttered.

"She's really sorry she couldn't come today."

"Why should she? I don't even know her."

He dismissed my question with a shrug. "She wanted me to give you this bread and tell you she grieves the loss of Jennifer with you."

Was this figure of a reverend in a green polo shirt and jeans something my loneliness conjured up? The bread smelled real enough. "Would you like to come in for a cup of coffee?" I asked.

Sharing a fresh pot of coffee with a minister was a new experience for me. Suddenly, I felt hungry and bit into the crusty bread. Ah, it was a better sedative than even the cigarettes. My tears dried up. A sense of aliveness I hadn't known since Jennifer died filled my body.

"Am I supposed to call you reverend or pastor?" I asked.

"Most of my parishioners call me Jacque, but if you prefer, use pastor."

"Jacque seems easier to me."

"Good. I don't want to hide behind a title. Ten years before I became a minister, I was an electronics engineer and I enjoyed that life, too."

"An electronics engineer? That's what my husband is, too."

"I'll look forward to meeting him."

With my tears on hold and bread in my stomach, I felt ready to talk. "In a way, he's all science and math. Both of us—we've never believed in God."

"I understand. You can't prove God with an equation."

"So it's too hard to talk with him about this. But last night, I had a vision."

He stirred his coffee, and then looked directly at me. "I believe you told me that on phone."

"I know I did. But I don't know what to make of it myself. I don't believe in visions or any other paranormal stuff, angels, spirits speaking and so on. I know mentally ill people experience hallucinations. Maybe I've gone nuts. I saw a ghostly figure in the rose trellis and it touched me. Does that mean I'm crazy, or what?"

"Had you been drinking when you saw this vision?" Jacque inquired in a matter-of-fact voice.

"No." My cheeks smarted with embarrassment. Probably he could smell whiskey from the dirty glasses that still lay around the house. "My brother Ben brought some alcohol, but I didn't drink it. Do Lutherans believe alcohol is sinful?"

"No. But let's stay on the topic of Martha, not Lutherans. Had you gone days without sleep or food?" he continued.

"No."

"Had you used any medicines or drugs?"

"No. Why are you grilling me? Are you some kind of church police?"

A belly laugh rolled out of his mouth. "No, no, Martha. I'm asking these questions to see if your vision was authentic or caused by alcohol or medication. The most important question is *How did the vision affect you?* Did it make your life better or worse?"

"Better, I think..." I tried to grasp my own feelings. "I had a sense of peace this morning, even made waffles and got the kids off to school...felt clean and energetic. But seeing an angel or God or whatever I saw in the rose trellis is pretty kooky."

"Martha, I can assure you, you're not crazy. You asked God to help you so He sent you a vision to comfort you. But it's hard for you to trust God. That's ok, too, He understands." He smiled and added, "May I change the topic a little?" I nodded yes. "Tell me how have you been feeling since the memorial service?"

Something about his presence—his voice, his caring, the sky-blue of his eyes—overcame my shame and fear. I trusted him. I pressed my hands in front of my mouth to whisper, "The truth is, I really want to kill myself."

He spoke in a matter-of-fact, how do you fry eggs voice. "So how would you take your life, if you were going to?"

"Phenobarbital. My husband takes it for his high blood pressure. I'd swallow a hundred or so, put a plastic sack over my face and go to sleep forever."

"So what prevents you from taking your life?"

"Hal and the children. I don't want to hurt them."

"You have chosen life and you and your children will be blessed. Listen to God speak in this Bible verse, "...I have set before you ...life and death. Now choose life, so that you and your children may live...and be blessed."

"But what kind of a mother am I who can't even keep her baby alive?"

For a few moments, he rested his chin on his hands. "Martha, I see a very intelligent mother, one who is safe and well-grounded in life. You have already chosen life, but spiritually, you are still a child."

I nodded uncertainly.

"I'd guess it was the child in you who needed a vision. Do you mind if I sing to you the way I do for my children?" Jacque asked.

I nodded again. If he wanted to sing, let him sing.

He knelt on the floor to be eye level with me and warbled in a slightly off-key tenor:

"Come into my heart,

Come into my heart,

Come into my heart today,

Come in to stay,

Come into my heart, Lord Jesus."

I hid my face in my hands. Hal and I had promised each other to be humanistic and never fall for some phony religion. But these simple words and tune slipped through the cracks in my heart. I wiped away my tears and desperately told Pastor, "It sounds so beautiful, letting Jesus in. But don't you see, I can't leave Hal. I can't take a different path than he does. Hal and I are one."

He sighed deeply. "Oh, Martha, every soul is separate. And the path you're walking doesn't seem right for you. Do you mind if I pray aloud for you?"

I wasn't sure how to respond. I shrugged my shoulders. "You can, if you want." I braced myself to endure the embarrassment of Jacque's prayers. Maybe he'd pray about my smoking or the whiskey bottle on the sink.

He bowed his head, I studied his face. He looked like a medieval portrait of a saint. A golden glow surrounded his head. Could it be possible that medieval painters actually saw halos? Were halos real? Did one circle his head?

Saint or not, he prayed away. I listened while he thanked God for the Sarkissian's happy home and Jennifer's brief life. He ended, "And Lord Jesus, forgive Martha's sins and show her a new path in life. Amen."

Sin. An ugly word! I carried a long sack of guilt with me and I did need forgiveness for my many mistakes. I couldn't even think of that mean, narrow-minded word trumpeted in the witch trials: *sin*. I sure needed forgiveness for my greatest mistake. I closed my eyes and bowed my head and prayed silently. "Forgive me for not checking on my baby that night and letting her die. Forgive me for not stopping Dad from going out the night he died." I halted to ask a question out loud. "Pastor, do I need to ask your Jesus to forgive the stuff I did at college, or as a child?"

His eyes were still closed and he still glowed. "The Holy Spirit will bring to your mind what you can pray about. But remember, the forgiveness covers all your missteps, not just the ones you remember."

I plodded on in silent prayer. "Forgive me for making fun of the Christian girls in the dorm. Forgive me for smoking and drinking, especially after Gladys Kinney prayed that Jesus would save me from my father's sins of alcohol and tobacco." Now, prayer was ripping the scabs off my inner injuries. I didn't like this process. This was madness. We had to stop.

But I had already opened Pandora's Box. The hurts I caused as a child spread through my mind like a wildfire. "I'm sorry I bit my brother Ben when he threw my Oz book in the mud. Forgive me for making fun of Cecelia when she gave our teacher a bouquet of dried weeds, instead of florist's flowers. And Oh, Jesus, I called our maid, Fanny, 'nigger' for a quarter paid me by my brother--disgusting child I was—forgive that child." My mind wearied of counting failures, big and little, and finally shifted into a neutral place.

Jacque sensed this and ended my prayer with the words "As a minister of God and by the authority invested in me, I hereby declare to you the complete forgiveness of all your sins."

I lifted my head. The blue lips of my baby no longer accused me. Instead, the elfin blue-eyed Jennifer gazed into my eyes and smiled. Gawky freckle-faced Cecelia put her arm around my waist and we skipped off together, pals. Gladys Kinney raised her arms in thankful prayer for me. Fanny beamed at her beloved child, my twenty-five cent betrayal forgiven.

Forgiveness tasted like the first swallow of cool river water, smooth and warm, like a baby's body, and smelled as fragrant as star-shaped magnolia blossoms showering perfume. Forgiveness sounded like a choir in a cathedral and looked like a Jennifer loving gaze.

The Pastor added, "Jesus has forgiven you but now you have a harder task. You need to forgive yourself."

CHAPTER 15

A Heavenly Secret

*D*oorbell chimes and cheerful raps on the front door pulled Jacque and me from a prayer state of consciousness. A high tide of boys and laughter washed into the entrance hall. Our eleven-year-old son Geoff sang out, "I'm home from school and here are the pastor's kids and Patrick, too."

Jacque Schweiss beamed at the boys. "Martha, I'd like you to meet my sons, Paul and Jon. Shake hands, boys." Small replicas of Jacque detached themselves from the mass and solemnly shook hands, then returned to joyfully pummeling their pals.

Patrick's mother, Gloria, the special ingredient that changed our neighborhood into a community, pushed her way through the crowd. She held Joseph on one hip. "I had a lot of fun keeping Joseph. When he saw all the kids and his brother Geoff were here, there was no keeping him."

She slid Joseph to the floor and he ran to the center of the wave of boys. "As long as we're all here, how about a potluck tonight?"

I replied quickly, "I'll make spaghetti."

The pastor grinned widely. "I'll call my wife, Solve. She'll bring salad greens and bread and butter."

Gloria shone with satisfaction. "Now I know why I bought a pie from the Helms wagon this morning. I'll bring it to the potluck."

"What time does your husband get home?" the pastor inquired.

"It really varies. I'll phone and ask him to come home early. Is this the God thing working, Pastor?"

His blue eyes smiled. "I think it's the choosing life thing,"

The front door banged again. Our oldest child, Julie, twelve, burst in the room and tossed a giant load of schoolbooks on the coffee table. She stared at the boys through her horned rim glasses and sensed the spirit of celebration. "Is this a party, Mom?"

"We're planning a potluck dinner tonight. I better phone Dad so he gets home early."

I left them chattering to phone Hal from the kitchen. Joseph followed me and scrambled on my lap. I drew an intoxicating breath of toddler and hugged him. I hadn't had a cigarette all day because of the pastor, so I lit one. After two deep drags, I snubbed it out, afraid of dropping ashes on my youngest son. I dialed Hal's company.

Hal picked up the phone himself. "Martha, what's up? I'm in the middle of a conference."

"You've got to come home early. We're having a potluck dinner with Pastor Schweiss and his kids, and Gloria and Pat."

"Have you forgotten? I'm in conference with President Allan, head of National Cash Register. He may buy us out."

"But Hal, Pastor Schweiss is here and we want—"

"For God's sake, Martha, what's that minister doing in our house? Does he like your big blue eyes?" His voice had fallen at least an octave and he sounded like a stranger. "Tell me, how'd he sneak into our home?"

Sound dignified, I warned myself. "I invited him. Pastors don't sneak."

"So one of those Viking types appeals to you more than a stocky Armenian, huh?"

"I needed someone to talk to."

"You can talk to me later. I'll be home at ten or so. But I don't want that Elmer Gantry after your soul or your body. You're my best friend, remember?"

That familiar sense of guilt crept through my body, deadening me. I'd disappointed my best friend. Why hadn't I told him the vision? Now he was jealous. I'd broken my word, too, for we'd promised each other we'd never engage in religious ritual. Yet, I insisted on a memorial service for Jennifer. So much for my promises. And as Hal predicted, I was hooked by a minister greedy for my soul.

With Joseph by the hand, I trotted back into the living room wearing an understanding-wife mask. "I'm sorry, but the potluck's off. Hal is tied up at work. He has a very important conference with President Allan of National Cash Register."

No one seemed particularly bothered, except me. Pastor Schweiss spoke smoothly, "I'd like to practice a little baseball with your boys. What if we all go out in the yard and toss the ball around?"

The tide of boys, with Jon leading Joseph by the hand, ebbed from the house.

"I'm going to see what the girls are doing." Julie crossed the street to the Burton house and her girlfriends, Penny and Pammy.

"I'll go get the pie for us, Chick," Gloria said.

The Helms coconut cream pie had a stiff golden meringue that resembled a snow bank at Lake Arrowhead. The slush underneath consisted of custard stuffed with grated coconut. Gloria lifted a trembling slice on to my plate while a rivulet of purple mascara ran down her cheeks. Gloria and I would never be done weeping. "Chicken, don't feel bad about Hal. My Clovis works every night in Gus and Charles's bar and the family has to adjust to it. Hal loves you."

"I wanted a chance while the minister was here, to tell him what happened last night."

"Hal has important business now, Chicken."

"All he cares about is that hunk of metal and switches they named MADDIDA. What about me? I'm not even supposed to cry."

Gloria wiped her own eyes. "What do you mean? Moms have to cry; it's the nature of the beast."

"Hal asked me not to cry," I mumbled. Hal's mother had never stopped crying. She had watched the Turks kill her husband and throw their baby on a sword and she wept and wore black all her life. The least I could do for Hal was not cry.

"You can cry all you want with me. But Hal loves you and he's trying to make a living. Why don't you tell *me* what happened last night?"

"All right, I will. Gloria—I had a vision." Gloria was Catholic and more used to visions and angels than the typical Protestant. When I finished all the details, including a cracked voice edition of, "Come into my heart, Lord Jesus," we'd become sisters in Christ.

"Oh, Martha, I want to celebrate your conversion. It's so beautiful. I knew Catholics had big experiences finding God, but I never knew Protestants did."

I grumbled, "Don't rejoice too much. I feel damned asinine as a convert. Maybe I made the whole thing up. Too much stress. I started seeing things. Maybe this God-thing is imaginary."

Gloria wiped pastry crumbs off her lips. "It doesn't matter if you're making it up. God doesn't care a bit. He just loves you. So do me, Chicken." She wrapped her motherly arms around me and drew my head down on her bosom.

I nestled there and whispered, "Gloria, the vision is a secret. I told you and the pastor, but I haven't told Hal and the kids. Don't tell anyone."

"That's okay, Chickie. It's a heavenly secret from now on."

I planned to tell Hal about my vision, but time, the tyrant in our household, blocked the way. Mourning Jennifer, business stress, three children, two cats, and a rabbit family left few free hours for Hal and me to wrestle with our beliefs.

We sought emotional release in music. Hal built his own giant stereo system before they became commercial, and Mozart or Beethoven became our comfort after the children were in bed. Hal loaded a stack of records on the turntable and dimmed the lights. I pulled the drapes over the windows and shut out the moonlit treetops, the tart tang of chaparral and a coyote's howl. We left a chaotic world outside, and clung to each other on our Naugahyde couch like shipwrecked sailors.

As my interest in Christianity grew, I continued to keep my vision a secret from Hal and the children. I told him frankly, "I feel split in two. I want to be Humanistic like you, but I experienced God and I don't want to give that up. It makes Jennifer's life more important. Why are you so against churches?"

He rubbed his chin thoughtfully, reflecting before he spoke. "Martha, I'm not against churches per se. In high school, I went to a Catholic youth group. A lot of fun! But as an adult looking at the larger picture, I see religion as a source of prejudice and violence." He patted my knees with his engineer's hand to soften the words.

I straightened up. "Are you trying to say that historically churches are a problem? Actually, I agree with you there."

He drew a shuddering breath before he spoke. "Armenia is the oldest Christian country in the world. There were a hundred churches in my mother's village. All the village wealth went into churches instead of an army for protection. The people were unable to stand against the Turks."

"I know, Hal. The same thing happened to Jews. They couldn't stand against the Germans—hideous! Ethnic cleansing. But the real reason for the killing wasn't religion. It was economic greed. Armenians and Jews owned a lot of property that the Turks and the Germans were after. Do you have to blame churches?"

He tightened his jaw. A vein in his neck pulsed. "The ruling class probably had economic reasons, but they used religion to motivate the common man to kill. The Turks and Armenians both believed they had the only path to God. The Turks employed their religious fables to justify their slaughter of Armenians, just as Christians once used their fables to justify the Crusades." He pressed his right hand over his left and pushed his knuckles. They crackled. "My mother lost her faith in God when she saw her husband and children murdered and she was thrown into the Syrian Desert."

I lost a baby in her crib; my mother-in-law watched her baby thrown on a sword. I could scarcely bear the pain. I kissed his fingers and swollen knuckles. "What you say is true and terrible and I hate it. But we are living in twentieth century USA. We don't have ancient feuds like Europe and Asia."

He sighed. "You're too naïve, Martha. Those feelings persist here today." He shook his head to clear his mind. "Okay, forget ancient history. Growing up in Fresno, I saw too many hypocritical Christians. I don't want you to join their ranks."

"When have you ever seen a hypocritical Christian?"

A faraway tone came into his voice. "In Depression days, my parents worked night and day to make a living in Leon's Armenian Grocery Store. Sundays, after attending church, customers would stream into our market. From the age of seven on, my job was to follow the customers around the store. When someone slipped a pound of butter or a can of tomato paste in her purse, I ran and whispered to my mom at the checkout. Then she added the item to their bill. They paid. We never lost a customer that way but I formed a different idea of churchgoers than you have."

"Honey, I imagine those customers were really hungry." I pictured to myself the little boy Hal dressed in a hand-knit brown sweater, trailing a covey of stout shoppers around barrels of pickles and sacks of rice. His beautiful dark brown curls tumbled on his high forehead. His expressive eyes captured every movement of a shopper. Then I looked at my husband and hugged him and pressed kisses on his fringed eyelids. "That was awfully hard on you."

He grinned. "Well, if you really want to join the church, go ahead. But if you take the kids with you, don't turn them against me." The phonograph records on the turntable ended. He walked to the stereo and turned over the stack.

I called after him, "Hey, Darling, I couldn't turn them against you if I wanted to. They adore you. And I want your beliefs and attitudes for them, too. Can't you see, I don't know how to organize myself now…after…." He gently closed the phonograph lid and Mozart continued. I stood up. We gazed into each other's eyes.

"I'll go to social events at church with you and the kids but not to religious rites, if you'll promise you won't stop loving me."

"I couldn't stop loving you, no matter what." We shook hands on the contract. I promised myself I would never forget his words and I never have. I needed his disbelief just as he needed my belief, for an emotional earthquake had erased the boundaries between my reality and a spiritual reality, and only Hal stood in the gap.

Nested inside this winter of my life lay spring, reminding me of the wooden Russian doll containing one doll inside another who conceals still another doll. With Hal's and my new contract in place to protect our marriage, I felt free to explore Christianity. I read the Bible and brought all the troubling tales of warfare and murder in the Old Testament to Pastor Jacque who attempted to explain the mystical meanings behind ancient texts. Then I pulled off the outer doll of theology to find the god doll inside. Elated, I told Jacque, "I want to join your church now!"

"Wait until you are more comfortable with Christian belief," he counseled. But I was too anxious a person to wait, fearing my faith might die any second and too rebellious to follow advice; why should he decide when I go to church? I focused on dressing Christian. I bought a felt lady's hat with a fake rose and dug out of my bureau a pair of gloves to wear to my first-ever church service. I carried my right glove to hide its ink stains and wore the left. A middle-aged usher, with a walrus moustache, greeted me at the church door. Too self-conscious to speak, I nodded and wobbled my way in high heels to a front center pew. A large gold cross on the altar forced my attention. Why did a symbol of execution loom so large in Christian life? Should it be up-dated with an electric chair?

I squirmed on the hard wooden pew hoping for a vision, an inspiration, something mystical, anything besides my fierce inner questionings. Pastor's tutoring had given me a sense of God, but the sermon sounded trite and the congregation appeared to be prejudiced, narrow-minded, middle-class people I wanted to avoid. I was a free spirit, a Berkeley girl. Whatever was I doing here wearing a silly hat and gloves?

The grey-haired organist pressed pedals on the Spinet organ and the congregation rose and sang "Just as I am without one plea, except thy blood was shed for me...." By careful listening, I learned this Sunday was called Communion Sunday, and that Christians practiced a type of symbolic cannibalism by sipping representations of their leader's blood and flesh. How morbid! I didn't take communion. Instead, I sat alone in my pew, shivering while the troops marched by. The service ended at last. I was trotting by the time I reached the door where Pastor Jacque stretched out a long arm and snagged me. "Martha, what did you think of the service?"

"I may come to church again, but I'll never take communion. Cannibalism is abhorrent even if it's symbolic."

His eyes twinkled. "I'm glad you're thinking of the significance of the bread and wine. The great majority of Christians are quite unconscious of what they are doing."

"I don't like it, anyway."

"Martha, Martha, I told you not to come to church until you were ready. You just weren't prepared for communion."

138

"I sure wasn't. I think it's awful!" I glanced over my shoulder at the line piling up behind us. Everyone wanted to shake his hand, but he didn't hurry.

He smiled down and explained, "In time, you may realize that humans have a need for sacrifice to appease their guilt feelings. A symbolic sacrifice is preferable to real blood."

"I'll—er—think about it Pastor." The very term *Pastor* curled my toes. Was I a stupid sheep and he the shepherd? Ugh! Christianity was too patriarchal for my taste. And yet, there lodged in my psyche, like a burr in my stocking, the concept that a bit of bread and grape juice might free me from the guilt of my father's and my baby's deaths. That's what churches were for. The flavor of forgiveness lingered in my soul.

So, on Palm Sunday, April 1960, six months after Jennifer's death, I joined the Lutheran Church, communion and all. Hal made great personal sacrifices. He forced his sons into white shirts and ties, donned his hated itchy wool suit, and sat with us all in the front pew. With special permission from her parish priest to attend a Protestant church, a radiant Gloria joined our pew.

When Jacque called me forward, I climbed the short steps to the altar making sure to keep my focus on Hal. Our after-the-kids-were-in-bed talks paid off wonderfully. He beamed and held up his thumb in a victory signal. I smiled back. Gloria baptized our church with her tears. More mascara rivulets—this time from joy.

Then the pastor called the children to join me by the altar. "Julie, twelve, Geoff, ten, and Joseph, five, learned about Jesus in our Vacation Bible School. Their sister Jennifer's life has drawn them to the church. They are old enough to reason for themselves and have declared their desire to be part of the fellowship of Pacific Palisades Lutheran Church."

The children faced the congregation cheerfully and promised to serve God. Gently, one by one, Pastor dunked their heads in water and handed them embroidered souvenir towels. The kids appeared to enjoy the ritual, but I felt squeamish when it was my turn. Perhaps they weren't as worried as I was about being honest. Would swearing the vows make me a hypocrite? How much did I believe?

Yet, reading Jung from college onward convinced me that life requires us to construct a spiritual framework to live in the chaos of the world. I recited aloud the entire beautiful Nicene Creed: "I believe in one God, maker of heaven and earth and in Jesus Christ, his only son, our lord...." In my inner mind I prayed, "I believe, help thou my unbelief." If I didn't believe, life was a random crapshoot. Faith gave meaning to Jennifer's life.

The organist struck a chord, the children and I hurried back to our pew alongside Hal and Gloria. The choir and congregation rose to their feet singing, "Fling wide the portals of your heart, Make it a temple set apart."

After church, Jacque cautioned me, "Remember, Martha, joining a church doesn't protect you and your loved ones from danger. Tough times will come. The difference will be that you will be aware of the presence of God." In the spring of my faith, I didn't want to listen to his prophetic warning. I was in love with the idea of God.

CHAPTER 16

The Little Armenian Man

I was given the gift of a year with Pastor Schweiss tutoring me, and the Women's Bible Study group nurturing me. A joyful and enthusiastic new convert, I awakened each morning to a sense of being God's child, until one night in May. I was stirring spaghetti with a wooden spoon when I heard Hal's footsteps. I turned to greet him. "I'm glad you got home for dinner. I was just going to feed the kids and wait for you."

Julie and Geoff were waging a battle of words over which TV program to watch while Joseph struggled to pull the guide from their hands. Hal ordered, "Kids, be quiet! I've got some good news to tell you." The TV Guide fell to the floor.

Hal looked very much the National Cash Register businessman in his long sleeved French cuffed shirt and red power tie. This uniform irritated him as much as a girdle and stockings did me, but he needed to appear as a proper National Cash Register manager. His face registered triumph as he spoke. "National Cash Register is moving to Orange County and we're all going to live there!"

This message tolled like a funeral bell in my ears. "You're kidding, right?" I stirred the sauce so vigorously that red sauce-drops rained down on the white stovetop.

The kids said nothing. I plunked a platter in the center of our plastic table and stood by with a pot of spaghetti. Hal himself had designed this kidney-shaped furniture. If we moved, we'd never again have such a kitchen nook. It would become a flimsy memory. Hal slid into his spot on the bench. "No! I'm not kidding. National Cash Register wants to move our division to Orange

County. Today, I signed a deal for them to purchase a bean field from a farmer named Segerstrom. What an interesting guy. I'll tell you about him at dinner." Hal twirled the pasta around a serving fork and slipped a nest of spaghetti onto the platter with a flourish.

His news stunned me. "You should have told me sooner." I pulled a salad out of the refrigerator. The cool air fanned my feverish cheeks. Move! We couldn't move!

"I did tell you." Hal sniffed the basil appreciatively. "The problem is, you didn't listen."

"I always listen to you," I snapped back. Inside, I worried. Had I been so stuffed with heavenly notions that I hadn't paid attention to earthly needs? Or did the macho Armenian layer beneath Hal's westernized self take over so he forgot to consult me?

He waved his hand. "Come on; sit down so we can talk."

Slaps and ouches filled the air. Just the kids, playing rock-paper-scissors again. Joseph's hand looked red. I hoped they hadn't slapped it too hard. I dished up their pasta and whispered *sotto voce*. "Go ahead and eat."

Hal plodded on. "I wish you'd sit down. You're always too busy to pay attention to what I say. When I mentioned the move, I wasn't sure I could find good property for the factory or I would have told you more. The Segerstrom thing just opened up today." He leaned back in his seat, very much the patriarch, and sniffed the rosemary sauce without a clue he was wrecking my life.

On duty, I monitored spaghetti eaters while attentively gazing at his face. He went on, "Today, the farmer Segerstrom signed the contract to sell their lima bean fields on Sunflower Avenue, Santa Ana, to NCR." He held up a thumb to represent victory. "Stick with me, Babe. We're going to the top. I'll be in charge of the National Cash Register Branch."

I spread napkins on laps, poured milk, and moved the spaghetti to a counter for safety's sake. Rock-paper-scissors might start up again at any moment. I addressed the back of his head so I wouldn't actually see his disappointment. "What gives you the idea I want to go to the top? I'm happy here. We have the church. The kids have their school and good friends. We can't interrupt their lives just like that." I snapped my fingers. "They've been through enough."

Triggered by my anxious words, Geoff and Julie tapped their milk glasses with spoons and chanted, "We won't move. You can't make us. We won't move. You can't take us." Joseph looked at them out of his brown eyes fringed with lashes almost too long for a boy. Then he grasped his spoon and screamed too, "You can't take us."

"Cut it out, kids." His alpha dog voice halted the riot. But the kids retreated. "I'm finished. Can I be excused?" Julie slid from the bench.

"Please excuse me." Geoff followed her.

"S'cuse," Joseph called from a face bright red with tomato sauce. I swiped at his mouth with a napkin and missed. He scrambled after the others. My vision of a family dinner with grace and pleasant conversation seldom became a reality.

"Wash your hands and face before you go out to play," I called after them.

Hal continued, "Try to understand. I make a living for all five of us from National Cash Register. President Allan will move our division to Orange County, whether or not that appeals to you. And you don't need to scare the children. It won't do any good."

"But Harold," He was Harold instead of Hal when I was mad. "There's actually enough land to expand the factory in Hawthorne. You just wanted to move, didn't you?" A pulse beating in his neck warned me to quit, but I couldn't stop my nervous rush of words. "Please, please, don't make me move. I'm just getting back on my feet."

My own words defeated me. I sank down on my chair, suddenly hating the cold spaghetti, the dirty dishes and the TV program blasting from the nearby dining room. Despite my strenuous attempts to be a good wife, I was still a mother in mourning.

Hal spoke deliberately. "My name is on that equipment. I am staying with it." The light left his eyes. Softness departed his face. He wasn't a loving presence.

"I'm only a flesh and blood wife, not an electronic brain like your MADDIDA, so I don't count, do I? You're the great engineer, the entrepreneur, the alpha dog. You're stubborn and you're going to do what you want—however it affects me and the kids." I attempted to swallow a spoonful of cold spaghetti but it stuck in my throat.

"Will you try to understand? This move is to help you and the kids. National Cash Register was losing interest in our product. I got their attention with my plan to build a great factory in Orange County and I found the perfect piece of property for it." I stared at my plate and stirred the red strings with a fork.

"Stop staring at your plate and listen to me. We decided not to move back to Dayton Ohio like Don Eckdahl, so I'm trying to make a go of it in California—for our family. I'll be the manager."

I spit the spaghetti into my napkin and choked back my sobs because he hated tears. I felt abandoned. "Why don't you just say MADDIDA means more to you than me and the kids."

"Garbage. I'm taking care of our future by moving. The case is closed." He patted me as if I were a pet dog. "Honey, you'll love Orange County. Maybe we can even live on an island in Newport Beach."

"I don't want to live there." Even to me, my voice sounded sulky.

"Come on, Baby, you love the beach. Give me a little kiss." He pressed his lips on mine.

I couldn't stand up to his masculine energy, so I conceded, "Well, I won't move unless you hire movers. In the last ten years, I've packed and loaded and driven enough to qualify as a Beacon's mover or a pack mule."

"You're a great little mule, but we'll hire packers and movers this time. We'll start a whole new life. And I promise it will be good. We need a change. We need to forget our grief."

"You need to, not me. I want to remember Jennifer."

Six months later, burly men in brown uniforms landed in our house like astronauts on the moon. The Beacon movers snatched our plates and packed them, sticky egg yolks and all. I poured Hal and me each a cup of coffee and then the pot, with its used grains, was wrapped and boxed. They moved everything, garbage in its pail, wastebaskets bulging with trash, empty tin cans and planks used as toys by the kids, kitty litter. *New Yorkers* disappeared from the coffee table. Whoosh! I watched my home dismantled. It was like viewing a speeded up movie of the Keystone Kops. And then I was standing in an empty shell of a house. Toots and Shadow, Joseph's cats, twirled around my legs and howled. Hal put his arms around me. "Time to go, honey. It seems hard now, but you'll adjust. You know people adjust to everything, even hanging by the neck."

But this house, our first real home, contained in its walls the memory of Jennifer and the memory of a vision in a rose garden. The neighborhood beyond our wooden garden gate held my first ever church and a network of friends who supported me daily. When the front door would be locked behind me and the wooden gate closed, a vital part of me would be left behind forever. Farewell canyon home, coyotes, chaparral. Farewell church, cemetery, friends.

Hal handed me Toots, who showed her teeth and hissed. He draped Shadow over his arms and loaded Julie, Geoff and Toots in the bright teal blue van. I climbed into the black Chevy with Joseph and Shadow. The kids stuck their heads out of the auto windows and yelled in unison "Wagons, ho!" We were on our way, caravanning to Newport Beach.

In the months that followed, Hal and I bought a house and agreed on a new marriage contract. Whoever had the worst problems during the day was entitled to speak first in our Before Dinner Discussions. For six months, I went first. Our open-plan house let me jabber away while preparing dinner. Hal perched at the counter and dispensed resolutions or comfort. The kids were in our view as they watched TV from the living room.

I told Hal, "The Lido Club to support developmentally disabled children rejected my application as member. I know I'd be a good volunteer. Either we don't have enough money, or they're prejudiced about Armenians."

"Your problem, Martha, is that you haven't lived in a barrio and you don't know how hard it is. Prejudice is everywhere, but the people on Lido greet me politely and that's all I ask. The law can protect us, but we can't change hearts."

Another night, another problem. "This morning, a girl asked Julie at the bus stop if she bought her clothes at Kmart, instead of Bullocks. We don't belong on this tight little island. We should live on the Bluffs, where people aren't quite so snooty and have more children."

Hal had an answer ready. "I'll get Julie to join the Girls Athletic Association so she'll meet her type, get the exercise she needs and not be so worried about her clothes."

When one evening Hal said, "I want to complain," my nerves sounded a warning. He didn't greet the kids. Fear lurked in his eyes. "I should have told you this sooner. President Allan has decided he doesn't want an engineer heading up the branch. He's sending Fred Bitterman to head it but I'll have the same salary and be in charge of engineering."

I hugged him and tried to erase the furrows in his brow with my fingers. I lied to sound positive. "We have enough money, Honey, and you love engineering. Sounds good." Inside, I wondered why this God I worshipped had let this happen to Hal.

He comforted himself. "Maybe it's for the best. Fred's a lawyer and will have some business insights I don't. After all, I'm only an engineer."

A month later, we welcomed Fred Bitterman, his wife, Debby, their two pre-teen daughters and their son, who was Joseph's age, to Orange County. I admired Debby's style and brains, although she put a distance between herself and me and I could see some kind of fear lurking in her eyes even as she laughed. I yearned to be her friend and to understand the anxiety she tried to conceal, but I knew I shouldn't probe—after all, her husband was the boss. Perhaps like me, she had lost a child. I hoped we would be good friends someday.

At first, only one habit of Fred's bothered me: he'd twirl his Phi Beta Kappa key. I wasn't sure if this was a nervous tic or an attempt to prove his intellectual superiority. Next, Fred started calling Hal "The little Armenian man." I hated his condescension but remained silent about it. After all, he was the boss.

Soon Fred Bitterman became the only topic of our Worst Problem of the Day discussions.

Hal raged, "I can't believe it. Fred's posted a regulation: no more coffee available in the factory and the water cooler will be removed."

"For Heaven's sake, why?"

"He says my gang of engineers spends too much time talking instead of working. He doesn't understand why engineers need to brainstorm. A computer is too complicated a project to be designed by one man. Fred's a Dayton, Ohio man. He doesn't understand California ways."

"He's weird. His wife isn't very happy."

"Don't escalate the problem, Martha."

I fixed Hal a thermos of coffee every morning. When I visited the plant, I noticed individual water bottles on the assembly line and on the desks. A glum silence prevailed.

Our next Worst Problem discussion began with Hal. "Save next Saturday for you and kids to come to the plant."

"Why? The kids have other plans."

"Fred has invited our family to watch carpet being installed in his office. He wants us all there."

Already disgusted with Fred, my rage grew. He had remodeled the factory office into two rooms, a large room for himself and a closet-sized one for Hal, with the only entrance through Fred's. And now was I supposed to watch carpet installation in Fred's office, while I knew Hal would be forever at Fred's command in the small joined office?

"I refuse to attend an office carpet laying ceremony. Only an egomaniac would even suggest it."

Hal answered quietly, "It's a command performance, not a request. Saturday at ten a.m. We're to be there with the children."

"I won't give up my Saturday to watch carpet being laid. It's my only free day."

But the following Saturday Hal, Joseph, and I drove to Sunflower as Hal insisted. The small new factory stood on red soil amid fields of lima beans. We scuffed our way through the red dust to the office. Then the Bitterman family appeared. I made my apologies, "I'm sorry, but Julie and Geoff had other engagements today."

The two small boys raced together into the fields. Debby and her daughters stood with me as workmen laid the carpet. Fred twirled his Phi Beta Kappa key faster than usual. Hal cracked his knuckles. There were no speeches, no refreshments, no bottle of champagne. The new carpet smell mingled with the odor of glue and the earthy scent of red soil. My stomach heaved with nausea, but I tried to follow Fred's logic. Did he want to impress the Sarkissians with the blue carpet and a new immense desk?

When we left the Bittermans and the factory behind, I told Hal, "Fred's narcissistic. Some sort of egomaniac." He didn't reply.

At Christmas, Fred insisted that all the engineers dress as clowns for a family party for workers and their families. Hal hated the idea. The painted sad white mouth on his face broke my heart. Something was terribly wrong. That night, I cornered Hal as we were getting ready for bed. "You've got to find a different job. Fred is killing your spirit."

"It's not that simple."

"You have a great reputation. Any of the big aircraft companies would hire you. I can't stand living under his weird domination."

"I've told you before. My name is on that equipment and I am staying with it."

"Well, I'm afraid you'll end up with no job and no prospects because he's crazy. I'm going to enroll at Long Beach University and get a teaching credential so we have some security."

"Good idea. Three kids is a lot for me to support."

"I thought you didn't want me to work."

"That was before I had three kids and, as you point out, a nut for a boss."

Soon, Fred had Hal working every night till seven or eight and on Saturdays, too. Then Fred started phoning our home early Sunday mornings. Hal and I would be in bed sleeping or whispering, gently touching each other, enjoying the early hours of Sunday before church and tennis when Fred would call. The phone rang earlier every Sunday as Fred became more and more dependent on Hal.

One Sunday morning, the phone rang about six-thirty. I reached it from my side of the bed and handed it to Hal. He liked to sleep in the nude and I draped my arm around his shoulders to enjoy the feel of his skin and the warmth of his body. As he was listening intently on the phone, I felt drops of sweat break out on his body. I took an edge of sheet and tried to pat him dry. He sat up. With his hand over the receiver, he directed me, "Martha, get a pencil and paper and write down whatever I say. If you don't, I'll never believe what I'm hearing." I reached for paper and pen as Hal continued. "I'm repeating Fred's words: 'Hal, make a chart of the number of words a minute different women speak and plot the correlation between evil in women and words per minute.'" I wrote it down.

The talk went on and on until Hal shouted in the receiver, "I'll get right on it, Fred. Sorry, but I need to hang up." Hal and I stared at each other. "Martha, he's insane. Really insane." We were bewildered and unsure in our first encounter with mental illness.

I was the first to speak. "You really have to resign. Fred is mentally ill. He can't run a company. You've been getting depressed. You're moving farther away from the children and me. MADDIDA isn't worth it."

He put his arms around me. "Honey, it isn't about MADDIDA anymore. Fred is a sick man and I have to take care of him. Try to understand."

I wanted to scream--You can't run a company to please a madman. But I kept silent because Hal had his own guidance system and I couldn't change that. Every evening I listened to his account of Fred's daily rambles. An eerie feeling overcame me. I was leading Hal's life, not my own, and for the first time, impotent and helpless, I had to stand by and watch as Fred Bitterman wounded my husband's computer company. For years, Hal had steadied me with his sense of direction and balance and now he was slipping ever deeper into depression. I had no resources. No power. I was only a wife. I kept repeating, "Quit your job. You can get another. Don't go down with the ship. Hal, the kids and I need you."

"Fred needs me. I won't desert him. Remember, my name is on that equipment, too." He spoke in a heavy definite manner that meant there was no use arguing. I understood that my position as a sheltered wife and mom was coming to an end. I doubled up on courses at Long Beach College to earn a High School Teaching certificate. My mother's favorite essay was *Self Reliance* by Emerson and now I understood why.

With an engineer's precision, Hal documented Fred's disordered behavior by the hour, day and month, then flew to Dayton Ohio to present his documentation of Fred's Bitterman's condition to the NCR Board of Directors and President Allan. Three days later, I watched him emerge from the airplane tunnel a defeated man. "It's no use, Martha. Allan and his Board wouldn't even glance at my report. They accused me of jealousy. God, how could I be jealous of that poor man?"

Two months later, police detectives arrived at NCRs Orange County factory. Hal was working on the line with his men. The Detectives led him to his office. "Sit down, Sir. Bad news. We found Fred Bitterman dead in his auto on a side street in Irvine. Suicide. He'd put a rifle barrel in his mouth and shot himself. We'll need you to identify the body. His wife is waiting in our car. We'll accompany you."

After Hal and Debby identified the body, he brought her and her three children home to Lido. Julie, Geoff and Joseph played with the Bitterman children, while Hal and I listened to a tremendous outpouring from Debby.

"Four years ago, I consulted a psychiatrist because I believed I was going crazy. After two sessions, the doctor told me my husband, Fred, was crazy—not me. Somehow, Fred managed to convince me I was the crazy one. I was afraid if the children and I left him, he would destroy himself. And now, he has."

Unable to speak, I put my arms around her.

She sighed. "It's all right, Martha. He's at peace now. We can be at peace too. Six months ago, I took Fred to court for a court order to hospitalize him. His life could have been saved, but he pulled himself together and spoke so sensibly as an attorney that they believed him, just as National Cash did."

She turned and put her hand on Hal's arm. "I know you loved Fred, too. You tried to save him and I tried to save him, but we couldn't, dear friend." Then, wordlessly, she handed Hal a one-page letter penciled by Fred before he died. It described Fred's despondency and the forces of evil arrayed against him. The last sentence in the letter read, "No one has ever been kind to me, except the little Armenian man."

A month later, National Cash Register closed the branch on Sunflower Avenue in Costa Mesa. Hal was unemployed.

CHAPTER 17

Heroic Journeys

idden in the corner of the gleaming factory, I heard Hal's farewell
address to his employees: "National Cash Register is closing down our
computer branch here in Costa Mesa due to the sudden death of Fred Bitterman."

Groans and sighs arose like a wind from the men and women crowded
around him. "You have worked side-by-side with me to create the Magnetic
Drum Digital Differential Analyzer, our own MADDIDA. Let's each of us take
pride in belonging to the crew which built one of the first computers."

Tears wet the cheeks of the men and women clustered around him. He
breathed deeply and continued. "I will help you find employment by any means
I can. I'll write references, work with unemployment forms and résumés,
and call friends who are hiring. Some of you took lower salaries to be in on
this adventure. I'm sorry it worked out this way." Hal had once been a First
Lieutenant in the army. Now he straightened up into a military position to
announce, "We have one month with full salary to close down the operation.
Then the doors will be locked. I'll answer individually any questions you have."
While his employees huddled around him hugging, patting his shoulder, squeez-
ing his hand, I tiptoed out of the grieving crowd. We needed a memorial service
for the NCR Computer Branch, for our lady MADDIDA and for our dreams of
success and fame. I thought of T.S. Eliot's lines "This is the way the world ends,
not with a bang but a whimper." I crept out of the room.

A month later, Hal locked the door of the model factory behind him. At the
same time, he locked me out of his mind and passed his days sitting in his blue
recliner chair, thinking.

I attempted encouragement. "You're so well known in the electronics field, Honey, you won't have any trouble getting a job. I bet if you make a few phone calls...."

"Martha, leave me alone. I'm thinking."

I drove top-speed down an anxiety freeway looking for a turn-off. My journal grew fat with my ravings about big corporations. Why didn't they even look at Hall's scientific notations concerning Fred's eerie behavior? How could they label Hal jealous? They probably sent Fred to California to get rid of him. Why didn't they recognize Hal's honesty? Didn't they know he only stayed on at the branch to give Fred support? Why did they want to shut down an invention that would make them a leading power?

I couldn't hide my grief from my mother, who noticed the arrival of every new wrinkle in my face. "You'd have a happy life, wouldn't you dear, if it weren't for Hal's business."

"Don't forget, I lost Jennifer."

"I know dear, but that was a long time ago."

Not to me. I worked the 'ifs.' If only Hal had left when he first realized Fred's sickness, he could easily have found a great position. The general manager of a failed business doesn't have very good job prospects. What if he can't work! His blood pressure is hideously high! His doctor says he's a "highly organized nervous mechanism." Maybe his spirit's broken. If he can't work, who will support the three kids and me? How can I get out of this panic?

It was 1963. I read a book that turned a searchlight on my predicament, *The Feminine Mystique,* a newly published book by Betty Friedan. I suffered from what she called "the problem that has no name." Just because I was..."an American housewife with a dishwasher, dryer and washing machine, the dream image of young American women and the envy of women all over the world," didn't mean I felt happy and satisfied inside. I really wasn't Cinderella. Regardless of how hard I tried, the glass slipper could never fit me.

When I heard about the Freedom Riders, many of them college women who risked their lives for justice, I wanted to be like them, not an overprotected oversensitive plump goose. They inspired Martin Luther King to march and I wanted to join him. Imagine being able to strike a blow for justice!

"Your place is with your children," Hal said. "When we decided to have a family, we committed to them. You can't leave them behind and run away, regardless of the importance of the goal. I'm planning how to bring home a monthly paycheck and you want to quit, run away and be a heroine. You need to grow up."

"I want to be important, Hal, like you. Men climb Kilimanjaro, or paint pictures of God on a chapel ceiling or invent computers, but I'm not doing anything."

"Baby, it's your spirit that keeps this outfit going."

As I came to realize my desire to join the march stemmed partially from a desire to escape the fact that Hal was unemployed, I abandoned my dream of striking a blow for justice. If Hal couldn't support us, did that mean I should take responsibility for earning money? My unconscious erected a big green sign on my emotional freeway that pointed to an off ramp reading: Exit Anxiety Freeway. Work! Support your family!

This decision ripped me apart. Early in our marriage, Hal asked me "Honey, what happened to the spirit you had in Berkeley? You advocated for a bus for women and housing for Afro-Americans. Now, it seems, you don't talk about anything but the baby and some book you read. Where's your spirit?"

"You took away my spirit. You make all the decisions. You have a car, a group of men—I'm here alone—with my baby and my books. Of course I talk about them."

He looked dejected. "I got you a nice house and all the equipment you need—I thought you'd be happy."

"You have made me happy. It's my own fault if I've lost my chutzpah." The next day I wrote a poem that began,

"My spirit just lay down and died, somewhere, I think,
Between the stove and kitchen sink..."

I couldn't run off to hunt glory. My family needed my presence and they needed money too. My writing rarely sold and earned only a few dollars. Running around Orange County, begging for a job took more guts than I had. A wimp, almost too shy to give a waiter my order, could hardly step into the business world. Who hires English majors, anyway?

One wet afternoon a neighbor, Judy Rosener, invited me to her home for a cup of coffee. Her son Doug and my son Joseph were building a block structure in her living room as we sipped coffee and watched the boys play. When we reached the river of conversation, Judy's intelligence jumped from idea to idea: local politics, save the Back Bay; national politics, President Kennedy sent 3,000 troops to protect the protestors; international, Fidel Castro and Cuba and the missile crisis. She never slipped into the river of neighborhood gossip. Her grasp of political concepts electrified me. When Doug and Joseph launched a kinder-gartners' dispute concerning the placement of blocks, I reluctantly stood up. "I hate to leave, but I guess the boys are ready for dinner. It's been great talking. I haven't met many women like you on Lido Island. It feels so darn good to talk about real issues, not just recreation."

Judy laughed. "I have a big mouth."

"Now that the kids are in school, and Hal's tied up with his business, I don't know where to look for mental stimulation." NCR's closure and my need for a job felt too shameful to be mentioned at all. The boys traded pushes so I grabbed Joseph's hand and Judy grabbed Doug by his T-shirt.

She shot them a glare and then focused on me. "My boys are in school now, so I'm going to pick up a Master's degree at our new Cal branch, the University of Irvine. It's just opening. I don't know what I'll study, but I'll be there. I like to live on the edge--you never know what might turn up."

Judy's short-cropped hair and athletic build conveyed an image of a woman already on the edge and I, though short and plump, wanted to be there too. But I was sunk in a swamp of domesticity. Her Doug and my Joseph were both five. If Judy could return to college, I could, too. I'd get a high school credential and support my family.

Two weeks later, I stopped my daughter Julie on her way to the school bus. "Can you take a minute and check my clothes before you go?" My voice pumped up with pride. "I've got an appointment with the Dean of Education at Long Beach College. I'm going to study to be a high school teacher."

"Sure thing." Twelve-year-old Julie, in the role of fashion police, appraised my navy blue suit and ruffled blouse. "Yeah, you look like a teacher all right. But your nylons are crooked. Good luck, Mom." She raced for the school bus while

I straightened my stocking seams—just one of the trials I'd have to endure as a teacher.

After a long wait at the Dean's office, a sad-eyed rumpled gentleman beckoned me in.

He sighed when I seated myself in the straight-backed student chair facing him. "Do you think that at your age, Mrs. Sarkissian, you can keep up with the students and still fulfill your duties as a housewife?"

I felt as confident as a thirteen-year-old girl with acne, but I imposed a smile on my unwilling lips. "I'm sure I can. My children will help me with the housework." I knew I lied, but I needed an A+ on the interview.

He flinched. Afraid I'd start talking about my kids, no doubt. "Have you had any teaching experiences?"

"I'm a Girl Scout Leader, a den mother, and Sunday School teacher." That ought to impress him. Not many candidates have as much experience.

This time he sighed so deeply the papers on his desk shuddered. "Mrs. Sarkissian, teaching high school is no Girl Scout outing. But if you're determined, you might manage." He stamped and handed me a square of green cardboard. I felt like a steak graded A1 for consumption, not a scholar. "Take this with you to the Registrar and good luck. Thirty-six, a woman...hmmm."

It appeared that the university system in 1960 had not changed since the day I was in college in the forties and heard President Kerr of UC Berkeley announce in a speech, "Female students are not emotionally equipped for university studies." I guessed I should be grateful that the Dean of Education admitted me, even though he seemed dubious about a housewife and mother applying. Most high school teachers were men, so he was probably more used to them. I'd teach him a thing or two about the power of women.

My classes began the following week and, though I felt a bit awkward and out of place in Long Beach State, I handled the academic work well until I took a required course in Public Speaking. I was voted to chair a debate on abortion. I wanted to run and hide when I discovered my committee members would be seated at a long table, but I, as the chairman, had to stand alone and speak loudly. My legs turned to mush, my throat constricted and my voice became a whisper. Our instructor, Dr. Burroughs, dragged over a chair for me to sit in and offered me a glass of water. I gulped it gratefully and struggled to control the body processes so revealing of my lack of self-confidence.

Dr. Burroughs pulled me aside after our class debate. "Mrs. Sarkissian, have you had any previous experience in public speaking?"

"No, never. I've been busy raising a family."

He waggled his eyebrows. "I almost had to use smelling salts to keep you going. You shook like a falling feather."

My cheeks heated up. "I apologize. I'm sorry. I did know the material."

"We're not discussing information. You'll never control students if you are so self-conscious. Since you've been out of the academic world for a number of years, I'll give you a second chance, but if you can't present yourself as a poised, in-control instructor next Wednesday, I'll drop you out of the program in the wink of an eye." I felt ashamed and embarrassed, but made up my mind; I'd learn to be a speaker in a week. I thought of Demosthenes the Greek orator who practiced speaking over the roar of the ocean with a mouthful of pebbles.

So, without pebbles but with a fierce determination, I gave speeches to the bathroom mirror as I dressed for school. The garden weeds received discourses on the hot topics of the day. The dishwasher heard recitations of poetry as I loaded it. Poochie, our mongrel mutt, heard many an impassioned oration and appeared to enjoy the sound of my voice pontificating! I debated with the ocean, too. My confidence in myself and my speech was growing.

Several months later, as I wrestled with lesson plans at the dining table, Hal called, "Come here, Martha. I've made up my mind."

I lay down my pen and ran to him. "About what?"

"I've been kicking this idea around for a long time—an electronic vote tally machine! It'll make paper obsolete at the polls. A start-up business. How about that!"

Scarcely could I absorb his words. "That's what you've been thinking? You haven't been depressed just sitting there in your chair?"

"You should have listened to me. I told you I was thinking. I filled a couple of legal pads with diagrams."

"I've been so worried. I thought I had to support us," I wailed.

"I needed to work out a few details before I told you. But I'm telling you now. Are you willing to have us invest in another company?"

Inside, I thought I really didn't have a choice. This man of mine was too individualistic and stubborn to work for anyone else. "You do what you want. You're going to anyway, no matter what I say."

"Hey, you can't get away with 'Do what you want'.' I can't do anything without you backing me up. You can blow some of your prayers my way and in turn, I'll support your schoolteacher career—all the way. Remember, we're a new kind of marriage."

"I just—read you wrong. Thought you'd collapse without MADDIDA. We'll support each other. Okay. Let's shake."

We were back in sync as pioneers in new territory. To be together, he had to cross the border of a patriarchal Armenian society and I had to cross the state line of a conservative Victorian family. He was at the forefront of entrepreneurial engineers with start-up companies and I was a Betty Friedan woman, returning to college, becoming a professional. We were building a new kind of life.

However, despite this inspiring concept, every morning as I drove to Long Beach State University, I fretted. Would my children be emotionally healthy if I worked? Taking care of the family always took all my time. Where would the extra hours come from? That's what the Dean had wanted to know, too.

Then I'd take the opposite position. What if I didn't work? Maybe Hal couldn't support us? What if the strain of another wild engineering business killed him? I chain-smoked and gnawed my fingernails while my fears duked it out on the battlefield of my psyche.

About the time the Hal's new business, Major Data, had won some contracts and hired a staff, I reached the credential candidates' Mecca— student teacher with two unpaid classes of Junior English. My master teacher, Mr. Claiborne, left me alone to teach because, "You're actually a mature woman. You can handle a class without help, and I need free time to correct papers."

"My supervisor at Long Beach State said I should remind you it is against the law to leave a student teacher alone in class."

He shrugged and disappeared into the Teachers' Lounge, but always returned in time in time to examine the floor for spit wads after class. "Mrs.

Sarkissian, I see three spit wads on the floor today. If you nab a student the minute he tears a bit of paper to make a wad, I'll find none tomorrow. And please check the girls' hair-dos every day. Those beehive dos are perfect for concealing knives. Pull their skirts down as you walk the aisle. The view up the skirts drives my boys crazy."

I could endure this loathsome advice but when he added, "I'm glad to have a woman teacher aboard because you can patrol the rest rooms for smokers during recess," I rebelled.

"Mr. Claiborne, I received a BA in English with Honors from Berkeley. I intend to spend my time teaching, not patrolling." His fingers as well as mine had yellow nicotine stains. He didn't mention rest rooms again. My other master teacher, Mr. Wilson, modeled teaching for me as we shared his class of twenty students with IQs ranging 80 to 100. "Mrs. Sarkissian, every morning I ask my students the baseball scores. The kids may end up washing cars and they'll get better tips if they converse with customers."

"Mrs. Sarkissian, I am reading aloud the Nobel Prize winner's speech. Our students need to be informed about the world they live in."

"Mrs. Sarkissian, an artist in this class has our lowest IQ. I helped him to sell his paintings and opened a bank account for him with the money. He lives on his own. You never know where you will strike gold. Treat each student with respect."

I loved Mr. Wilson and could scarcely tolerate Mr. Claiborne, yet I depended on their joint approval for my credential. Every morning before I left for school, I had a fit of vomiting. I confided in Hal, "I'm afraid I'm too nervous to be a teacher. I'm vomiting every morning."

He shook his head disapprovingly. "You have a nervous system like an ox. You better visit the doctor."

"You know I'm nervous."

"Bullshit! You lack confidence and have some bad habits, that's all. Go see a doctor."

After a brief examination and a few questions, my general practitioner enlightened me. "Mrs. Sarkissian, you do not have the flu or food poisoning. You are pregnant!" After a miscarriage and a curettage three years earlier, a gynecologist told me "I'm very sorry, Mrs. Sarkissian, but you will never be able to conceive a baby again." Yet, I was pregnant—a miracle for sure. I had joined the elite company of Job. God restored his losses, and now God was restoring mine. Hal had a new vote tally business and I had a new baby underway.

That night, I pushed my chair close to my TV-watching husband. "Listen Honey, I don't want to shock you, but I saw the doctor today. He says I'm pregnant. That's why I've been so tired, vomiting and all. Oh, Hal, I'm going to stop working and stay home and take good care of myself and the baby."

"A new baby? Is that so!" Happiness erased his wrinkles and he looked like the First Lieutenant I loved as he embraced and kissed me. "We Sarkissians make good babies. Thank you for a new life."

"I'll be glad to leave behind the brown linoleum halls of high school. It's a long drive to Long Beach and I've been getting so tired and..."

He interrupted. "You must not quit because you're tired. You give up too easily. You'd be published by now if you worked at it."

"Maybe so. And maybe you couldn't design a vote tally machine if you took care of three kids and a house and garden. School's dangerous. Last Wednesday, two kids got in a knife fight on campus. I walked between them and hollered, "You guys cut that out!"'"

"Did they stop?"

"They did. One said 'Okay, Teach,' and they both put away their knives. Actually, they were relieved to see me."

"Honey, kids always respect you. You know how to manage them. Push yourself a little and earn that credential. And congratulations on the baby in the oven."

"Hmm. I'll see what my GYN says. Probably 'Stay home and think peaceful thoughts.'"

"Maybe so, but again, maybe not."

A week later, I consulted Dr. Browning. "...so I plan to quit teaching immediately to take good care of my baby." Expecting approval, I studied his kindly face across the expanse of a mahogany desk.

Instead, his face collapsed in worry lines. He moved uneasily in his chair with wheels. "Mrs. Sarkissian, I do not advise it. You are thirty-eight and have

had several miscarriages. You may end up with nothing--no baby, no credential. The activity of teaching will be good for you, keep your mind off your
past losses. I'm sure you'll be a fine teacher. Enjoy your work. I'll see you next
month." I felt cruelly abused by his words and terrified that I might "end up with
nothing."

When I announced my pregnancy in the teacher's lounge, Chuck Claiborne
reacted "It's against regulations to have a pregnant teacher. Too bad! I'll sure
miss the free period!"

Mr. Wilson snorted. "Hey Chuck, we can take it to the School Board. Times
are changing and she's too good to lose."

By September 1963, I had a Life Secondary Credential and a baby girl. I
watched Laura's birth in a mirror, thanks to a nurturing doctor and a new anes-
thesia, a spinal block that left me alert and cognizant. A reverent awe filled
my being when Dr. Browning lay the barely five pound baby on my stomach.
Dr. Trotter, our pediatrician, also attended her birth. President Kennedy had
recently launched a movement to screen newborns for PKU, so Dr. Trotter did
a special examination. "You have a normal baby---under five pounds, but not
premature, and free from PKU. Still, I'd like you to stay in the hospital for a
week. Once Laura Kay goes home, her siblings will bring her some germs along
with some lovely adventures."

Laura and I spent a blissful week together in Hoag Hospital. My book club
friend Bernice Sisson sent me a telegram reading "Welcome back to the wonderful world of the bottomless coffee pot." I sighed with relief that I could leave
behind the brown linoleum halls of Venice High School and become once more
a stay-at-home Mom.

Julie, Geoff, and Joseph helped us bring Laura Kay home from the hospital.
I settled her bassinet in the living room, but Julie, 15, moved the bassinet to her
own bedroom. "She's my sister, Mom. We're going to share a bedroom." And
they did.

Joseph's back-to-school night at Newport Elementary occurred two weeks
later. Terrified to leave this precious baby with a sitter, I hired a registered
nurse, an impressive figure garbed in white cap and uniform. But when Hal and

I returned home, an indignant Julie met us. "Don't ever hire a nurse again. She just let the baby cry. I changed her diapers and soothed her. I'll sit Laura whenever you want to go out."

With the arrival of a new spirit in the home, a sweet flavored breeze blew across our family. The children and I attended Prince of Peace church and it brought us new life, too. In appearance, our church resembled a child's drawing: a rectangular base, rectangular door and a sloping roof topped with a cross. Pastor Andy, farm-reared, father of five, embodied the characteristics we all longed for in a father. With his love and attention, the church became a community for families who'd survived World War II. Even Hal, strictly Humanistic, enjoyed their potlucks and the ambience. Our kids and I sang, "I've got joy, joy, joy, joy down in my heart...." We meant it. We felt good. Geoff and Joseph vied to carry Laura around the church lawn to show her off. The congregation admired the ribbons I taped to her bald head. One droopy-eyed church matron exclaimed, "I'd never trust my boys to carry a baby."

"I do." All of us Sarkissians needed a baby to love and Laura Kay was exactly the baby we needed: calm, happy, greeting everyone with a smile.

Hal and his cronies, Bill Saylor and Bill Speer, set up a honey of a cozy factory to produce vote tally machines. Many of Hal's former staff returned to work for him. Pastor Andy preached, "You never reach the top of the mountain of life. You find a plateau and rest and then climb on to the next plateau." Now that is an old-fashioned, stodgy idea, I mused, sitting on the hard wooden pew. We Sarkissians have reached the top!

One Sunday after church, Esther Olson, principal of the Prince of Peace Elementary School, stopped me by the coffee cart. My impulse was to dart away, but her steady gaze held me prisoner. "Martha I'd like you to teach our fifth-sixth grade class next September."

I choked on a swallow of burning hot coffee from the nearby coffee cart. "Esther, I'm astonished. You must be kidding! I have a high school credential, not elementary, and you must know I smoke." Driven by pure nervousness, I plucked a doughnut from the cart and took a giant bite. It seemed likely that this lady, who had been a missionary to Asia, who had survived the Bataan Death March and who had established an elementary school at Prince of Peace in Costa

Mesa, was so saintly and dominating that she could drive me crazy. I considered myself a free spirit.

Esther carefully studied me. "I don't care if you smoke. When I saw you teach Sunday School, I made up my mind to have you on staff." Her violet eyes sparkling with mischief and the charming lilt in her soprano voice let me see beyond her missionary persona.

Turning my gaze from her to the rolling church lawn, I pondered how to refuse graciously. "Thank you. You're very kind. But I plan to work in Santa Ana when Laura is a little older. I want to help underprivileged children."

"Rich children have souls, too. Some are so materialistic that it takes a very special person to break through their shell. I think you are the one."

Tenderness appeared in the cold blue fiords of her Norwegian eyes. Her strength of will tugged on me. My bottom line: I couldn't give up cigarettes. "If I didn't smoke, I'd join your staff. But after all, isn't a teacher supposed to set a good example?"

"You're a good example. A whiff of smoke isn't going to blow that away. Promise me you will, at least, think about the idea."

"I'll think about it."

She started down the path, then turned her head and called out, "Eileen Shoup, wife of our assistant pastor, lives a block away. She'll baby-sit Laura."

How could I give up my tranquilizer of choice? In my first flush of enthusiasm as a convert to Christianity, I quit smoking until our family physician told me, "Mrs. Sarkissian, a cigarette is the cheapest most socially acceptable tranquilizer. I suggest that whenever you feel like crying, you smoke a cigarette." I took his advice. Vivid media memories tied me to cigarettes. When he was eighteen, my brother Ben leaned back on the piano bench and blew smoke rings and played "Dream, when you're feeling blue. Dream. That's the thing to do." I promised myself when I grew up, I'd blow smoke rings like Ben's.

In the forties, a voluptuous woman on a billboard convinced me to "Reach for a Lucky, instead of a sweet." I was fifteen and I could lose my baby fat, look as sexy as Marilyn Monroe—just by puffing on a Lucky. Lucky me! Varoom!

According to the 40's culture, it was as easy to strike up a conversation as to strike a match. "Pardon me, I seem to have lost my matches," Lauren Bacall murmured.

"Care for a light?" Humphrey Bogart placed two cigs in his mouth, lit them, and then placed one between her heavily rouged lips. It worked!

It was as easy as pie to talk to a guy if you asked for a light.

"Lucky Green has gone to war," announced the radio during World War II. No cigarettes were available in the drug stores near Berkeley, but we gals were creative. We made cigarette butt holders out of our bobby pins and sucked in every last puff we could. We felt patriotic and tough as soldiers. We epitomized Phil Harris's "Smoke, smoke, smoke that cigarette. Smoke, smoke yourself to death. Tell St. Peter at the golden gate, that you hate to make him wait, 'because you got to have another cigarette."

For 23 years, I relied on cigarettes to create an image of a sophisticated, alluring, in-the-know gal. What would be left without my Luckies? Why did that missionary lady think I'd give up cigarettes to teach her pampered little kids? Give me a break, Miss Olson. Me, a parochial teacher? Ridiculous. I was a free spirit addicted to cigarettes, and I liked life that way.

My breakfast always ended with a cup of hot coffee and a cigarette. The following Sunday, I hunted in my bathrobe for a coffin nail. Nothing there but tobacco crumbs. I must have had a pack somewhere, but gosh, I was too lazy to hunt for it.

I never got around to finding a cigarette every day that week. Not even when Rock Hudson's mother, who lived across the street, offered me a smoke with her coffee. By Saturday, bewildered, I asked myself, what's going on? Why were unopened packs of Luckies piling up in drawers and cupboards and pockets?

On Sunday, Hal held me in his arms and sniffed my hair. "Honey, you don't smell bad anymore."

"What do you mean? Do I usually smell bad?" So much for Johnson's Baby Powder and Evening in Paris cologne.

He proceeded gently. "Well, you usually smell pretty strong of cigarettes, but I guess you can't smell yourself. Right now, you smell awfully good to me."

My brain had changed. I didn't crave cigarettes. Either Miss Olson's prayers "worked" or my subconscious had such deep longing to be a Lutheran school-teacher that I stopped. Smoking is very addictive, but I never smoked again.

"I'm sorry—sorry I've been smelling so bad," I sniveled.

"Hey, cut that out! You were okay. You're just better now." He kissed my nose and bouncing a tennis ball on his racquet, he strode off for the courts like a happy kid. Our children clustered around me. "Neat! You won't have gruesome lungs like they showed us in science class," Geoff said.

"Pretty cool. You knocked out an addiction," Julie added.

Joseph pressed against me and I tousled his hair.

One evening I told Hal, "I signed this contract, and now I'm worried. Pastor Andy preaches against mothers pursuing a career, but he also urged me to sign this. I don't know what's right!"

"If you really don't want to teach, we can get out of the contract, I'm sure. If teaching creates a moral dilemma for you, just do what you want. No one knows what's right."

"After I read *Feminine Mystique* I felt sure, but Pastor…"

He interrupted. "Martha, it's time I explain something. I've been scared to death at being the sole support of four children and a wife! You've decided to help financially—that's great."

I hugged that familiar warm body and kissed the dimple in his cheek. "Honey, you're some man."

"And you're some woman. You gave me the emotional support to start another business. Now, it's time for me to back up your career."

For my first day as a teacher, I spiffed up in a purple and black chiffon dress, a gift from my mother. With a trembling hand I printed legibly on the green board, "My name is Mrs. Sarkissian."

"We know. It's an Armenian name," the class chorused.

"How did you know?"

A round-faced boy grinned. "Miss Olson asked us last year to pray for you to be our teacher. We've been praying ever since."

"Oh, my goodness," I gasped. Miss Olson's prayers were dynamite.

A lanky blonde girl added, "We prayed you wouldn't smoke and that you'd be our teacher because you are very intelligent."

The classroom fell silent. Twenty pairs of eyes stared at me.

In my shock, I completely forgot my lesson plans. "Well, thank you. But I don't feel so smart right now. I'm too excited to know what to do next." The kids smiled. I'd connected with them. The round-faced boy raised his hand. "Mrs. Sarkissian, we usually start the day with the flag salute."

"Good idea. What's your name?"

"Ronnie Tye."

"Okay, Ronnie. Will you lead us?"

He nodded and walked to the front of the class.

"I pledge allegiance...." My school career began. I had no idea that I'd diagnose Ronnie's academic problems as due to his eyesight, and that a referral to an optometrist would save him from impending blindness, but I did know that I was in a place where events occurred with purpose. Soon I loved every boy and girl I taught and poured my energy and strength into teaching.

As the years passed, Laura deepened the joy Hal and I found in our family. When Geoff married Sarah Post in 1972, once again our joy deepened as Sarah became our third daughter. After a year in Germany, they returned to the states to attend college: Sarah at Occidental College as an English major, and Geoff at Fuller Seminary as a PhD candidate in psychology. When Joseph enrolled in Evergreen College, Washington as a chemistry major, we believed he'd soon be a scientist. Our daughter Julie, working in the in Seattle Health Department, received a grant for a new procedure to save the lives of the babies of HIV positive mothers. When I slid out of bed in the morning, I felt a new sense of harmony with God and life. My definition of success was to raise children who would contribute to the ultimate good of the world, and this was in process, though I never forgot Jennifer's tragic death. Over the phone, I told my daughter, "Dad's ship is coming in at last."

She chided me. "Mother, you've been saying that since I was five. Try to be a little more realistic."

Even Julie, though, grew excited when I told her that Major Data had received a Letter of Intent from Bakersfield County to purchase the Vote Tally system with two conditions: First, that a real election would be used to prove the system. Second, that Hal would personally manage the operation. Elated over this break-through opportunity, and eager to show off his brainchild, he invited me to accompany him on this historic occasion.

In a froth of joyful expectations, I rushed out and bought a gold lamé dress. Of course, this dress was out of our budget and not at all like the simpler clothes I normally wore. But *this* was an occasion! I would surprise Hal and impress the newspaper reporters with my glamour. Gram, my mother, moved into our house to look after the kids while I was away.

When the voting polls closed at 8 p.m. in Bakersfield, police escorted trucks with the completed ballots to a warehouse for the automatic counting. By midnight, all marked ballots had arrived at election central. Worn out by the excitement, I walked across the parking lot to our motel for some rest.

Footsteps awoke me at 2 a.m. Peering out the window through a heavy fog, I glimpsed a new car parked in the lot, but all was quiet now. I slipped into my new lamé sheath with its low-cut neckline and prettied my face with a make-up kit, an unused gift from last Christmas. The lady in the mirror smiled at me. She no longer resembled an ordinary Lutheran schoolteacher, but a Mademoiselle Magazine sophisticate. When I stepped out of the motel, I stepped into an impenetrable tule fog that lay across the parking lot like a snow bank. I couldn't see anything. If only I could hang onto Hal's arm. But walking alone is the price of having an important husband. After all, the contract was valid only if my husband ran the election. What a man he was!

Usually I dressed plainly, but on this election night, I looked like the wife of a VIP. Of course, this dress cost too much and the night was cold, but just thinking how Hal would love me in it warmed me up. The neckline alone would turn him on. It was one to die for.

As I stumbled alone through the fog in high heels, I tried to keep up my courage by dialoguing with myself. I'd been smart to take a nap. When the last vote had been counted, I'd still be up and running, ready for a victory dinner. This was 1965. Women had some freedom. It was safe here with gobs of police hanging around. Was I heading in the right direction? I didn't know. Darn this fog.

I heard footsteps. Panic crept down my back. My mind shifted into anxiety mode. Two men were following me. Who were they? Did Hal send an escort for me? I peered desperately at two black blobs. They didn't look like the staff. I couldn't run in high heels. My dress glowed through the fog leading those men to me. A flashlight shone on my face. I tried to scream "Help, Hal!" My voice wouldn't come out.

A flashlight blinded me. Something jingled. Something cold clicked on my wrists!

"Lady, show us your ID," broke through my panic.

I laughed with relief. The blobs were police offers, not gangsters.

"Oh, sure. I have a driver's license. It's in my purse." I was handcuffed. I did not have my purse. I wasn't wearing a coat. The lamé neckline was cut deep. Maybe this wasn't so funny.

I stammered "M-my purse—it's in the Election Bureau. O-over there." I pointed in the direction of the Bureau. "We're running the vote tally count for elections."

"I bet she's running a tally," one officer sneered. They grabbed my arms, one of each side and pulled me along. I stumbled across the tar top and into the Bureau. "Am I arrested?" I asked, but they didn't answer.

Inside, a grinding noise as cardboard ballots moved along on a belt toward the computer, made conversation difficult. Hal spotted me and sprinted over. "What crazy thing has my wife done now?" he yelled.

"Your wife?" an officer asked.

"Yes. My wife, Martha. Why is she in handcuffs?

The policemen looked at each other. "Sorry, sir. The way she looks, and all, and being a lady alone in such a place—and at 2 a.m." He unlocked the cuffs.

The other finished the sentence. "We don't see many ladies looking like her in Bakersfield—gold dress and all. Thought she was a lady of the night." He seemed to be chuckling, but luckily, the assembly line drowned him out.

The losing political candidate demanded a recount, alleging that the vote was rigged by secret code in the equipment. The hand recount vindicated the electronic count over and over. But suspicion and political acrimony so dominated the conversation that election officials were afraid to go forward, and the county backed out of the purchase agreement.

While there would be many more election nights for Hal and his equipment, I stayed at home. The lamé dress hung in my closet for years.

In 1976, Joseph decided to take a semester off from Evergreen College to rest from what had been a difficult fall term. Hal distrusted Evergreen. "It hasn't required enough prerequisites for Joseph to take advanced chemistry. I think he's working above his level. Of course he's tired."

"I know, but the English give their kids a gap year and Joseph deserves one. He worked darn hard on a project to make the labs safe by discarding poisons."

"Yes, but I'd rather look at grades than a folio of what he did. Joseph needs more structure. Maybe he can change colleges—after his gap year." Hal looked more satisfied.

"Yeah, maybe. But it's the seventies. Just because a kid takes a semester off, doesn't mean he can't do the work. Joseph is smart! There's nothing wrong with taking off a semester, is there?" Hal grunted one of his *ummms*. He had nothing more to say.

Geoff and Sarah invited Joseph to live with them and offered to help him start a gardening business. So Joseph moved to Pasadena. Sarah with her fine artistic talent soon created a flyer they distributed in their neighborhood. Strangely, Joseph disappeared at the time that he was to meet with the first customer, but Geoff put on Joseph's gardener shirt and kept the appointment. Joseph had a customer.

The next month, Geoff phoned. "Mom, I'm awfully sorry, but we can't keep Joseph. He left a hose running, didn't close a gate. The dog got out, and he mowed someone's Astroturf lawn. He's lost his customers. He doesn't bathe so he smells, too. We can't stand it. I'm sorry."

This triggered the sense of guilt that always lay below my emotional life. What did I do wrong raising Joseph? He always took a shower and smelled good. He always remembered to close gates and not let the dog out. What had gone wrong? A deep purple cloud of danger enveloped me, but I ignored this grim alarm. I told myself firmly, God has restored our family. All was well. I did not dare think that Joseph was in peril.

"Well, thanks for trying, Geoff. Maybe he can get a job around here." Our entire family was a bit absentminded. Forgetting to close a gate—that's really natural. The smell? I assumed Joseph was working so hard he didn't have time to bathe. I'd make sure he showered when he got home.

So Joseph returned to Lido Isle and soon found employment at a paint factory on Bristol Avenue. The owner liked him. They played chess together at noon. Joseph showered every day and I did his laundry. When we celebrated the New Year, 1997, Joseph decided to return to Evergreen for his junior year and register as a double major, art and chemistry, which Evergreen permitted. Hal said nothing more about his own dissatisfaction with that university and I didn't want to raise any problems. Joseph drove to Tacoma for spring semester in February, and moved in with his sister who had settled there.

After a few weeks, she phoned. "Mom, you know Joseph sleeps in the attic and he's just a little bouncy for me. I've asked him to move because I hear him clumping around all night. I can't sleep."

"Don't worry, darling, he'll find another place." I didn't put the pieces together; both brother and sister found Joseph difficult. Joseph was different, a nature boy, a lover of the environment who walked the beaches to pick up trash. He helped build an environmental center at his high school. He had a mischievous sense of humor and a genius IQ, but he didn't fit in just anywhere. I hoped he would find his right place in life while making pots in ceramics class and experimenting in science at Evergreen.

The first of March, Joseph phoned. "Hey, Mom, I've got an apartment on a lake, a super roommate, and a job, lab assistant to a famous scientist. I'm making vases too."

"Oh, Joseph, that's wonderful. I'm so proud of you."

Joseph had settled down. Hal's business was truly improving even without the Bakersfield contract; Laura was finding new friends in junior high. All was well, and all was well, and all was well.

PART III

Mosaic Mind

CHAPTER 18

The Angels of Pierce County Jail

Tacoma, Washington, March 2, 1978

*A*lone, I flew from California to Pierce County Jail, Tacoma, Washington. I stood paralyzed on the stone steps, crushed between my need to save my son and my impulse to run for the comfort of my family and my job, Director of the Lutheran Learning Center. At last, I tugged on the oaken door of this granite citadel. The stench of despairing men engulfed me.

A guard's voice challenged me. "Make up your mind, Lady. Are you coming or going?"

Through forced lips, I said, "I'm coming." I made my legs step over the threshold and marched to the end of a line of women. In loud voices, they cursed and called out. If only I could keep a distance between those other women and me.

They stared at the clock on the wall. When it pointed to 10 a.m., the women charged down the corridor with the intensity of racehorses. I ran after them. The doors of a jam-packed elevator were closing. I jumped. I fell against a buxom woman.

"You 'all got your elbow in my stomach," she yelled.

Her words broke the dike holding back my emotions. "I'm sorry. I don't know what I'm doing. They locked up my boy. He had a nervous breakdown."

As the elevator creaked and shimmied its way upward, I remembered the phone call—it was only last night when Joseph's roommate Bill phoned and told Hal and me, "Joseph had a breakdown. He wandered nude around campus. They've locked him up in a Tacoma jail. The police said I shouldn't let you know, that you should forget Joseph. He's over twenty-one so they don't notify parents."

When I hung up the phone, I began packing. I'd fly to Tacoma and not come home until I brought Joseph with me. Hal had a contract to close, but he'd fly up soon.

The elevator stopped with an impact that threw us jail visitors even harder against each other, generating moans and cusswords. The door slid open. The women, in jeans and sneakers, galloped out. I trotted after them, hobbled by my skirt and slippery pumps. Only five feet tall and the last to reach the visitor's room, I couldn't see over the women crowded in front of the single viewing window. I stood in the rear and listened to the chorus of their voices.

I won't bail you out this time. You go to hell."

"You hearin' me, son? I love you."

"Yo baby's cryin' fo you, sweetheart."

"Bastard!"

"Lover!"

"The dog ain't et since you gone."

Joseph needed to see me. I had to let him know I'd get him out of there somehow. I remembered jumping rope with the kids at school. Though short and plump, I could jump really high. Up in the air I sprang. I scanned a blur of unfamiliar faces before I thumped to the ground. No Joseph.

"Where are you, Joseph?" Jump! Jump!

Sally yelled, "Who you jumpin' fo', Chil'?"

"My son! He's somewhere in there." I prayed *O God, let me see my son.*

"Her son in there. She need help!" Sally bellowed.

A cluster of women walked toward me. Together they lifted me above the crowd. Sweat patches showed through their T- shirts, yet they stood firm. I scanned the men behind the window; men with overflowing stomachs, men with sunken eyes, men with faces mashed against the glass.

Sally explained, "This here a holdin' pen. No judge said dey guilty yet."

I spotted my son. "Joseph, I'm here!" The women shifted their bodies toward Joseph and lifted me higher. I got a clear view of my son. His hair hung in curls to his shoulders. A beard half-covered his face. A skeletal body, yet truly my son. "Joseph, don't give up. Dad and I love you. Dad's coming. We'll get you out." A half-smile lit his face. He waved his hand with a thumbs-up sign.

A whistle blew. A guard yelled, "Visiting hour is over." As one body, the mass of prisoners turned their backs on the window and marched away.

The women lowered me to the floor. Just an hour ago, I feared them. Now my heart swelled with gratitude for these angels who lifted me. I hugged Sally. I half-bowed to the others. "Thank you, Ladies. You gave up your precious time with your men to help me find Joseph."

"You sure welcome!" Sally grinned.

"Ladies, move along," the guard ordered.

In the elevator, my chorus of women prepared me for the hard journey ahead. Sally patted my back. "Remember you got guts, Chil'. Fight for your son."

Another voice rang out, "You'll snatch Joseph out of this here nasty place!"

A teenager chanted, "Go, girl, go!"

These angels of Pierce County Jail gave me confidence in a woman's power and a fighting spirit strong enough to do whatever it took to bring Joseph home.

Hal flew in at three that afternoon and our daughter Julie, who lived in Tacoma, joined us in our hotel room. While Hal unpacked, Julie and I lay across the double bed. Scenes of Joseph's childhood ran through my mind like slides on an overhead projector. "Julie, I can see Joseph in his rose-colored corduroy suit with the feet in. Remember it? And now I see him with his cats, Toots and Shadow, hanging from his arms. You used to say he had eyelashes too beautiful for a boy—oh, now I see him as first clarinet in the marching band the time they went to the Rose Parade. Climbing mountains with those crampons and ropes…how strong and happy he looks…."

Julie listened. Her attention and her presence comforted me. Finally, I wound down like a music box. "Seems impossible—Joseph in jail."

Julie patted my hand. "You have a lot of great memories of him."

Hal had finished unpacking and laid a yellow legal pad on the desk for notes. "Let's decide on our plan of action."

Julie opened her brief case. "I've asked all my friends, and they have given me a list of attorneys. Do not use the public defender. Everyone says, if you do, Joseph will lose his case"

"I always thought the Public Defender was..." I began.

Julie interrupted. "Noble? Well, they aren't. At least nobody seems to think so. I've studied psychology and work for the Health Department. No one likes dealing with the mentally ill. You need to hire someone who will work hard for my little brother."

Hal nodded agreement. "We'll pay what it takes. That's why I'm keeping my business going. Joseph's care will be costly." I managed a smile for these two, father and daughter, so much alike. Julie left me with my memories while she dialed names on her list of attorneys. Each time a voice on the other end of her line refused her request, her voice grew a little more determined and edgy. She had guts.

Hal paced in the narrow confines. "After Julie finds a lawyer, you should come home with me and return to your job."

"Prince of Peace School gave me a leave of absence for as long as I need it."

"I know. But Laura doesn't want to live with her friend's family and I want my women back." Hal rarely spoke of his emotional needs. I longed to return to my role of wife and mother at home but my Tiger Mother instinct on a rampage overpowered any doubts as to where I belonged. "I won't leave Washington until I bring Joseph with me. The connection between Joseph and his family is too weak. If I abandon him now, I'm afraid he'll be lost to us forever."

Hal kissed me. "You do what you need to do."

Before Julie left, she handed me the name of an attorney, Norman Gleim. In a fifteen- minute consultation with Norman, we offered what little information we had about Joseph and handed over a $3,000 retainer fee. The next morning Hal called a taxi for the airport. "I'll be back next weekend. Maybe sooner. Keep your pecker up!" he joked. I ran after him to kiss him goodbye, but I wasn't fast enough. The taxi whizzed away down the street with my man. I threw a kiss at the vanishing auto.

The next morning, already a veteran of the system, I arrived early at the jail, the first visitor in line. "I'm here to visit Joseph Sarkissian." I slipped my ID through the slot in the bulletproof window. The guard frowned. "No prisoner of that name here."

"But he is. I saw him here, yesterday. I'm his mom." My own sense of reality was crumbling. Had he escaped somehow? Was he dead? Was I asleep in a never-ending nightmare? He was my son. I felt his despair. Every cell in my body was connected to him. I shrieked, "You have to tell me. I'm his mother!" I felt the warmth of the line of women forming behind me and heard their murmuring voices. "I won't move until you tell me." They could throw me in jail for all I cared. If Joseph was dead....

The guard smiled. "Down the hall, Ma'am, to Room 103. They'll look him up. Next?"

"Thataway." A woman pointed her thumb at a hall to the right. Today I wore sneakers and I could run. I found a window into an office marked *103*. I peered in and watched a clerk shuffling papers. I rapped on the window. He looked up briefly and continued shuffling. I yelled into a mail slot, "Where is Joseph Hunter Sarkissian? He is my son. Has he died?"

The man studied a paper. He looked my way. I pressed my ear to the slot. "Transferred to Western State Hospital, Lakewood, Washington, Ma'am," he shouted. The secrecy of this transaction laid down a new layer of horror in my mind.

I had to phone Hal. I escaped the jail. Inside a glass telephone booth, a woman dripped tears on her polka-dotted dress. I waited. A line formed behind me. When she emerged, I stepped inside. The phone felt wet from her tears. I emptied my coin purse on the little shelf. "God, make this enough money to phone. Newport Beach, California." Ridiculous prayer. God can't multiply coins like He did fish. Can He?

I dialed Hal's business. "Major Data. Sarkissian speaking."

"Thank God you're there. They transferred Joseph to Western State Hospital in Fort Steilacoom. I'm stuck in Tacoma. No car. Don't know what to do!"

Hal threw a rope into my emotional abyss. "Hold on, Martha. I'm glad he's in a hospital. That's where he should be."

The operator interrupted, "Please deposit two dollars and fifty cents." I fed the phone the rest of my coins. On their way to the operator, they clanged like a streetcar in a traffic jam. Why didn't Hal speed up a bit and talk faster? Didn't he know I was running out of coins? Why did he always take so long pondering every detail?

The line of desperate women outside grew longer. Hal's voice rose above the snapping static. "I'll take the first plane I can to Tacoma, snag a rental car at the airport, and be at your hotel tonight. We'll figure out our next stop together."

The operator's voice broke in, "Please deposit fifty cents to continue." I was out of coins but I could hear Hal's voice above hers. "Tomorrow we'll visit Joseph together, talk to his psychiatrist. Learn what we're facing."

I breathed a kiss into the receiver just before we were cut off. As I stepped out of the box, I told the women cued up for the phone, "Sorry I took so long. My husband's in California and I...." They nodded with understanding. More angels from the Pierce County jail.

Hal arrived that night. We were the only customers in a diner where we shared our grief. A waitress with a road map of wrinkles above a ruffled apron brought us the Special, chopped steak with mushroom sauce. She hovered nearby, pouring countless cups of coffee. We felt safe in her care. Hal slammed his fist on the checkered tablecloth. "It's hell not understanding Joseph's condition." The waitress looked alarmed and headed toward us. I waved her away. "My God, we've got to fight for Joseph. Can they put you in jail for taking off your clothes on a university campus?" He drew a shuddering breath.

"Thanks to Julie, we've got a lawyer working on it," I answered.

The waitress persisted in friendly overtures. "More coffee?"

"Keep it coming," Hal said.

"When Joseph is released, Geoff will drive him home."

Hal gulped a swallow of coffee and smiled. "The kids really are going to bat for us. We've got each other. Let's try to be *cool kids.*"

"I almost lost it today when they said Joseph wasn't there and wouldn't give me any details."

"Poor Honey. It's the confidentiality law. He's over twenty-one. They aren't allowed to give out information. You used Mommy power to find his whereabouts."

"I can't stand it. What can we do?" I wrung my hands in despair, just as my Mother did.

"You can visit him in the hospital and we can make plans for his care. Hal hung on to his slide-rule mentality to keep from slipping deeper into a chaotic swamp. "I'm an engineer. We need the facts before we make a plan. First, 'breakdown' is not a medical diagnosis. I know enough, though, to understand this is going to be expensive, starting with the lawyer. We've always saved for a rainy day and, Martha; this is the time to use our savings."

While Hal wrestled with an action plan, I tried to visualize a satisfying life for Joseph apart from college. "Joseph grew such a great vegetable garden here last year. Maybe we should buy a farm for him. Or, let's set him up as a potter. That pinch vase he made, the one with brown and gold glaze—it's my favorite vase."

"You're dreaming, Martha. Joseph is sick. He needs medication and a psychiatrist."

"He needs us and the rest of his family. He'll get better when we take him home. Everyone at church is praying...." Like a sailboat tacking back and forth, we were actually moving forward.

The waitress stuck her head into our conversation as she gathered up our plates of gravy-soaked steak. "You two must have some big troubles. Can't even eat your dinner. Well, I'm bringing you both chocolate sundaes on the house."

Hal's face lit up when she plunked in front of us balls of ice cream soaking in pools of chocolate syrup. We grinned at each other like kids. Hal took a spoonful. "Martha, if Joseph got injured in an auto accident, we'd get all the info about his condition we could and look after him—without blaming ourselves. Try to look on Joseph's illness as a cosmic accident."

"I'll try, Hal. But when you give birth to a baby, you feel responsible for it all its life."

"It would have been some miracle if I had a baby, but dads feel responsible too."

"I know. But a woman's hormones...I tried to be a good mother...but it's my fault if my child...."

"Cut it out. The difference between us is, I don't feel guilty and you shouldn't. This has happened and we'll both deal with it the best we can."

As we left our refuge, the waitress patted me on the shoulder. I felt her kinship. All the angels weren't in Pierce County jail. At least one was in a

Washington diner. In the darkness of our despair, nameless ordinary women and men lit candles of compassion for us.

The following morning, Hal drove the eighteen miles from Tacoma to Lakewood, Washington where Western State Hospital stood on the grounds of the former Fort Steilacoom. Trees ablaze with pink blossoms lined the curving driveway. An American flag waved in front of a chunky, cement block building. We parked. "This must be the place," Hal announced. Near the hospital, we noticed two signs: one pointed west to a cemetery for soldiers who died in Fort Steilacoom Hospital. The other pointed east to a cemetery for mental patients who died in the same building after it became Western State. I shivered. Had those patients died of old age or had they committed suicide?

"Keep your pecker up!" This idiom for "be brave" brought a smile to my face, as usual. We linked hands. We pushed on the heavy double-door and crossed into a vast reception room where we read a notice posted on the bulletin board nearby.

Center for Forensic Services, Western State Hospital Washington

Patients enter the forensic (legal) unit in the hospital through the criminal justice system. Evaluation and treatment services are provided for adults prior to their trial, after they are convicted, or after they are acquitted by reason of insanity. The Center also provides services to certain individuals under the mental health laws that require the security of a legal unit.

"Criminal justice system! Hal, Joseph isn't a criminal," I whispered.

Hal took my arm. "That's what we're going to prove in court. Let's go."

We headed across a linoleum floor that smelled of antiseptic. "At least, it doesn't smell bad here like the jail," I commented.

"And the nurse in charge looks professional," Hal noted. We moved closer to a curved desk where a wiry woman moved rapidly through a pile of papers, pen in hand. She wore a gleaming white uniform and her brown eyes looked kind through her horn-rimmed glasses. The edge of my icy fear melted. Joseph was in a safe, clean place. I smoothed my hair and tried to smile.

Hal whispered, "Let me talk to her. If we want to get any information, we need to act professional. I bet she's up to here," he ran his hand across his neck, "with hysterical parents."

I swallowed my tears and nodded agreement. "Concentrate on collecting information, Martha. So far, all we really know is what his roommate Bill told us."

After my baby died, I constructed a dam to hold back the flow of bad memories. This new trauma reopened the floodgates of sadness and guilt. "Hal, if you'd been home the night Jennifer died, you would have heard her cry and she'd be alive today."

His voice had a cutting edge. "Martha, let's take one problem at a time." We'd reached the nurse in charge. Hal spoke in a commanding, yet gentle voice. "Good evening, Ma'am."

Her brown eyes flickered over me and I sensed some sympathy or pity in them. I tried to smile through my trembling lips.

"Can I help you?"

"I'm Joseph Sarkissian's father." Hal spoke in a pride-filled voice, unashamed of the illness and proud of the son. "And this is his mother, Martha. Our son is a patient here. We'd like to speak with his psychiatrist. We're hoping to receive some suggestions for Joseph's care."

She riffled through her papers. "Since he's twenty-four his records are confidential. I can't give out any information about him." I wanted to protest, but Hal squeezed my hand to quiet me.

"I understand. You need to respect the regulations." Hal stood motionless, smiling pleasantly across the desk.

I tore at the cuticles on my fingernails. I wanted to scream at this nurse but I tried to copy Hal's pleasant demeanor.

She leaned forward conspiratorially and whispered, "Dr. Halliburton is your son's psychiatrist. He'll be stepping out of that elevator over there in a few minutes. Try talking to him there. Big man, big heart." e'He She bent back over her papers.

I gushed, "Oh, thank you so very much. We just have to learn more about Joseph—Joseph's sickness."

Grief is a thirsty business. Hal and I gulped mouthfuls of ice water from the fountain by the elevator and waited. I fretted. How would we ever recognize

Joseph's psychiatrist? Should we go back and ask the nurse what he looked like? But the minute a two hundred pound, six foot something man, exuding importance and kindness, stepped out of the elevator, I knew *this* was Dr. Halliburton.

Hal approached him. "Dr. Halliburton, we're Joseph Sarkissian's parents, but no one as yet has explained his condition to us."

The doctor nodded thoughtfully. Then he stole ten minutes from a demanding schedule. His gentle eyes and the occasional pats he gave my husband, a much shorter man, softened his words.

"Joseph's diagnosis is paranoid schizophrenic. Schizophrenia is a brain disease entailing a profound loss of connection to reality. He has delusions, that is, he has false ideas of reality, which means he perceives sensory impressions that are not part of reality. An inner voice prompted him to wander around nude playing a flute on Evergreen campus. Perhaps the flute was magical and protected him. It might be a flute from an ancient Greek myth or from an Aztec culture. Strange beings urged him on. Too bad. He's a fine boy."

A surge of love for this big bear of a man filled me. Dr. Halliburton viewed Joseph as a fine boy despite Joseph's strange distortion of reality.

"He was doing research with Dr. Kutter at Evergreen when this thing overwhelmed him," Hal explained.

Dr. Halliburton nodded. "A female student at Evergreen reported him. She might not bring charges. She understood his condition."

I burst out with "Charges of what?" Now I understood there were greater charges than a misdemeanor for wandering on campus playing a flute. I repeated, "What charges? Joseph is a good man. He'd never hurt anyone."

Dr. Halliburton did not answer. We stood there silently until Hal picked up the dialogue again. "What is the prognosis for Joseph?" My question fell into the dust.

Dr. Halliburton replied, "Impossible to tell at this point. One third of persons with schizophrenia recover from this brain disease without intervention. One third recover with the help of medications. One third never recover." He patted Hal's arm.

"What should we do to help Joseph?" I asked.

"Officially, his prognosis is poor. But I'm counting on Joseph. He cares about people. He reacts favorably to medications. If you can make sure he takes his meds

— I think he'll be ok. Without meds, he'll relapse. Don't get your hopes up too high. Always remember, Joseph is special and don't give up. Good evening." He strode away, a tired, caring man, aware of his own and others' limitations.

The next morning, I phoned Jean Barraclough, my principal at Prince of Peace. "Can you extend my leave of absence? Joseph is in Western Washington State Mental Hospital. Hal has to return to North Carolina but I intend to stay near Joseph. I don't know where, but I'll stay."

"We'll extend the leave of absence as long as you need. Remember, all the teachers are praying for you. You'll find the right place to stay." aal is leaving Sleepless, I lay in bed, composing a rosary of the people who helped me. I prayed, "Bless Bill, who called us despite the police advice; bless Dr. Kutter who trusted Joseph; bless Sally and the women who lifted me up in the jail; bless the guard who smiled a little; bless the waitress who gave us sundaes; bless Dr. Elizabeth Kutter who phoned me with the compassion of a mother; and especially bless the nurse in charge and Dr. Halliburton, who dared to go against regulations." I paused, then added, "And bless Laura and my husband and Julie and Geoff. I couldn't live through this without them, and without You."

I awakened the next morning to a ringing phone. Judy, the daughter of our school kindergarten teacher, was on the line. "Martha, you can stay with Tom and me as long as you like. We're just a few miles from the hospital and Tom can drop you off on his way to work every morning. "

Before Hal left for the airport, he drove me in his rental car to Judy and Tom's home in Lakewood, eighteen miles from Tacoma.

At Judy's, I dined on rhubarb pie and fell in love with their children. In the morning, three-year-old Maranatha climbed into my basement bed singing, "Jesus Loves the little children, all the children of the world" I added "including Joseph." A feeling of ease coursed through me. I wanted to stay forever in my basement apartment, where backpacks and teddy bears surrounded me and Maranatha sang hymns in the morning.

I was savoring homemade waffles with maple syrup when Tom stuck his head in the kitchen. "Come on, Martha. It's time to go to the hospital."

CHAPTER 19

Ring the Bell

An entry hall with no doors and no receptionist confused me. How could I find Joseph in this vast hospital? I studied the quiet carpeted box of a room and slowly the outline of an elevator detached itself from the beige background. I pushed a button. A door opened. I stepped inside.

A leaden silence filled the elevator. I held my breath as I slowly rose to the second floor of Western State Hospital. I exited the elevator to face a forbidding metal door. A sign printed in large black letters read, "Ring the bell."

"Eat me," read the sign that greeted Alice in Wonderland. Was it safe to follow the sign? Twisting my head left and right, I searched for some indication of human life and found none, except the sign. I forced my shaky second finger to ring the bell. A long wait ensued.

The door opened a crack and a resonant voice spoke softly, "I.D."

I handed over my driver's license. The door swung open wide enough for me to squeeze in and closed with a snap behind me.

"Purse," the guard demanded.

I handed him my puffy handbag and watched as he undid its leather straps, unzipped the fake alligator exterior and burrowed inside. His eyes narrowed. "What's this?" He held a plastic wrapped lump in the air.

"Banana bread." He ignored my forced smile, which I hoped proved I was a wholesome, bread-baking sort of woman and a Lutheran school teacher, to boot, and hurled the bread in a trash can. It landed with a forlorn thump. I opened my mouth to protest, but just then glimpsed Joseph in the distance playing checkers. He wore clean pants, a faded clean T-shirt, and was smiling.

"There's Joseph," I told the guard. As he walked with me through this community room, I noticed a viewing window in the left side. I peered in and saw a dormitory with layers of men sleeping in triple bunk beds.

"Why are all those patients asleep in the daytime?"

"The brain repairs itself in sleep," he intoned in a melodic voice. That phrase still lingers in my mind.

I pushed a folding chair over to Joseph's table. "Hi, Honey." I spoke as normally as possible.

"I'm playing checkers now, Martha," he admonished me.

The other player, a med tech, looked directly at me. "Joseph is doing very well. He's already beaten me in one game."

"When he was only eight, he used to beat me in checkers." Joseph looked over at me and smiled shyly.

"Are you his mother?"

"Yes, I'm Mrs. Sarkissian."

Joseph stared at me and chanted, "Sarkissian. Carcinogenic. No mother. Other." His black checker hopscotched across the board and he scooped up the reds.

Joseph's salad speech alarmed me. Best for me to keep quiet. I took a seat near the table. From time to time, Joseph glanced at me out of the corner of his eye and smiled. A part of him recognized me as Mom, even though another part didn't.

An ageless woman, in a pink-flowered housedress and fluffy slippers, stopped by our table. "My name is Molly. Do you want to see a photo of my children?"

"Pull up a chair. I'd love to see them." Since Joseph barely acknowledged me, I welcomed her presence. She handed me a wrinkled photo of four little children, two girls in ruffled nylon dresses, two boys in long trousers and white shirts. They had eyes like blue marbles and hair like dandelion fluff.

"Why, they're beautiful, Molly. How their hair shines."

She moaned, "They took my children away from me."

"I'm sorry." My heart, broken by Joseph, broke again for Molly. How many times can a heart break and pump on?

The next day, Tom again drove me to Western Hospital. This time my son, focused on painting a picture of Harbor High cheerleaders, barely noticed me. The energy of the cheerleaders' pom-poms and prances vibrated in the hushed room. Too engrossed in his painting to talk, he recognized my presence with his smile.

Once again, Molly joined me and displayed her photo. She laid her head on my shoulder. I patted her back. The tech led her gently away. "Come on, Molly. Visiting hours are over."

"Joseph, it's time for me to leave. Is there anything I can bring you tomorrow?"

He looked at me from the absorbed eyes of a painter. "Tomorrow, borrow, sorrow. Where the wind goes who knows."

I spoke more slowly and clearly. "Joseph, what do you need?"

He imitated my slow clear speech. "Mar-tha...I need a tube...of teal blue... acrylic."

"I'll bring it tomorrow, Joseph." Now the guard took my arm and gently led me toward the exit. I wanted to say, *Joseph, let me give you a goodbye hug,* but I did not dare break the holy silence of the room. I waved a silent kiss in his direction and I thought he lifted two fingers in farewell.

That night I scribbled a poem in my journal, hoping it would ease my grief.
What happened to Molly O'Mallory's children?
Why were her little ones taken away?
Wearing a wrapper and pink feathered slippers,
"Look at this photo," is all she can say.

What happened to Molly O'Mallory's children?
The children with blue eyes and corn tassel hair?
She knows they are dressed in their best and smiling,
She has a photo to prove that they're somewhere.

What happened to Molly O' Mallory's children?
She knows she has children gone, gone away.
She can prove she has children. She holds up a photo.

"Look at this photo," is all she can say.

What happened to Martha Sarkissian's son?
"Look at his photo," is all I can say.
See his alertness, intelligence, kindness.
How could these qualities vanish away?

On my third visit to the hospital, I clutched a tube of teal blue acrylic paint in my hand and envisioned Joseph, like Van Gogh, continuing his artist's life though confined in a hospital. Now that I'd witnessed the respect the staff showed the patients, I no longer feared empty elevators and metal doors.

I showed my ID, handed over my purse, and spoke cheerily to the guard. "I brought my son some extra paint today to finish his painting."

"Son's name?" he asked.

"Joseph Sarkissian."

"We have no one of that name here."

"You must remember him. He was the man painting the Harbor High School cheering squad. He smiled while he painted pom-poms."

The burly attendant stared dully at me. "Uh, how long was he here?" he finally asked.

"Two and a half days."

"I only remember my regulars," he replied.

The med tech that played checkers with Joseph just two days ago joined us. I looked pleadingly up at him. "You remember Joseph, don't you? Yesterday you told me he beat you in checkers."

Silently, he shook his head no.

My gut contracted with a now familiar lump of pain. Alone in a mental hospital searching for my son, that was the stuff of nightmare. But, I reminded myself, Hal is on a work contract in North Carolina. He can't be here. You can do okay by yourself. Locate a carpeted office with a desk and you'll find an administrator. Psych techs speak warily and keep their eyes on their patients.

I wandered through labyrinthine halls searching for offices with name-plates. At last, I came upon a room with a bulletproof window that met my prerequisites. I rapped loudly.

"Come in," a neutral voice responded.

An administrator in an oatmeal colored suit nodded at me across a mahogany desk. With every hair on his head combed into place and every piece of paper and pen neatly arranged, he was a model bureaucrat. I recalled Hal's advice to speak professionally, not like a hysterical mother. "I'm Joseph Sarkissian's mother. He's a patient here, but I can't locate him."

In a cool packaged voice, he informed me, "Your son has been declared sane and returned to prison."

I sagged into a plastic leather chair. Words from *Alice in Wonderland's* tea party popped into my mind, "Clean plate, move down." Insane yesterday. Sane today. Move down to jail. "How can they move him when he obviously still needs medical help?"

He spoke in his unfeeling, almost robotic voice. "Since he reacted well to medications he is declared sane and sent back to jail to stand trial."

"Why didn't you phone me when you moved him? I'm his mother. I need to know where he is."

He bit his lower lip and stared firmly over his desk into my eyes, a dog-training technique. "Your son is over twenty-one. We have neither obligation nor authorization to inform the parents. Now if you'll excuse me...."

He continued to stare pointedly at me. I arose from the chair and stumbled out of the room. Apparently, motherhood was not a value at Western State Hospital and sanity and insanity were states of mind decided by a judge. I hated to move from Judy's loving home, but now I had to find lodging near the jail so I could watch over Joseph and soon bring him home. Hal flew in to drive me to Tacoma and find an apartment for us.

"1 bdrm, kit. liv. near Pierce County Jail. $11/day. Aspen Motel." I held in my hand the small newspaper ad, yellow and damp with my sweat, while Hal unloaded my suitcase. Too soon, he was waving goodbye through the car window. "See you next weekend."

The ad failed to mention walls painted a funeral black or a bilious green stove that leaked gas, or a green refrigerator, coils on top that hummed like a beehive. I'd told myself, "I'll take it. I'll stay here until my son is released from jail and I can bring him home."

The place met my qualifications: five blocks from jail, and cheap. I would not think of my lovely home by the sea in Newport Beach or my classroom of eager bright-eyed children. When Hal came on the weekends, his presence would transform the sordid rooms into a home. e I filled the rickety bedroom bureau drawers with my belongings and fell into an exhausted sleep on a thin lumpy mattress. Whenever my nervous system went on overload and another cup of coffee or a prayer or a telephone call didn't help me, I slept. "Sweet sleep that knits up the ravell'd sleeve of care."

The next day when I appeared at the prison, I learned I did not have permission to visit the person they called *the prisoner,* who was my son. I called daughter Julie to complain. "I need visitation rights at the jail. Joseph isn't even allowed to talk on the phone and that's illegal. We've paid all this money to the attorney you recommended and he doesn't even answer my calls. Julie, what can I do?"

"Be patient, Mom. Norman is a good attorney and a good guy. He'll look after Joseph. It takes time." My messages to agencies and departments and Norman Gleim were piling up everywhere and no one ever answered or called back. How could the prison system strip Joseph of his rights? What had happened to justice? What had happened to God? What was happening to me?

Finally, Mr. Gleim phoned. "We're set today for a visit with Joseph at two p.m. at the jail. I'll meet you at the front entrance."

Doors opened and guards smiled more widely than usual when Mr. Gleim led me to a small splintery table. I seated myself by Joseph, and Mr. Gleim took the bench across from us. A guard stood at the door.

I yearned to hug Joseph, but he glared at me through his thick black lashes and I hesitated. His curly maroon hair reached to his shoulders. He looked fragile, breakable. I reminded myself he was broken. "Is there anything I can get for you, Joseph?"

His words fell like stones. "I don't want anything from you, Martha."

I touched him gently on the arm. "Darling, don't call me Martha. Call me Mom, like you always have."

"I won't call you Mother. You aren't my mother. You adopted me in Switzerland as a baby. I know all about it."

"Joseph, please, I'm your mother."

Mr. Gleim interrupted. "Ahem. We have a few business matters to discuss." Dressed in a gray gabardine suit and maroon tie, he looked far too handsome and well groomed for the shabby smelly room.

Joseph suddenly focused. "Business. I need to talk to my brother Geoff on the phone."

"Sorry, Joseph, I can't arrange that," Mr. Gleim answered.

I burst forth, "Mr. Gleim, there's a law in this country that every prisoner is entitled to three free calls. Joseph loves his older brother very much. You have to arrange a phone call for them!" Was this a Gestapo prison, or America? How could the jail simply take away rights? "Sue the jail. My father was a lawyer. I know our rights."

"Mrs. Sarkissian, you must listen to me." He leaned forward, elbows on the table, and looked directly into my face. "If I grow legalistic about the phone calls, the guards will take out their anger on Joseph. That's the way it is."

I pinched my arms fiercely to keep back the tears. I couldn't even arrange for my son to talk to his brother. Oh, if my attorney father had been alive, it would have been different. He would have waved the Constitution and the Bill of Rights in their faces. He wouldn't permit this outrage to his grandson. But I was impotent.

Joseph leaned toward me and whispered hoarsely, "Did you know they put me in a cell with a murderer?"

Mr. Gleim replied quickly. "I had you moved there for your own protection, Joseph. Some of the guys in the tank would hurt a handsome kid like you. But Hugo is a really kind man. He caught his wife in an act of passion and killed her but he doesn't have a killer's nature. You can trust old Hugo."

I gasped. Joseph's life depended on the actions of this lawyer and the kindness of a murderer. Our world had become unsafe, unpredictable. I murmured, "Thank you for protecting my son."

Joseph waved his hands above his head as though chasing mosquitoes. "Radio waves –I don't want to hear them—turn them off."

I kissed Joseph on the cheek. "I'm your mom, and Geoff is going to drive you home when they release you. Dad will be here soon, too. Our family is with you. Do you understand?"

"Off! Stop! Stop!" He waved his arms again.

A guard poked his head in. "Time's up," he said.

Norman told me he could not arrange any more visitations to the jail, so my major occupation became waiting for the trial. I phoned Norman "When are we going to court?"

"I'm delaying as long as I can. The longer we wait, the better Joseph's chance will be."

So waiting was good. Joseph was safe in his cell and I, in mine.

Then, three weeks later, Norman phoned me. "Be at court tomorrow morning at 8:30. I'm expecting a good outcome, because the young woman on the library steps that night has refused to testify against Joseph. She said she feels sorry for him and realizes he is mentally ill."

With such short notice, neither Julie nor Hal were able to come to court with me, but since there was no one to testify against Joseph, hope spread its wings again. Joseph would be coming home with me soon.

I wrapped my hair in curlers the night before the trial and in the morning, donned a new pant suit, black crepe with a ruffled white collar. Wearing this outfit felt adventurous and brave, because my principal, Esther Olson, had just given permission to teachers to wear pant suits the week before Joseph's break-down. I talked to God as I walked the five blocks to the courthouse.

Oh, Lord, forgive my lack of faith during these weeks. My world fell apart. I couldn't believe in You, or in our lawyer, or even in Hal. Please let me know in some way that You are with Joseph and me in court today.

I imagined myself testifying for my son in court. "Your Honor, our son, Joseph Hunter Sarkissian, has always had the finest character. Newport Mesa School District employed him as an assistant bandleader for Harbor High School, in charge of the instruments, practice and field trips. Active in Luther League, our youth church group, and an environmentalist, he set an example for high school students. Dr. Elizabeth Kutter, the renowned DNA scientist, employed him as her lab assistant at Evergreen and she told me, she would again if it was possible."

The sidewalks and shops of town glittered and shone after a rainstorm in the night. In my imagination I could hear the Harbor High band playing the Marine Hymn and Joseph, the shortest player, setting the pace, his clarinet pressed on his lips, his cheeks puffy with air. The music carried me all the way to the stone courthouse.

I stepped inside. The golden oak interior and wooden pews evoked a church. The railing, known as a *bar,* that separated judge, jurors, and prisoners from the gallery reminded me of an altar railing. A raised desk for the judge, called a bench, brought to mind a pulpit. No cross, of course, but the American and state flags hanging behind the judge's seat recalled the American and Christian flags in my church. A sacred silence prevailed in the golden brown room. I chose a seat three rows from the bar and bowed my head in prayer. *Comfort and protect Joseph through this trial and set him free. Help him to become the man you created him to be.*

The bailiff walked down the aisle. "All rise. The court is now in session with the honorable Judge Abbot Clearwater."

I stood. No one else in the audience stood entirely alone. This shamed me. What had I done wrong in my life to be abandoned?

"Kleenex?" a voice whispered in my ear.

Pastor Schweiss had entered my aisle from the other side and now stood beside me. I held up my head and looked into the sky blue eyes. "Pastor. You're here. A miracle."

I wasn't alone anymore. I clutched his arm, desperate for the touch of another human being to sustain me. Pastor Jacque Schweiss had brought me the gift of hope twenty-one years earlier when Jennifer died and now, in a time of even greater need, he was with me again.

Pastor whispered, "Your daughter Julie phoned me. I moved out of Seattle years ago, but she tracked me down. I do a lot of volunteering in jails nowadays. Thought I could help you."

"Oh, Jacque, I cannot bear this. God has abandoned me."

"No, Martha, God will never abandon you. He's here now with you and Joseph. Your heart and mind are so filled with grief you cannot sense him. But believe me. He is here and he is weeping for Joseph." I saw tears escape from behind Jacque's gold-rimmed glasses and knew he, too, wept for Joseph.

The judge in his ancient black robe strode to his seat in a business-like fashion. The audience sat down. The judge pounded his gavel for silence.

"Where are the jurors?" I whispered to Pastor.

"This isn't a trial. It's an arraignment. The judge will decide if it should go to trial."

I had been rehearsing in my mind again and again defenses of my son in front of an imaginary jury. What a fantasy. I hadn't even understood what was going on. Had Norman tried to tell me and I not listened? "This is better than a trial, isn't it, Pastor?"

He nodded yes.

The judge told the bailiff, "Bring in the prisoner."

Joseph, a dark mirror image of himself, appeared, his eyes burning like coals, his wavy auburn hair lank and lifeless on his shoulders. A bulky orange jail uniform overwhelmed this thin and fragile handcuffed man, my son. My stomach cramped, my head pounded, my chest contracted, my body could scarcely contain the pain I felt.

When our lawyer, Norman Gleim, approached the judge's seat and tilted his head to look up at the mighty judge, my heart sank. In his pale blue suit, Norman seemed too young to confront the powers that be and he mumbled as he spoke, "Your Honor, may I address the court?"

The judge acknowledged him with a quick nod.

Then Norman Gleim read from a paper in a very rapid, low voice. I strained every nerve in my body trying to hear, but his voice was too soft. The judge banged his gavel again. His words rang through the hall: "I declare Joseph Miller Sarkissian not guilty by reason of insanity."

"Not guilty! Not guilty!" The liberty bell rang in my heart. I jumped from my bench and ran down the aisle to the bar that separated Joseph and me. I held out my arms to embrace him. He moved toward me. "Joseph, darling," I called.

A rough hand clamped on my shoulder and dragged me away. "You are not allowed to touch the prisoner."

"He's my son. He's been declared not guilty. Didn't you hear the judge?"

The judge banged his gavel and ordered, "Bailiff, remove this woman from court."

Pastor Jacque, who had followed me down the aisle, asked, "May I address the court?"

The judge nodded permission. "I am Mrs. Sarkissian's minister. I am requesting an opportunity for this mother to speak to her beloved son."

The judge nodded again and told the bailiff, "See that this woman has a few moments upstairs to speak to her son before he is locked up."

Then I understood. Joseph was not guilty, but he still was a prisoner.

CHAPTER 20

The Escape

*A*s I explained to Miriam the details of Joseph's incarceration, tears and mucus streamed down my face. "That jail! Its smell. I was forbidden to visit Joseph. Even today in my eighties, it hurts, it hurts."

"How long did you wait for his release?" Miriam asked.

"The physical details of the mental hospital, the court, and my apartment are clear in my mind but the time is just a blur. I can't get hold of it."

"You were in a state of shock."

"Yes. Over and over, Joseph's arrest plays in my mind. I remember a message I left on Norm Gleim's phone. 'It is illegal to keep someone in jail who has been declared not guilty. Why won't they let me visit Joseph in the prison? Please return this call.' He never did."

Miriam murmured, "You were a courageous woman dealing with severe trauma. I hope by now you appreciate yourself for rescuing him."

"I don't know what I did. I was panicked. "

"Do you want to tell me what happened next?"

"Why should I go into this now?"

"Telling your story to someone else helps you learn how to handle the strong emotions you experienced and separates you a little from them. Your son is a fine man today and you no longer need fear he will take his life. I'm glad you are writing your memoir because that is another telling that will help you to separate a little more."

"In a way, I have to tell this story. I want everyone to know how much damage our legal system causes when it throws the mentally ill in jail instead of arranging for treatment and care in a hospital. This experience of Joseph's affected everyone in our family. Hal's business and health suffered, Geoff may have left the study of psychology when his loving care, and the Anne Sippy Clinic, failed to help his brother. Laura became depressed and unsure. Our children felt concerned about the possibility of a genetic effect of schizophrenia on their possible future children. "

"If you choose to tell me what happened next, I will be listening."

In a hurricane, the winds become light and almost calm as, whirling counter clockwise, they approach the center. Miriam's presence created a calm center in my emotional storm and I told my story.

The Escape

Hal commuted from Orange County to spend weekends with me at the motel. One Saturday night, he decided on a new tactic. "We're spinning our wheels. A teacher and an engineer don't have enough political power to get Joseph released. We need to tell our senator, Barbara Boxer. Her slogan is 'I give a damn' and I bet she does."

"Let's write her a letter. Now!" I pushed the dirty dishes aside and Hal plopped his yellow legal pad on the table. "I'll draft an outline, you work on wording sentences."

I struggled with the intro. "We are writing to enlist your aid in freeing our son, Joseph Hunter Sarkissian, from Pierce County jail." How many people were similarly imprisoned like Joseph? "Hal, I think I should do research in the library. This problem may be more common than we know."

We never finished our letter. More than a knock or a rap, a weird pounding shook our warped door. Hal and I exchanged fearful glances. Who pounds at night on the door of a rundown motel five blocks from the jail? I jumped up to clear our table of steak bones and curls of fat, vestiges of our weekend festive dinner. Hal waved me to my chair. "Stay seated, Martha. I'll get the door."

He opened it slowly. Step by step, in a measured pace, four sinister figures approached the dinner table where I sat. I could not discern their features with only the weak light of an old lamp with a pleated shade. Two men wore business suits and the other two wore police uniforms; they seemed to have masks hiding their faces. Perhaps it was the poor light casting shadows. Perhaps these four apparitions stood here to report Joseph's death. Regrets and questions flashed through my mind. I should have found a lawyer to sue the county for Joseph's release. Perhaps Joseph could not bear living with his terrible illness. The sight of the four strange men sent me on a sudden mental trip speeding down a mountain on gleaming silver tracks to Joseph's death, my guilt, and despair.

"FBI." A tall suited man showed his identification. I didn't look at it but Hal did.

The other FBI agent stepped forward. "If you will just sign a few papers for us, Mr. and Mrs. Sarkissian, we can arrange to release your son."

Hal and I spoke simultaneously.

"Has Joseph been injured?" I was scared to death that Joseph would kill himself.

At the same moment, Hal inquired, "What is the content of the papers?"

This apartment must have been created for criminals plotting crimes, not loving families. The appliances were sinister. The grease-covered stove leaked gas into the fetid air while the green refrigerator moaned and sighed. The unadorned black walls-no calendar-no painting of flowers or ocean-belonged to darkness and secrecy.

"Your son is alive. We are here to arrange his release," the tall FBI man answered A tornado of emotions---fear, anger, joy, hope, relief, suspicion---whirled me about. Could these men really release Joseph? Why did the police keep their hands on the shafts of their guns? Did we look dangerous? Why were they from the FBI instead of Pierce County? Why so late at night? Why on the weekend? Maybe they had the wrong family. Maybe this was a big mistake!

Hal remained silent. It was up to me to identify us. "Uh, sir, you don't need guns for us. My husband and I—we're just a Mom and Dad. I'm a Lutheran schoolteacher. Hal's an engineer."

I felt the pressure of Hal's fingers on my arm. These men weren't joking and I shouldn't say anything unless asked--I knew that's what Hal was thinking.

None of the men smiled.

The tall agent sat down with us; Hal moved our rusty standing lamp closer to the table and sent me a wink as if to say, "Hang in there, kid, we're winning."

"This meeting is confidential." The tall man spread out papers.

"Yes, sir." Hal's voice blended cooperation and caution.

"They called us in on this case because rape is a federal offense and a rapist has been operating on the Evergreen Campus."

I took a sharp intake of breath. A rapist on campus. Now I understood that suspicion had fallen on Joseph, who had been nude the night of his breakdown.

The agent continued in a low rapid tone. "It was clear that Joseph was not the rapist. They have no evidence of his ever having touched anyone. The girl who reported Joseph's nudity refused to witness against him. She expressed sympathy for his condition."

The shorter agent explained "Pierce County jail kept Joseph in prison in the hope that the real rapist would be found before they released him. Public opinion is in a lynching mood. The county is trying to protect your son."

I doubled over in pain from these revelations. Joseph suspected of rape! My idealistic young son hated by a lynching crowd. Hal patted my arm. "It's going to be all right. The gentlemen are helping us." We held hands while the FBI men took turns speaking in hoarse whispers.

"Joseph will be released from prison under these conditions. You must agree to a probation, which includes taking Joseph home to California and supervising his medical care for schizophrenia. Also, you must guarantee that he will never return to the state of Washington."

My tongue clung to the roof of my mouth. Even Hal, the great poser of questions, remained silent. His forehead wrinkled. That meant he didn't like a secret deal; he wanted justice in the light of day. But he nodded agreement. We had no bargaining chips. Hal read the paper carefully, signed with his fountain pen and passed it to me.

The second man continued, "Pick up Joseph at 3 p.m. the day after tomorrow. This is the name and phone number of his probation officer in California. Phone her on your arrival home."

There were no farewells, no 'thank-you' or 'have a nice day.' No rejoicing over Joseph's release. We were supposed to forget these men who hastily stuffed their papers into brief cases while the police stood ready to draw their guns. Then the four disappeared mysteriously into the night. I noticed two copies of the orders we had just signed lying on the table. We had promised to get Joseph transferred to formal probation in California, and to prevent him from ever returning to Washington.

"Hal, can we manage this?"

He was studying the probation conditions and didn't reply.

Two days later, our oldest son Geoff joined us in Washington. He picked up Joseph at the jail as the agents had arranged. Hal and I flew home to be with Laura. Geoff drove Joseph and his possessions back home, all fitting into the old Chevy van Joseph had used in the gardening business.

Hal and I arrived at Lido Island first, and both of us returned to work without hearing from Geoff. One afternoon as I drove home after four days back at work, I spotted the old rust-colored van parked by our open garage.

Geoff, brown haired and trim in a flannel shirt and jeans, lifted a box of textbooks out of the large vehicle. Like a fog over the sea, a sense of gravity lay on his face. His younger brother, dressed in grimy Levis and a black t-shirt, glared as I ran toward him.

"Joseph, I'm so glad you're home." Planning to hug him, I touched his rigid body as he drew away, suspicious. Something was clearly wrong with his legs or feet. When he stepped, it looked as though he walked in glue. He struggled to lift one foot and then the other. I tried to keep my face calm.

Geoff handed a carton of books to Joseph. "Put them in your room," he said softly.

Joseph's arms shook as he took the box. Then he walked with a peculiar gait through the garage toward the patio. He'd yank a foot loose from the floor, lift it high, and then slowly, slowly set it down, leaving it stuck to the floor. His progress was slow. Sweat trickled down his face and back.

When he managed to reach the patio, Geoff whispered, "It's the Haldol, his meds, that makes him walk like that. I took the responsibility of cutting his dosage in half, yet he still can hardly walk."

"Oh, is it ok for you to change it?"

"Mom, I'm working on my Ph.D. in psychology. I know about the medications. They've overdosed him. He wouldn't even be able to move if I hadn't cut the amount."

Now thirteen-year-old Laura sauntered through the garage and sidled up to me. "Mom, what's the matter with my brother?" she whispered. Her green eyes held tears. A blotchy rash appeared on her pale magnolia skin.

I steadied my voice. "It's his medication. We'll get it adjusted soon."

"You can help us unload," Geoff told her.

We were more of a funeral possession than a family welcoming home a son. Laura and I kept pace with Joseph's slow fearful tread. We lugged framed photos of Yosemite, ceramic pots and vases, and garbage sacks full of clothes through the kitchen to Joseph's bedroom. Geoff and Joseph worked together to reassemble a redwood table that fit together like a jigsaw puzzle. This glue-less nail-less wonder stirred a mix of emotions in me, delight in Joseph's artistic talent and sorrow over his losses

Over the next weeks, Joseph's bedroom gradually became a container for his madness. Every day he added new amulets; an Incan flute, mosaic tiles, bird nests, butterflies, signs in his secret language, an abalone shell radiating rainbows, cardboard squares, chalk drawings, charred black notebooks. The floor held heaps of dirty clothes, shoes, clay in a plastic sack, pebbles, bed sheets, blankets, paper clips, a confusion of objects I could not process or count.

At first, he joined us at the dinner table and silently wolfed down his food. When we attempted dinner table conversation, he replied in *salad speech,* his private language. "Hurricane quadra zunder zietag danger." His amulets, flute and magic signs couldn't keep his fear at bay. It became a formidable task for us to cope with this man who responded principally to the bizarre demands of his confused mind, but who was also our son and lived with us.

Laura grew silent at dinner, but Hal and I plodded on, trying to make family dinner normal. It didn't work. After several months, Joseph stopped eating with us. He took a walk at dinnertime. Late at night, we'd hear the refrigerator door bang and knew he served himself a plateful when we were in bed.

In the morning, Hal and I sat close to each other at our over-sized dining table. *The Kiss,* a print by Klimt, hung on the wall. A man and woman dressed in fantastic cloaks ornamented with rectangles and circles, kissed. As they did, none of the world existed for them except the plot of grass and flowers where they stood and each other. I nodded to the picture. Like the painted figures, Hal and I used to live in our own universe when we were together, but now Joseph made such intimacy almost impossible. Everything was affected by Joseph's presence, and not for the better. We sipped our coffee and exchanged pieces of the morning newspaper. "Hal, it's April and time for 'Take Your Daughter to Work' day. Clinton's taking Chelsea. Are you going to take Laura?"

"Laura's been at Major Data a lot. I don't think she'd like to miss school for this."

"What's the news about Clinton?"

"He's signed a bill against cloning humans. I guess that's a good thing."

We grazed on our newspaper until I couldn't restrain my emotions any longer. "Hal, we can't live like this. Joseph doesn't pay any attention to me, but he does respect you. I can't reach him, but you can. You have to make him eat dinner with us. Dirty dishes are piling up in his bedroom. Tell him he must follow family rules if he lives here."

Hal sighed, and lay down the paper and his coffee. "He's home now. I'll talk to him." I followed Hal to Joseph's door. He knocked forcibly. No answer. Hal pushed open the door and stepped inside. Joseph tossed a half-finished chalk drawing onto the heap of belongings on the floor. We stared at him. He stared back, a tiger in his jungle.

"Stay out of my room," Joseph spoke menacingly.

Before Hal could speak, I blurted out, "Joseph, dear, we need to be sure you're all right."

Joseph shook his head in confusion. A mass of glorious auburn curls tumbled about his shoulders. "Leave me alone." A suffering saint.

Hal, in military mode, stepped forward, and spoke in a firm voice, leaving a space between words for Joseph to process them. "While you live with us, we expect you to eat your meals with the family."

Joseph tugged on the curly black beard he'd recently grown. "Hmmm, radio waves surround us." An Armenian priest.

Hal recognized the futility of speaking in our language to someone living in the land of his subconscious. He smiled and nodded at Hal. "Yes, we'll keep in communication."

A smile transformed Joseph into our son once more. Hal had interpreted Joseph's code; radio waves meant communicating. Joseph had signaled us from his planet.

Our breakfast forgotten, we tiptoed out and sank down on our saggy couch and let our bodies rest against each other. We drew comfort from the smell and warmth and touch of our bodies. "He isn't taking his medication," Hal announced.

"I know."

"He isn't seeing his psychiatrist. No one's helping him. We have to face the fact that we can't manage him. We may not be able to keep him here." His measured tones beat a funeral dirge on the drum of my heart.

"He's our son. He needs us. He'd be living on the streets without us and...." I choked up. "I shouldn't have asked you to talk with him about family dinner and so on. He isn't a teenager. He's a troubled man who needs compassion."

"We've tried. I don't think we're helping him."

"It's my fault for asking you to help and now you want to throw him out."

"No, I don't. I want to find a way to help him and so far—we haven't."

CHAPTER 21

A New Marriage Contract

"Will you stop crying, Martha! This isn't the end of the world. We've still got each other and three other kids."

I dabbed at my eyes with a soggy Kleenex. "Can't seem to quit the tear thing. When you start talking about throwing Joseph out and I think of him—on the street, no resources." The tears recommenced. "I can't help it."

"I think you can. Suppose for a minute Joseph had been injured in an auto accident. We'd adjust and take care of him and ourselves. Now, because his disease is mental illness, we've let it unbalance us. We have to work together to make our marriage stronger and our life calmer."

"And how in the world do you propose to do that?" My eyes still oozed but he'd caught my attention.

He continued solemnly, "We have to promise each other not to blame each other, no matter what happens. If it should turn out Joseph cannot live here, we won't say I should have done X or you should have done Y. We'll take the attitude that an accident has happened and examine what we can do about it. Not examine why it happened or whose fault it is."

I hugged him and nuzzled his shoulder. "I'll never blame you for Joseph's sickness," I promised.

"And I will never blame you. Schizophrenia is a cosmic accident and neither of us is to blame."

"Yes, Hal." I kissed his cheek.

"And now we also have to promise not to blame ourselves." He shrugged off my kiss. Hal treated our agreements like a business contract and expected me to, also.

"That's not so easy to promise. I'm the Mom. Moms are to blame for everything, aren't they?" I peered into his eyes.

"Not just Moms are always to blame. Don't you think I'm wondering if it's my fault he had a breakdown? Maybe I went on too many business trips. Or maybe schizophrenia is in my genes because my half-sister is ill, or a hundred other things. We gotta let blame go. Don't blame us or anyone else. It happened, and we'll do what we can."

"It's different when you're the Mom. Lots of psychiatrists believe schizophrenia is caused by over loving mothers."

"Baloney, Martha. Just remember, you were my wife before you were a mom, and I don't want a wife crippled with guilt. Can you promise not to play the blame game?"

"I promise to try. We've always set up our contracts and this is the hardest, except for the original *I do.* I'll try. That's it." I took a deep breath and held out my hand. "Let's shake, partner."

Hal seized this moment to tack on a rider. "One thing more, while we're at it. All we ever talk about is Joseph. Let's allot him one hour a day and spend the rest of our time together talking about stuff for living—like we used to. You know, our other kids, your work, my work, music, recipes, ball games. We need to keep our balance."

I had my bargaining chip and it was my turn now to set a condition. "I agree to keep the Joseph talk down to one hour and out of the bedroom, on the condition that you attend meetings of the National Association for Mental Illness with me. This group really helps me."

"I don't know. I'm very committed at work and..."

"Talking to each other one hour a day will be absolutely useless unless we know what we're talking about. I'm learning about brain disease at NAMI. If you aren't willing..."

So we argued, raising our voices, sometimes even jokingly punching each other. Finally, I snatched a blue sofa pillow with an embroidered lighthouse and held it over his face. "You are a prisoner and I won't set you free till you agree to come to NAMI."

I could barely hear his voice through the pillow, "I promise to go to NAMI if you promise you'll never talk about Joseph in our bedroom. Save the bedroom for sex," he added.

"That one's an easy yes," I eased into his arms. "But can we do NAMI and talk one crisis hour a day in addition, not in the bedroom."

He counted downward, "5,4,3,2,1, sold."

From then on, Wednesday nights at seven we joined a group for relatives of persons with mental illness, one of the first NAMI support groups formed in Orange County. We met under the guidance of Dr. Eugene Ericson in the basement of Hoag hospital. Energy-saving lights imparted a mysterious yellow color to the evenings. I accepted this group at once as a necessary ritual. In the beginning of time, our ancient ancestors gathered in a similar circle around a glowing fire presided over by a great chief. Now we gathered around the psychiatrist Dr. Eugene Ericson. When his mother had died from unknown causes, Dr. Ericson left a position in Boeing's space program to pursue a career in clinical psychology. We parents of mentally ill children all tapped into the peace and energy this great man radiated in our small group.

As I listened to the other family members, I realized some parents had more severe problems to deal with than Hal and me, although Joseph, young, unmedicated, and artistic, stirred up the most creative messes.

Eleanor Hobson, a fellow Lido-ite, asked Dr. Ericson "Is it true that mental illness hits persons with high IQs more frequently than average people? As you know, my son, Peter, was a talented ballet dancer and a genius. Now he just sits around in odd pieces of clothing. Doesn't dance. Does nothing at all." Eleanor's hair, a coiffed yellow helmet, and her jeweled fingers told me how much agony her son's peculiar dressing must cause her.

Dr. Ericson replied, "Other people in this group hold the belief that mental illness hits the intelligent more often than others. It seems true because Hoag hospital is in an area with engineers, teachers and other successful people who are intelligent themselves and who reared these children. But mental illness hits equally across the IQ range and national borders. You'd find if we started a

NAMI group in a less educated area, the patients with mental illness would be less educated."

Eleanor looked disappointed. "I always thought Peter was a mad genius."

"He probably is." Dr. Ericson regarded her with such loving kindness that she visibly relaxed in the stiff hospital chair. "Mental illness cuts across the bell shaped curve," he added.

Next, he turned his attention to a quiet woman who cuddled her plastic purse in her lap as though it were her baby. "Do you want to tell us how Abraham is doing now?" he asked.

She shifted the purse in her arms and smoothed her rumpled blouse. She began shyly. "Abraham's never been very smart like your children. He's a little bit retarded and a little bit mentally ill. Since he's got both diagnoses, each agency sends him to the other. I guess you call it 'falling through the cracks.'"

A moment of silence followed. What pride Hal and I once had in Joseph's achievements. How little they mattered now. Mary's round face shining with tears glowed from a mother-place inside her. Abraham's being a little retarded and a little mentally ill made her love him the more. I bowed my head and prayed silently for this son who didn't fit any diagnosis. "God, help us to love our children, smart children, slow children, children with hallucinations, children with fear. Help us to accept them."

Dr. Ericson stood and handed his card to the weeping woman. "Phone me. Bring Abraham in. I'll see he gets care," he said.

Then a tide of hopeful comments washed over the room. "...a medicine is being developed ... new brain scans show exactly what part of the brain is different in schizophrenia...HUD apartments...job opportunity...a new day on the horizon...a different psychiatrist...a new medication...." We all had hope for Mary's child and for our own. There had to be hope. There had to be a new better way. We had gathered together not to despair, but to hope.

When the tide of helpful suggestions ebbed, Dr. Ericson spoke to an old man waiting quietly. His wife, crumpled by sorrow, leaned against him. "You sound a bit down today, Tom. What's happening with your son?"

"Well sir, it's bad. Our Freddy's been living with us in our mobile home for thirty years now. Used to be, he'd eat with us. Then he started taking the food from the refrigerator to his room to eat." His words stabbed me. Joseph, too, had stopped eating with us and had already reached the refrigerator stage.

Tom continued, "Nowadays, we lay his food out by his door like you would for a dog. He gets it at night. But last night, we saw him when he crawled out for food. His leg's bad infected. Can't walk. He needs a doctor."

Tom's wife raised her head. Her thinning fluffy white hair formed a kind of halo. She peeked at us from violet, red- rimmed eyes. "I'm afraid he's going to die. I've been an LVN. I can see the streaks from blood poison creeping up his leg. He won't let us help him. I can't bear to let him die."

Dr. Ericson's voice sounded assured. "You are prisoners of your son and Freddy is a threat to his own life. That means the police can place him in a hospital for treatment without his permission. You must call the police. You've got a window of opportunity now to save your son's leg and yourselves. While he's in the hospital, you can plan a better living situation for Freddy."

"Tom and me, we could never call the police on our own son."

"Not even to save his life?" Dr. Ericson asked.

The magic circle grew very silent for a few minutes and then a stream of emotions poured forth. "You'll save his life and your own." "There's only tragedy this way." "Talk about killing with kindness. Remember tough love."

Tom looked at his wife with a face full of love. "We have to do it, darling. It's the only way left. I'll do the phoning for us."

"The only way left," she agreed.

I stored this memory in my mind bank for future use. Hal and I must not end our lives as senior citizens unable to care for their son or themselves.

"How's Bill Junior?" Dr. Ericson turned his attention to our closest friends in the NAMI circle, Bill and Gretchen. Bill, founder of a successful electronics company and Gretchen, his wife, a retired nurse who volunteered at UCI to assist in research on brain disease, appeared much more able to cope emotionally than the rest of us. Bill aimed an all-inclusive grin at the group. "We bought

Bill Junior a new car. He's got a job now as a roofer and promises to pay us back. Things are going well."

We all congratulated the lucky family, but I felt a surge of jealousy. We didn't have the money to cheer Joseph with new cars, and he didn't have the courage for a dangerous job, like a roofer.

While I brooded, a tall striking woman in a beige linen suit told her story. "My name is Aiya. I was born in Iceland. I'm a single mother, an office manager. I can't afford to lose my job." She twisted a ruby ring on her well-manicured finger. "Every week, my daughter Brenda phones me at work. Says she is going to commit suicide. I rush from the office to be with her and prevent this tragedy. Today my boss said he sympathized with me but he needed my full attention on the office. I am the sole support of Brenda and myself."

Dr. Ericson leaned forward and spoke in a soft almost motherly voice. "Aiya, my dear, you need to realize that if Brenda is truly determined to take her life, there is no way anyone can prevent it. When she phones, you need to tell her how much you love her but that if she is determined to take her own life, you will not stop her. Tell her that she is an adult and she is able to make the best decision for herself."

The circle drew a sharp intake of breath and sighed.

"Oh, Dr. Ericson, isn't that dangerous?" Aiya asked.

"It is a dangerous situation. But you need to put her in charge of herself. You will not always be available to come to her rescue."

After a time reflecting, Aiya decided. "I'll do it."

I examined my psyche. Did I have the toughness to take such a risk with my son, even if it were the only way to save his life? I didn't know. Bowed heads, cracked knuckles, and silence indicated the magic circle felt the same.

The next speaker, a thin anorexic woman, described how her brother with schizophrenia had sexually abused her when she was a child. She had recently told her parents but they refused to believe her. I felt a wave of sympathy for this tiny bony woman whose parents failed to protect her. I resolved to be the kind of mother my Laura needed, regardless of the cost.

At last, Dr. Ericson said, "Let's hear from the Sarkissians."

Hal went first. "We're having difficulty establishing rules with Joseph. We have not yet gotten him to a psychiatrist and on medication. This situation is frustrating for our family."

Dr. Erikson replied, "You will, sooner or later, need to offer Joseph the alternatives of living at home with you under medical care or leaving home."

"Tough love," the Greek chorus of parents breathed.

"We're trying. But I'm not ready to take that path yet."

"What about you, Martha?" Dr. Ericson asked.

"I just need to learn how to live with this Joseph. Any little thing angers him. I can't even ask him if he wants a cup of coffee."

Dr. Ericson replied, "Persons with schizophrenia do not like to be questioned. Remember, these individuals are living much of the time in their unconscious. They have a secret world they are trying to protect. He is afraid you're after his secrets."

Heads nodded agreement.

"But I have to ask Joseph some questions," I protested.

"Try something like, 'Coffee's here if you want some'. I think of persons with brain diseases as being inside a space bubble. If I come too close, I'll pierce their bubble."

There was nervous laughter from the circle. "Hey doc, you don't think you're getting a little schizo, too, do you?" a portly gentleman teased.

"Martha, is there anything else I can help you with?" Dr. Ericson asked gently.

"Joseph won't believe that I'm his mother. Says he was adopted from Switzerland. I even dug out his birth certificate and the beaded bracelet they put around his wrist...." I was weeping. The circle offered us parents a time and place for mourning. We would all be brave later on. "Even though I had his baby bracelet, he doesn't believe me. Won't call me 'Mom.' Only calls me Martha. So cold. I'm his Mom."

Everyone gazed at me with love and understanding. They knew. Dr. Ericson explained, "Of course, Joseph doesn't want to admit you are his mother. He loves you too much for that. He knows how hurtful his condition is to a mother.

So he simply decides you are a kindly stranger who won't be so hurt. Mentally ill persons often deny their identities so they don't bring disgrace on their family."

"But I want to be recognized as his mother. After I showed him all the proof, including baby photos he said 'Martha, I believe that you believe you are my mother.'"

Dr. Ericson threw back his head and laughed. His deep guffaws were contagious and soon we were all laughing. "You have a very intelligent son, Martha. He's learned his lesson well from his counselors."

When we stopped laughing, Dr. Ericson added softly, "But Joseph may have a bit of an idea, there. You need to distance yourself a little from him and give a little more attention to other matters."

"Oh, no, I couldn't. I made up my mind to take care of Joseph, and I will."

"If you distance yourself a little, you'll still be able to love him and help him. But if you become too entangled with Joseph, it will be hard on both you and him."

Hal took my hand and squeezed it to let me know he understood my feelings. Dr. Ericson added, chuckling, "I think we can all use Joseph's phrasing: I believe that you believe...." And the laughing recommenced and our session with Dr. Ericson ended. But Joseph's special activities had only begun.

When I finished my story, Miriam responded, "I hope that you appreciate yourself for finding Dr. Ericson and bringing Hal with you to his group."

"Uh, well, I really loved Dr. Ericson. He had an ability like yours, to listen to sad stories and turn them, just a little, to bring positive aspects into view. He showed me how to appreciate my sensitive and loving son more."

Miriam looked thoughtful and a bit wistful. "Schizophrenia is a very complicated disease and not much was known about it in the seventies."

"We had an awful time then. Under Reagan's order, many mental hospitals closed. Joseph could only be held in a hospital against his will for 72 hours. So, he cycled from hospital to hospital, never spending enough time anywhere to become stabilized. County agencies, which were created to close the gap between a person with mental illness and specialized care, weren't well funded or organized. I couldn't get a social worker for Joseph. After six months, the

210

probation officer stopped coming. NAMI became our only resource for dealing with our son with untreated schizophrenia.

"In our circle, one man spoke of taking his daughter to a mental hospital where they refused her service. She had been living crawling in a gutter looking for scraps to eat. The hospital staff claimed this emergency wasn't *life threatening*. She walked out of the door and crawled off in the gutter."

Miriam shuddered. Closed her eyes for a moment, thinking, then spoke. "Martha, you have managed to keep your son safe and alive in these circumstances and now he leads a contented life. How did you manage this?" This comment I viewed as a ruse to turn my attention from the social problems of mental illness, to me.

"I didn't keep Joseph alive. Joseph's core of being had a rock-like center that held the determination to be well and independent. He was a rock climber, remember? Can I read you a meditation he wrote at that period? I found it crumpled up in the trash can."

"Of course you can read it. Remember, this is always your time to do what you want to do."

I read:

Meditation on Rock Climbing
By Joseph Sarkissian

Why does a climber love his rope?
Because the rope smells like the Rock
And decayed Rock is the foundation
Of the world holding and nourishing nature.
Rock symbolizes freedom. Rock is strength,
You depend on rock to sustain life.
Rock displays the weakness of man
in the face of the worst of nature.
Rock is the quintessence of ecstasy
the climber feels while climbing,
not to conquer—but to live.
Rock symbolizes reliance on self and when you fall,
Reliance on fellow men.

Below that, Joseph wrote in large letters with a calligraphy pen that oozed drops of ink like blood:

"Something is pulling me. I must go."

Miriam asked, "How were you feeling when you read this to me?"

"I could smell his red and blue climbing ropes that hung in his closet. He'd started climbing with his brother Geoff when he was sixteen. It frightened me then, but reading it now I'm glad he knew that ecstasy. I'm glad he learned reliance on self and others."

Miriam looked at me tenderly. "And how did you feel when you read that last sentence?"

"It broke my heart, of course. His hallucinations were pulling him away from us. He had his own language, his own world and we couldn't even visit it!"

"Do you think he has hallucinations now?"

"Maybe sometimes. I see him moving his lips silently. Maybe he's just rehearsing what to say. He seems very sane. But before he took medication, they were realer than reality." I paused to pull my thoughts together and continued. "There was a letter he wrote in the trash, too, and a crumpled photo of Dianna. She wore big boots and a bright checked flannel shirt. In his letter, he said 'the craziness (on my last visit) was that I was hallucinating and thought you were, or at least might be someone you aren't. These hallucinations led to an eventual nervous breakdown. They got worse as time went on. ...' That showed me he had some understanding of his illness. I asked him if he ever saw Dianna anymore and he glowered. 'No. She's evil.'"

"How did that affect you?"

"I agonized over his words 'she's evil.' His hallucinations isolated him. The tragedy of schizophrenia is aloneness."

Miriam repeated my words thoughtfully "The tragedy of schizophrenia is aloneness. Yes, Joseph was alone in his own world. How did this affect your feelings?"

"Joseph's illness melted down my entire mental framework of the world-- churches, hospitals, jails, justice, human rights. My mind became a mess."

"You have a lovely mind. You write beautiful poems which I've enjoyed hearing. I feel you reach your deeper emotions in your poetry."

"I did write a poem about Joseph. I can recite part of it, if you want."

"I'd very much like to hear it."

Mosaic Brain

A mosaic brain shattered
And scattered rainbow tiles
That lay heaped and broken on the floor.
A note from Quetzalcoatl's flute
Lingered in the air.
He stooped and gathered them
And spoke in unknown language
Trying to restore
A pattern to fragmented tiles.
"Speak to me, Joseph, I am your mother."
Louder, "I am your mother."
Softly, softly, "I am your mother."
'I am your mother' disappears
Into the rubble of rainbow tiles."

I glanced at Miriam's plain brown clock standing on the table. Its readable face displayed ten minutes after ten. We'd gone over time. Embarrassed about the time, the poem, and me, I grabbed my purse and scuttled out as quickly as possible.

CHAPTER 22

"Ma'am, Is He Mental?"

M iriam tapped pointed to a page on her clipboard. "Last week, you felt your entire framework of the world melted down, including God, church and family."

"That happened. The world became a dangerous place for me when Joseph had his breakdown. They locked him up without a legal basis. A society I believed in whole-heartedly, family, church, physicians, psychiatrists, could not cope with one fine young man with a dreadful illness. How could the prayers, even of saints, hold back the flood of schizophrenia? Chaos ruled."

"Yet, you taught school in a church surrounded by spiritual people and Hal was building a successful business. You loved each other and your children. Perhaps chaos didn't rule everything."

"Hmm. Of course, you're right. It was like patting your head while rubbing your stomach. I suffered the chaos of the world while I poured energy and love into my school teaching and yearned for a hiatus between emergencies. The phone on my bedside table was like a bomb with a short fuse. I always answered it, even at 2 a.m. with "Hello, Sarkissian residence.""

"This is security, El Toro Marine Base. Do you have a son named Joseph Sarkissian?"

The words pumped adrenaline into my system. My heart beat double-time. "Yes! Is he all right?"

"He sure is, Ma'am. He's sitting here with me in the guard house, petting my cats and drinking coffee."

Flashing lights in my vision signaled the throbbing of a severe headache and the recognition of a dilemma. Mentioning schizophrenia might end up with

Joseph in prison, but without labeling him, how could I explain his appearance at El Toro? Hal would say, *Never tell more than you have to.* "Uh, thanks for giving him the coffee."

"Well. Ma'am, I think your son was playing CIA man. He came here trying to take over the Marine Base. Said he came to warn us about a dangerous enemy."

Hal reached for the phone. I shook my head no. "It's good of you to take care of him," I answered.

"Ma'am, is he *mental?*"

A demeaning term—"mental." The caldron of anger simmered in my aching head but I told myself: *Words don't matter. The guard is kind. O Lord, make me sound like a nurturing mother who takes care of her sick child.* "Yes sir, he is. He lives with me and my husband."

The guard's tone became firmer. "Ma'am, you and your husband get right over here and take him home and take care of him. I'll keep him till you arrive. He's taken a liking to my cats."

"We'll be right there."

"Yes Ma'am. I won't press charges, you understand. Just keep him safe at home. Okay, Ma'am?"

A wave of gratitude calmed my bubbling anger. "Oh, yes. Thank you, Sir. Thank you."

Not long after this event, Joseph found an apartment on the Balboa peninsula and moved in with a roommate, Jed. We fully expected that Joseph's leaving home would bring a measure of peace to our family, but the phone rang again.

"Is this Mrs. Sarkissian?"

"Yes, it is."

"I'm Joseph's roommate. I just called 911 and they took your son to Hoag Hospital. He overdosed on drugs."

"We'll be right there. Thanks for telling us." Hal and I pulled on our sweat suits that lay across a chair, handy for night rescues.

When we entered a curtained alcove in the emergency room, a surprisingly clean and rosy-cheeked Joseph lay on an emergency room cot. A solicitous physician bent over him. "Your son is not having a problem with an overdose of drugs. I have diagnosed him with schizophrenia."

Hal laid his finger across his lips meaning we shouldn't give a history, but let the doctor prescribe an anti-psychotic. Perhaps a door of opportunity for Joseph opened when his roommate brought him to Hoag. With medication, Joseph could commence building a new life.

The physician continued, "I have convinced Joseph to sign in with us for two weeks of care. Joseph smiled, enjoying his fourteen-year-old personality, until the doctor handed him commitment papers. He took them happily and lay in bed reading. Then he suddenly sat up. All at once, his features tightened and his eyes grew wild. He hurled the papers on the floor and jumped to his feet. In a clear and resonant voice, he declaimed the Lanterman-Petris-Short Act: "If you are not a danger to yourself or others and are not gravely disabled then you have the constitutional right to be psychotic. I claim that right. I'm leaving."

Calm and cheerful, a man in control, he strode from the emergency room.

"There's nothing more we can do," the doctor declared. The dark circles under his eyes seemed to deepen. "Our hands are tied by that darned 1960 law. But good luck with your son. Perhaps at a later time, he'll decide on treatment."

We thanked the overworked physician and hurried after Joseph who, now in his young-prince persona, casually directed us. "You can drop me off at my apartment."

Frustrated and angry, I snapped, "Joseph, the landlord won't let you back in that apartment. The landlord never even signed the sublease. The paper you two scribbled on isn't worth anything. You have to come home with us."

"In that case, Martha, you may drive me to my rooms on Lido Island. I'll see my lawyer about the apartment. I believe our contract is legal."

When we reached home, Harold groaned. "Come on, you two, stop quarreling. It's 2 a.m. Joseph, your mother and I have to go to work tomorrow."

Suddenly, our fourteen-year-old Joseph appeared before us, cheerful, respectful of his father. "Sure thing, Dad. See you tomorrow."

Hal and I sighed together. We could never tell which Joseph would appear.

A few weeks later, just before dinner, Joseph pulled on his blue knit stocking cap. "I'm going for a walk." He stormed out of the house, slamming the door behind him. Hal and I didn't protest. Though we worried about his being in danger, we'd gradually slipped into survival mode where we simply tried to exist alongside Joseph. That left Joseph in charge, an uneasy situation for all of us.

A few months later, the bell tolled at midnight. "This is the Newport Police. Your son's been in an auto accident."

Adrenaline pumped wildly through our bodies. Like firemen, we jumped into rescue mode. We met the police by a cement barrier wall. Our Peugeot now resembled a crumpled toy car. Joseph had wrecked it. But the police officer raised his voice above the freeway roar to correct our suspicion. "We're not giving your son a citation. Another car forced him to dodge and he hit the wall. Hadn't been drinking. Just an accident."

This crash terminated weekly drives to Pasadena where Joseph had been in therapy with Dr. Martin, a psychologist who didn't use medications in his practice. To our disappointment, the visits to Pasadena hadn't lessened his hallucinations and it did not seem that psychotherapy did any good. Instead, the unconscious world where Joseph dwelled was gaining an ever stronger grip on him.

Joseph somehow convinced us to buy him a motor scooter. "I drove one in high school, remember? I don't want to ride with you, Martha, because you cringe your way through Costa Mesa."

I thought, "Of course. Joseph needs to express his manhood by independence and we need to trust him more."

A few months later, the bell tolled, this time at 6 p.m. "This is the Costa Mesa hospital. Your son has been in a motor scooter accident. The scooter's destroyed, but the police didn't cite him. He's refused treatment here. But because of his injuries we cannot turn him away unless someone takes the responsibility for his care."

Hal snatched the phone from me. "We'll be there in fifteen minutes," he promised.

Fifteen minutes later, Hal and I, bodies as stiff as the plastic chairs, waited in the emergency room lobby until a folding door swung open. Joseph, disheveled, frightened, oozing blood and motor oil, stood there too disoriented to even see us. The whole room reeked of a wrecked motor scooter. A nurse waved papers under my nose. "Please sign these papers to release your son from our hospital. Otherwise, we are obligated to treat him."

Blood dripping from his legs and arms formed little puddles on the floor. "How can we take him home like this, bleeding all over the place?" Not a glimmer of pity shone in the slate gray eyes of the nurse. Joseph must be the last straw in her legendary burden.

All at once, my imagination transformed this bleeding wild-eyed man into Joey, our 5 year old. He cried and stamped his feet in the pediatrician's office at the idea of a shot. How did our pediatrician, Dr. Trotter, calm his fears? "Joseph, would you consider seeing Dr. Trotter?" I asked.

A funny little smile appeared on his face. "Yes, let's see Dr. Trotter."

The entire family loved our pediatrician Helen Trotter MD, a birdlike woman with a soft voice and slim gentle hands. Whenever a Sarkissian turned 18, she passed him/her on to a G.P. It was after office hours now, and Joseph was an adult but I found a quarter for the pay phone. "Dr. Trotter, we're here at Costa Mesa hospital with Joseph. He's been in a motor scooter accident. Could you break with protocol and treat him?"

No quivers or hesitation sounded in her voice. "Of course I'll treat Joseph. I'll go open my office and meet you there as soon as you can make it." She didn't question his age or mental condition or her office hours.

Joseph agreed to wash his hands and face before seeing her. Embarrassed about his wounds, he wrapped paper towels around his legs and arms. We scribbled our names on an official paper and the granite nurse looked pleased as we left, even though we left a bloody trail on the tiles.

Hal and I held hands and took turns worrying in Dr. Trotter's waiting room while she cleaned and bandaged his abrasions. When she and Joseph returned to us, her face glowed. "We're lucky. His wounds are simple abrasions and I can treat them here."

Hal hurried Joseph off to the car, but I lingered a few minutes to question Dr. Trotter. "Why didn't you ever spot any symptoms of schizophrenia in Joseph? I brought him in every year for a yearly physical and you often treated him between times."

Dr. Trotter smiled "Because Joseph had no symptoms then. He was well." She cocked her head as if to decide she dared say more, then continued. "Martha, hang on. There will soon be new medications for mental illness and Haldol will be a thing of the past. Don't give up on Joseph. He's a good man."

"I promise you, I'll never give up. But Dr. Ericson says I should detach from him. How can I? He needs me to find an apartment, and a psychiatrist he'll work with and a social worker, too. We can't keep him at home with Laura. With all of this, how can I detach?"

"Dr. Ericson means for you to detach emotionally while still delivering services. But I'm not a bit emotionally detached from Joseph myself, so it'll be even harder for you."

At home, the three of us ate a late omelet dinner. Joseph seemed to be more the young boy tonight than the angry man and we all smiled a lot. He went to his room and Hal and I racked the dishes in the washer while we talked.

"Isn't it amazing how Joseph pulled himself together when Dr. Trotter treated him."

"He always pulls himself together in an emergency. Remember, Doc Erikson said danger releases adrenaline in the brain which stabilizes the mentally ill for a while."

"I guess I need adrenaline too."

"You do okay in an emergency."

I whispered in his ear, "Thanks for thinking so, but I'm actually scared to death."

He whispered back, "Me, too."

We curled up together in our queen-sized bed and attempted, once more, to fall asleep. Nowadays, we never had enough sleep. Like Sisyphus, whom the gods compelled for all eternity to roll a boulder to the top of a hill where it escaped and rolled to the bottom. All of our rescues of Joseph ended with the two of us pushing the ball back up the hill again. Even in our sleep, our bodies stayed tensed, waiting for the phone to ring.

When summer came, with a vacation for teacher and students alike, balmy weather urged me to stretch out on our patio chaise lounge and doze in the sun. Once more, the phone demanded my attention. I heard Joseph through a static-filled connection. "I'm in the Newport Beach jail, Mom. Fell asleep on the grass in the park. Meter maid hit my feet with a stick. Scared me. Waved my arms. I didn't do anything evil—honest, Martha."

"Of course you didn't...." The line went dead.

At once, I called Allen Wilcox, our attorney and a faithful friend familiar with Joseph's history. "Allen, you've got to help us. Joseph phoned from Newport jail. He hasn't done anything wrong..."

"Calm down, Martha. Newport Beach isn't Pierce County. I'll go to the jail now and get details. They're pretty decent here."

Allen called that night. "I can get Joseph released from jail right away, if that's what you want. They never should have picked him up. But I have a plan. Since he refuses to take medication, I can talk to the judge and we could ask for probation to a hospital."

"I hate him being in prison—for even one hour. But I'll talk to the family tonight."

Hal came home early from work and we sat close together on the couch where the nearness of the smell and feel of my husband steadied me. He listened intently to my story.

"...so Allen can get Joseph released today, or he can get a judge to grant him probation to a hospital or clinic for the mentally ill. What should we do?" Hal mulled this over while I nervously chewed on a fingernail.

Deliberately he answered. "It's a good idea to release Joseph on probation to a hospital or clinic, even though it will be on his police record. The way I see it, this is our window of opportunity. We must try anything we can."

"I've already talked to Geoff. He thinks the Anne Sippi clinic is the best care in southern California. They don't use medications. Joseph would like that. Instead, they have counselors available 24 hours a day."

Hal cracked his knuckles. "I'm only an engineer and not so certain what's best in this area. But Geoff must know. We'll go with Anne Sippi."

I stroked Hal's hands, grateful for his ability to weigh the consequences of such a decision that pitted a life-long prison record against a possibly healing environment. His knobby red knuckles held the stress he suffered.

The next day, Hal and I drove to Anne Sippi Clinic, Pasadena. I had imagined something lovelier than this long narrow house surrounded by cement and cradled in the noise of Los Angeles traffic. A stocky, bearded man met us at the door. "I'm Dr. Goldman, you must be the Sarkissians." He herded us into his small office and seated us across from his desk.

Eager to cooperate in this new venture, I started out, "I'm so happy to be here and meet you, Doctor. Our son Geoffrey has told us a lot of good things about you. I'd like to give you a brief history of Joseph."

Tightly wound and with his own agenda, he interrupted. "Before we discuss Joseph, we need to consider the terms of his treatment. It's $2,000 a month, which includes a private room, all meals, and counseling whenever the client requests it. We will not medicate your son."

Hal gave me a reassuring glance before he spoke. "Several hospitals have told us Joseph responds well to medication and that he is lucky in that regard. I'm afraid he'll be unmanageable without meds."

The doctor's black eyebrows waggled up and down. "In such a case, I will phone you and he can receive medication then."

Whether he wanted to or not, this mysterious doctor needed to understand the tragedies of Joseph's childhood so he could heal him. I blurted out, "When Joseph was only four, his baby sister died. They shared a bedroom and..."

Dr. Goldman gestured with his hand and arm as if pushing me away. "My dear, I will make my own assessment of your son. Many authorities believe the over loving mother is the underlying cause of schizophrenia, so we don't want you involved. We have a rule that the patient doesn't see or hear from his family for thirty days. But let us finish our business details before we discuss your son."

Me! Underlying cause of schizophrenia. My fault. Another rock of shame landed in my sack of guilt. So it had been wrong to sit up at night rocking Joseph! What should a mother do when her baby cried? My muscles could barely hold me up. I slumped in my chair. Tears pressed against my eyelids. Bright lights like fireworks shot off in my peripheral vision. Over loving mother! Schizophrenia. A doctor more interested in payments than in Joseph.

Hal took over. "The Anne Sippi Clinic looks like it will be helpful for Joseph, but I still need to be informed of your procedures for dealing with an unmedicated client who is not conforming to your rules."

Dr. Goldman stared deeply into Hal's eyes. "You can trust me. I'll see he gets medication if he needs it."

The check crossed the table. Goldman jumped to his feet. "It's been a long day today. If you'll excuse me…."

Bent over with pain, I could barely walk to the car. Hal took my arm. "Don't believe that BS about mothers. No one knows what causes this illness. We have to stay balanced, honey." His face brightened. "Hey, I've got an idea. You have thirty days while Joseph is in the clinic. Everyone's been asking you to chaperone Laura's Bell Ringers on their Hawaiian tour. Why don't you go with Laura?"

Hal's words beamed a light through my emotional fog. I quavered, "Well, can we afford it? There's the clinic…Laura's ticket… something might happen while I'm gone."

"We've still got savings. Think of the trip as a type of medicine. You need a break from the Joseph syndrome. I go on business trips. Now it's your turn to get away. You can ride the waves and enjoy the kids. What could be better?"

CHAPTER 23

Aloha to Paradise

$\mathscr{L}$ ike an old-fashioned music box, my voice rattled away, gradually wound down and finally stopped. I leaned back against Miriam's couch cushions.

Her voice seemed to come from another world. "You and your husband certainly had a therapeutic relationship." My mouth found a smile. Miriam, like a miner panning the river, always found at least a grain of gold. "You realize, don't you, that many families fall apart under the continual stress of caring for a handicapped child, yet you and Hal strengthened each other. It's quite remarkable."

"We didn't have the fun we used to, but he sure comforted me in every crisis—until he died."

"And you comforted him. You did much of the hands-on effort which left him free to do much of the planning."

"He was a lot more intelligent than I. He knew what we should do."

"I would say you were *as* intelligent, but had a different type of intelligence."

I shook my head no and looked down at my clunky tennis shoes. Although in awe of Hal's brilliance, a new warmth spread through my body in hearing that someone else believed that I was pretty smart too. But since I paid her to believe in me, could I trust her evaluations? Yet in an attempt to prove *intelligent,* I added, "I'm writing the part about Joseph in my memoir now."

"Excellent. Writing helps you to put a little distance between yourself and the events and helps you to gain a new perspective. I hope you continue in this project."

"I will." Like a wilted tomato plant in a spring shower, I came alive as Miriam sprinkled me with her positive ideas.

At our next session, I arrived with a handful of papers to read. I told her, "I don't think I'm getting everything about Joseph in the right order. So much happened. A lot of it's clear in my mind but it's like looking at a pile of separate photographs. Jerky, not sequenced exactly right."

"Sequence isn't important. Discovering emotional truth is. As you share your memories they will have less power over you, too."

"Well, here goes."

Aloha to a Bit of Paradise

In Hawaii, I felt like a kid on the first day of summer vacation. I waded out in the crystal blue waters, waited for the just right wave with a curve to settle in. Then the wave flung me high in the translucent sky and I coasted to shore with only my body for a surfboard. That was ecstasy. When finally I returned to the golden shore, my young Bell Ringer charges lay spread on towels, sound asleep in the sand. Blessed be the thirteen-year-olds who find peace in sleep.

We were staying at the University of Hawaii dorm. After a luau, we trooped into the gym for folk dancing. A buoyant kid-out-of-school mentality lifted my spirits like the waves. I folk-danced with Bell Ringers from near and far, fending off thoughts of Joseph that clustered around me, pecking like vicious birds. *Shoo, birds! Joseph is in good hands.* Junior high students and chaperones held hands in a huge circle and spun to the right in a grapevine step. The energy and freedom of the Bell Ringers were contagious. I rode so high on a wave of music I didn't even see the floor beneath me. I crashed in a wave of pain.

"Come on, Mom, we'll help you up." That was Laura's voice.

"You tripped on a rolled carpet on the floor. Are you able to stand?" asked Eleanor Prichard, my roommate and fellow chaperone.

My head cleared. "Sure. Of course." Leaning on Eleanor and Laura, I hopped my way to our room. I heard Laura's voice say, "See you later, Mom. We're going back to the dance." Almost immediately, I fell asleep and the sleep became a dream of pain. The next morning, when I limped into the dormitory bathroom, I fainted on the black and white tiles.

When I awoke, I stared into the face of a med tech and a hazy background of anxious Bell Ringer faces. I tried to say "I'm okay!" but it sounded like a mumble. My fellow chaperone, Eleanor, tapped my shoulder. "Stay awake. Hang on. The ambulance will be here in a few minutes."

My pajamas, cold and wet, slapped around my legs when the paramedics lifted me onto a gurney. I showered myself with shame as I realized I'd wet myself. I sighed. How many of Joseph's weird words or actions came from a mysterious deep place inside himself, like pee, and couldn't be stopped?

In the informal Hawaiian hospital, I was okay enough to munch on the huge mustardy hot dog Eleanor brought me while a doctor encased my leg in plaster foot to hip. The shouts and giggles of Hawaiian children playing tag in the halls and the strains of ukulele music eased my pain, but not my guilt. "Eleanor, I'd better go home. I can't keep up with the kids wearing all this plaster on my leg."

"It's a walking cast and you can use crutches, too, for balance. You'll be all right," the doctor said.

Eleanor handed me a coke. "The kids love you, Martha. You don't have to chase after them. They'll come to us when they need something."

The cool drink slithered down my throat. "I don't want to be a drag on you."

"We'll be one short on chaperones if you leave. If you stay, you and I'll have a darn good time together." I wanted to hug Eleanor, but this tall, efficient lady seemed out of reach.

That night, before we went to bed, I steadied myself on crutches and made a reverse charge phone call to Hal in Newport Beach.

"I think I better come home, darling. I broke my ankle folk-dancing and I'll just be a nuisance here."

His voice, determined and angry, froze me. "Don't come home Martha. Stay there."

Didn't he want to see me? "Why are you talking to me like this?" I felt like a child rejected by her mother.

Hal sounded miserable. "I wasn't going to tell you till you got back from Hawaii. Joseph smashed a window at the clinic. Used a baseball bat. Wanted to get out of there. The day after you left, Dr. Goldman moved him to Camarillo

Mental Hospital. He's on meds in Camarillo now." His voice broke. "I want you to get away from the problems for a while. Hop on one foot, whatever it takes, but stay in Hawaii, have some fun. If you come home, you'll just sit alone all day and brood."

"I can't stand it, Hal. The psychiatrist promised Joseph would get medication if he needed it and then—he dumped him in Camarillo." I swelled with rage. I might explode any minute. "We trusted him. We paid him to look after Joseph. He's a…"

Hal interrupted my rant. "The clinic couldn't handle Joseph—that's all there is to it. They didn't kick him out on the street. So don't get too worked up about it. Stay in Hawaii with the kids."

Dr. Goldman's belief that mothers caused schizophrenia lingered in my mind like a slow-working poison and made me doubt my instinct and lose faith in myself. But I followed Hal's advice to stay with the Bell Ringers. I wrapped my cast in a garbage sack and crawled out on a coral reef to bask in the ocean spray. Laura and Carol told the airline, "We have doctor's orders to stay with our mother as we island hop." So the three of us rode in a forklift to the airplane's cabin.

By the time we reached Maui, my cast had shrunk from the ocean spray and my toes turned black. Eleanor and I taxied to the hospital on Maui where a doctor sawed open my cast and re-plastered my leg. I rode in a pedicab to restaurants. On crutches, I limped down a muddy trail into Waimea Canyon, Kauai. As a chaperone at the Bell Ringer Ball, I fell asleep with my head on a table. Eleanor woke me at midnight and dragged me to our room. The next morning the other chaperones wondered how the dancers "got loose" and "ran all over the island." I kept my mouth shut. When my head hit the table, the bell ringers left the dance and paraded around the university. "But they all got back safely by 1:00 AM," Eleanor told me.

Ten days after I left home, I returned to Lido Island, my leg in a hip-to-toe plaster cast, brain groggy from jet lag, spirits high from luaus, ukuleles, barbecued pork and time with Laura. While I unpacked, Hal packed to fly to North Carolina to fulfill a contract for his vote-tally equipment. The next day, Laura, sun burnt and happy, dropped back into the world of Horace Ensign Jr. High

School, and Joseph's med tech at Camarillo Hospital phoned. "You are a lucky woman, Mrs. Sarkissian. Your son has made fine progress here. He reacts very positively to medication and he helps the other patients. He will be discharged tomorrow. Can you pick him up?"

"Oh, I can't. I broke my right ankle and I'm in a heavy cast. Can't drive now. My husband will be home in a few days and he…"

Mark's genial voice became threatening. "If you don't pick up your son tomorrow during the day, he'll be given five dollars and put on a bus to Los Angeles tomorrow night.

"To LA? We live in Newport Beach. Will five dollars cover the bus transfer to Newport Beach?"

"We don't run a transportation service here, Ma'am. He'll be put off in Skid Row. He'll have to figure out what to do next."

"No one can survive in LA with only five dollars! Let me talk to your superior."

My head pounded. It'd crack open any minute like an old Halloween pumpkin and spill my brains, not seeds, on the floor. "You've got to help me, please. Release him Monday. My husband will be home then and he…"

"Ma'am, I have to follow orders."

Hal believed you should talk to the top man in charge when you had a dispute so I cranked up my nerve. "Please transfer me to your supervisor."

After a speaking to a number of minor officials, I reached the director of Camarillo Hospital. "A terrible mistake is being made. At present, I'm in a plaster cast, toe-to-hip, can't drive, but your hospital plans to release my son tomorrow night anyway. They claim they'll put him on a bus to LA with five dollars. That isn't true, is it?"

"Madame, regrettably it is. As you may know, President Reagan closed many mental hospitals. Every bed available is needed for patients far sicker than your son. So if you do not pick him up, we'll put him on the bus at midnight. Perhaps you could meet him in LA and help him find a bus to Orange County." His voice, sad and dismissive at the same time, cut off further arguments.

"Thank you," *for nothing* I whispered under my voice, and hung up. Thousands of severely ill men and women were adrift in the sea with only a

227

few frail lifeboats left. Yet, there was no sense in blaming this tepid administra-tor for a problem arising from the President's office. The agency of last resort, my church, Prince of Peace Lutheran, answered my plea for help. Pastor Don Brentro offered to drive me to Camarillo, pulling a U-Haul to bring home not only Joseph but also his possessions: his grandfather's desk, a chair, books and clothes, which had been abandoned in his move from the clinic to Camarillo.

Pastor Don's little old Ford looked too frail for the task, but we rattled along that morning to Camarillo Hospital, a fortress set in the rolling landscape of hills draped with yellow mustard. Pastor Don dropped me off at the entrance. "I'll wait for you here." The drive from Newport Beach through Los Angeles to Camarillo had exhausted him so he rested and prayed while step-bump, step-bump, I moved slowly on crutches down a long crowded linoleum hall.

Camarillo, like many programs of that era, used cigarettes for behavior modification. In the hallway, patients stuck out their hands and pleaded for cigarettes. Lost as if in a beggar scene set in East India, I thumped along the corridor. It was hard to believe I was in a hospital in the scientifically advanced United States. All the patients appeared young and desperate (perhaps the older ones could not push their way into the hall). Their skins varied from shades of black, brown, red, yellow, to pinkish white, freckled, or plain, but they all longed for the touch of a woman. Their eyes, shades of blue, black, brown and hazel, all expressed the same terror and wildness as did Joseph's eyes. They all were my sons. At times, I leaned my crutches on the wall and shook their thin bony hands, large fatty hands, hairy hands. I yearned to bake them chocolate brownies or broil them steaks or pass out the cigarettes they wanted, but all I could do was clump down the hall on my crutches, step-bump, and shake hands.

Joseph and the Med Tech, Mark, materialized in the crowd. Dressed in a clean green sweater and clean faded blue jeans, Joseph looked cheerful and waved above the throng. At my side, Mark encouraged me, "Your son is doing just fine, Ma'am. As long as he takes his meds, he'll be okay. There's a few papers for you to sign and you'll be on your way." Joseph and I signed without reading.

"Let's go, Mom," Joseph urged. At last, I was Mom again, at least for the moment. We set off together step-bump down the corridor where men still called and begged. But we could not help them. Step-bump. It was a long way back to our little yellow house on Lido Island.

Telling this story had taken me back in time to Dr. Goldman's office. I told Miriam. "Deep inside, I've always felt I was to blame for Joseph's illness. When Dr. Goldman forbade me to see him for 30 days and explained that my over loving attitude caused his schizophrenia, I believed him, though Hal said that was bullshit."

Miriam answered calmly and cheerfully. "Dr. Goldman's belief was the norm in those days. I think physicians then didn't realize how a highly organized nervous system in a child might signal a mother to be especially kind and loving. So, in a sense, they turned the effect of the brain disease into the cause."

"I bet you're right. Hal used to watch TV football with baby Joseph lying on his lap and he'd rub his back to soothe the colic. Later on, Joseph had nightmares and I used to just crawl in bed with him and we'd talk until he fell asleep again."

Miriam beamed. "But I hope you realize now that you and Hal were good parents, and that schizophrenia is a brain disease."

"Intellectually, I know it, but my feelings are something different. When I was in Dr. Ericson's NAMI circle---it was in 1980, I think---he recommended a seminar on the brain at the University of Irvine. For the first time, Hal and I viewed slides showing the damage to the frontal and temporal lobes of a person with schizophrenia. Then we realized schizophrenia was a brain disease, not something caused by an over loving mother. Intellectually, I accepted that, but deeper down inside me, I still felt at fault for either having been too loving, or not loving enough."

"I believe that you have a type of compounded guilt. Each tragedy in your life, starting with your father's death, didn't just add guilt, it multiplied it."

"We talked about that a year ago and I don't feel that way now."

"So, you don't feel guilty about Joseph's brain disease anymore?"

I lifted my bowed head to her concerned face and nodded. "Yes, I guess I don't feel guilty any more. I mean…it's hard to absorb…mothers always feel guilty…but I.…"

"Martha, I am certain both you and Hal were very good parents. Do you think writing these stories is causing you to relive too much?"

"Oh, Miriam, I can't stop writing them. They are my—life."

All at once, she looked energetic, out of time, moving forward. "Well then, write on. And when will I see you next?"

CHAPTER 24

The Quest

I had to wait two weeks to see Miriam, a decision that fit my budget but not my emotions. When I finally sat once again on her couch, I commented, "I'm so darn glad to see you. The two weeks between visits seem to drag, but maybe the hiatus is good for me. I really mull things over in that stretch of time."

"And I'm so glad to see you. While you were mulling, did you congratulate yourself for chaperoning your daughter and her friends, despite your broken ankle and the trauma of Joseph's situation?"

"It's hard to feel too great about my chaperoning. Remember, I fell asleep and the kids ran all over campus."

"You're hard on yourself, Martha. No harm done and the kids had fun. You must realize that you acted in a courageous manner when you coped with Camarillo Hospital on crutches and without the support of your husband. I believe you are much stronger than you ever suspected."

Her lavish praise always embarrassed me. I looked away from her and down to my shoes. But it felt good too. "Thanks. The whole focus of my life has been on creating a loving family. I took a real nosedive when I realized everyone in the family was miserable. Hal, who used to call himself 'a cool kid,' was cracking his knuckles, and I was tearing at my fingernails. Worst of all, Laura's beautiful hair was falling out. I tried to get her into counseling but she flatly refused. I had failed my job as mother of the family. But I still believed all could be forgiven and Joseph would flourish, if only I could find the proper housing for him so he could be independent, an artist as he wanted, but near enough for our supervision. The Bible says 'In my Father's house are many mansions'.... so surely, there had to be a just-right apartment for Joseph. Hal and I called around, hunting an apartment for Joseph." Such difficulties, I told Miriam, were like an exhausting medieval quest.

The Quest

One kindly landlord, a grandfatherly man dressed in suspenders and a white shirt, went misty-eyed as he explained, "I'm sorry, Ma'am, but I have to evict your son. I wanted to help the poor fellow but I have to consider the other occupants. Joseph has been bouncing a rubber ball against the inside walls for hours at a time. Too much noise. The other tenants have complained."

He stared at the dirty living-room carpet with watery blue eyes. "And he's got artist's paint on the rug. Looks like he wanted to paint a picture, but the carpet needs cleaning. And he never reported the leaking sink. Now the flooring in the kitchen is rotted and needs to be replaced. This has been going on for a long time. I'm sorry, but we need to keep the cleaning deposit. Joseph must leave."

I react to crises by growing numb and paralyzed, like a deer caught in the headlights. So I nodded dumbly and stared straight ahead.

Joseph smiled, and endlessly bobbed his head. "Thank you, thank you, and thank you."

The manager waited. I mumbled, "Fine about keeping the deposit. Let's go, Joseph."

"Thank you, thank you," Joseph intoned as we gathered his belongings, including the acrylic paints and the ball. The manager's look of pity and his misty eyes live on in my memory.

A month later, a tiny ad in the *Penny Saver* one morning propelled Joseph and me down the freeway to a cluster of brown condos. The manager scarcely glanced at us before processing my credit card for first and last month's rent and damage deposit. If Joseph bounced a ball or made a ruckus here, it would never be noticed. The families in the courtyard didn't speak English, so Joseph's salad speech would pass unnoticed. The rent was doable.

When I finished teaching school on Fridays, I dropped by Joseph's apartment to take him marketing and to clean his condo. A silence like a heavy quilt fell between us, smothering conversation.'

Each week, his moods darkened. A few weeks later when I arrived at his house, the food we'd purchased the week before had putrefied. Steaks turned blue and smelled foul. Yogurt grew grey beards. Potatoes leaked gas and sprouted.

A NAMI poster condemned me. It showed a sad man alone in a bleak room. Drops of rain leaked through the ceiling onto the floor. Its title read *Neglected man in a Neglected Apartment.* Joseph needed a better life. I railed at myself for my inadequacy and powerlessness. With mental hospitals closed, promised community centers never opened, and some psychiatrists, though not Dr. Ericson, still blaming mother for mental illness, where could I turn?

On arrival at his condo one afternoon, a space where his handmade redwood table once stood shocked me. "Joseph, your table!! Where is it?" I cried.

"Threw it out."

"Joseph, you can't do that! It's a masterpiece—no screws, no nails, no glue. It's your work. It's amazing."

Every week, as I rubbed his table with linseed oil, it offered proof of Joseph's genius to me. "Where is it? What happened? Were you robbed?"

"I threw it away. Mexican guy next door pulled it out of the Dewey Dumpster."

"Joseph, you can't throw it away. I'm going to get it right back."

Before he could protest, I ran outside. Night had suddenly come upon us but a slice of moonlight and headlights from the boulevard lit up his neighbor's rickety door. I pounded on it. A tired looking Mexican man opened the door a crack.

I tried out my feeble Spanish. "Buenos noches. Por favor, la mesa…"

The bewildered man shook his head, He rapid-fired in Spanish. I caught the word *basura,* trash, and the word *ladron,* thief. He was explaining he had taken the desk from the trash and was not a thief. He would return it if I wished.

I stepped inside the house followed by Joseph. "That table belongs to my son. *Mi hijo.*" The room smelled of chili and tortillas. Four children sat at Joseph's table and stared at me from round brown eyes. Every bit of the wood in that table was precious to me. Why were these children eating on it? My unfathomable brain had substituted Joseph's masterpiece of craftsmanship for his flesh and blood. "Give me that table!" I demanded.

This tired looking father turned his head from Joseph to me. Compassion and understanding overspread his face. "Senora, I give you the table." The children slipped out of their seats. One little boy threw his arms around his father's legs.

Joseph stepped toward me. "No, Martha. The table is evil. Out! Out!" He yelled, waving his hand at me. "Get out of here, Martha!"

That familiar paralyzed feeling overcame me. I wanted to flee but my legs felt like pillars of cement. I forced myself to move them, thump thump across the room. At last, I heard the latch on the door slide shut behind Joseph and me. The worker's compassionate face lived in my mind like a painting. I skipped the cleaning job that night.

When I came a few nights later, I glimpsed this neighbor wearing the down jacket we'd given Joseph for Christmas. I didn't mention it. The jacket, like that table, had become evil. I cleaned in silence.

One night a few weeks later, I answered the phone and heard Joseph cry, "Help!" Then the line went dead. Had someone attacked Joseph? Should I call 911? No, I'd force my numb body to act. I ran to the car, sped to his condo and burst into his living room. Joseph stood handcuffed between two policemen. One on each side held an arm. My tiger mother self came to life and raged filled me. I yelled at the intruders, "Do you have a search warrant to be in my son's house? If not, take off those handcuffs and let go of his arms. My son is not a criminal!"

Amazing, the power I had. The police removed the handcuffs. Joseph rushed to my side and put his arms around me and we hugged. He whispered, "Thanks, Mom." I drew a deep breath. My rage and fear subsided like an ocean wave come to shore. Joseph loved me. The police had responded to me.

One officer even smiled. "Ma'am, we asked for his identification and he refused to show it."

"It was stolen from him. I told Joseph we needed to get new ID."

"Ma'am, a drug king lived in this apartment, number 4G. We've had a stakeout of his place for a week. We didn't know the dealer had moved out and we thought your son—who didn't have ID—was the drug king."

My husband Hal arrived and after a brief hug for Joseph and me, he stepped outside with the officers to fill in necessary forms. When the police departed, we three sat down and shared tea, Oreos, and heart-felt relief. But I had learned that an apartment and my services were not enough to save Joseph.

Not long afterwards, unable to cope with the terror he experienced in the hands of the police, Joseph was hospitalized for 72 hours. As usual, he turned down an offer of a two weeks' stay and when I brought him home again, I felt scattered and unable to cope. Yet I was very much in charge, as Hal spent long hours running his business.

When September came, bringing Laura's birthday, I determined to focus my full concentration on this youngest child. I detested the anxiety that often filled my consciousness with grief and pain.

I knocked timidly on Laura's white door. "Honey, can I come in so we can plan your birthday party?"

"Yeah, come on in, have a seat." She gestured to a twin bed where her special stuffed animal friends and a Harbor High School band uniform waited for her attention. A magical unicorn sticker, purple and pink, covered her closet door and posters of Chuck, a rock singer, hung on the wall. An edition of *Transactional Psychology for Teens* loomed large between Oz books and *Wilfred the Pig*. What a delightful mix of childhood and adolescence. Not long ago, she favored pink little girl clothes, and now she wore olive drab. I yearned to give her a magical birthday party. "Would you like a scavenger hunt, Honey, or we could have a dinner party and rent a movie..."

"You forget—I've grown-up. We're high school now. No Mommie games or food. Just get us Diet Cokes, M&Ms, and onion dip with chips. That's our Mood Food. Red is for...."

"Spare me; keep your M&M secrets, but I'd like to cook a lovely feast for you."

She shook her head no and her hair flew in the air. "Please, mom, we don't want Mom and Dad helicopters hovering over a buffet. Think chips, dips, CDs and M&Ms, okay?"

"Okay, honey, with one exception. I want to bake a birthday cake special for you."

"If you want to bake, okay. But keep Joseph out of the way and don't you and Dad hang around."

"Okay." Lately, Laura had seemed out of reach, more like a porcelain doll than her chattering giggling self. Her crowd of friends and her determination to do her party her way really pleased me. "Dad and I will stay in our bedroom most of the time so you can do your thing. But I can't leave a party of sixteen-year-olds on their own."

She hugged me. "Love you, Mom. Just don't hover."

The night of her party, we gulped a quick family dinner of sandwiches. I felt relieved when Joseph pulled on a navy blue stocking cap, and muttered, "Going for a walk." He didn't seem to notice the birthday cake on the kitchen counter or the packages of M&Ms and chips.

The evening belonged to Laura. Her pale skin, green eyes and cloud of maroon hair bestowed on her a unique beauty. Her mantra, "I'll never work in fast foods and get my beautiful hair greasy," amused Hal and me. She was not usually vain and we enjoyed this conceit.

When the doorbell rang for the first guests, Hal and I ran for the master bedroom, so that no Essence de Parents spoiled the party. I comforted myself with the words, "At least we're nearby in case of emergency, Hal."

"Emmm," he commented.

Eavesdropping through the wall, we learned that eating a green M&M meant you were fertile; a red, you were in love. The shrieks and laughter prevented our learning more. The discordant squeaks of the boys with changing voices, and the continual giggles of the girls assured us the party was going well. From time to time, Hal or I strolled through the house to replenish the dip, chips, and M&Ms and enjoy the sweet ambiance. Kids filled the couches and armchairs. Some stretched out on the floor. One boy and girl held hands. We returned to our bedroom and listened in on a Sonny and Cher CD. The front door slammed. Hal startled. "Probably some kids went for a walk to see the bay," I told him.

A scream pierced the air. I rushed into the living room panting with fear. Joseph, with an uncombed beard, dirty Levis, and stocking cap, clutched Laura's friend Megan around the waist and was pressing an unwanted kiss on her lips.

"Joseph! Put her down!" My controlling parent voice filled the room. He abruptly dropped Megan and she slid to the floor. Laura and her friends gathered protectively around her body. Joseph headed for the door in the kitchen that led to his quarters--a room, a bath, and a small study. Emboldened by the potential effect of that unwanted kiss on Megan and Laura's lives, I grabbed Joseph and shook him. "You must never touch Laura's friends!" Someone in the family room turned up the stereo.

A wistful smile transformed Joseph into a young man. "Calm down, Mom. It's my sister's birthday. I thought her friends would like a college man's attention at a party."

I let go of Joseph. Space and time passed between us. No way to explain to Joseph that he had changed from a desirable older brother into someone who roused fear and distaste. I couldn't speak.

He looked confused. "I just wanted to have fun with the other kids. Is something wrong?"

Words evaded me. I leaned against the wall to keep from falling. Joseph ducked into his room and slammed the door.

This thirty-year-old memory still devastated me. I stopped talking but listened to Miriam's voice. "That scene at Laura's party must have been especially difficult for you with your history."

Her words brought me out of the past. I straightened up, curious. "What do you mean?"

"As you told your story, I recalled your junior high graduation party. Your father appeared intoxicated on the balcony above the party. You suffered deep embarrassment from his behavior."

Her words hit me in the stomach. I felt sick. "Yes, yes. I knew my father had an illness and couldn't help himself. Probably, like Joseph, he wanted to be part of the party. But oh, I felt such shame for my father and for Joseph. I wanted to protect them and the guests too and I couldn't."

"You protected Megan. You did what you had to, while loving and understanding Joseph's behavior. The suffering you have endured has made you a very strong person."

I managed a smile. "I sure don't feel strong."

"Do you want to continue your story next week?"

"In two weeks. After I tell you my story, the shame and guilt diminish."

"A different perspective is running through your stories now."

"I'm beginning to have some empathy for myself."

"Good for you. You and Hal certainly had a difficult decision to make."

CHAPTER 25

Tough Love

"*S*ometimes when I'm down and all alone…." The song wriggled its way under Laura's door and trickled into the kitchen, where I washed dishes and Hal crushed Coke tins for recycling. "Martha, Joseph's behavior at the party is not acceptable. We cannot let him live here any longer."

Aimlessly, I stirred the soapy dishwater as if the just right words might show up amid the bubbles. "Joseph said he only wanted to have fun with the other kids. He wasn't angry. He looked about fourteen when I talked to him." I kept my face averted to avoid the outrage in Hal's eyes.

"I'm sure that's true, but since he isn't fourteen, we can't let him live here. It's too hard on Laura's development."

I employed a chirpy tone to reply. "After school tomorrow, I'll hit the local ads for apartments to let. I promise you I'll find a place for him to live."

Hal crushed more cans, waggled his bushy eyebrows up and down. Finality sounded in his every word. "We are enabling Joseph's illness. He lives here rent-free and refuses medications to control his illness. His life has no structure. He's digging deeper into fantasy every day. You can find an apartment for him, all right, but you can't make him able to live in it."

"Would you put a person with cancer out on the street? He's our son. He'll die on the street."

"He has his SSI disability. I hope he's capable of living on his own. Let's see if he can."

I wrung my slippery soapy hands. "Hal, I can't do this. Give him one more chance. I'll find another psychiatrist. Dr. Trotter will help me. I'll make him go to appointments. One more chance."

"If I agree to one more try, will you accept that he must leave here if he still refuses to see a psychiatrist and take medications?"

"I promise."

We shook hands. Neither of us felt that sense of togetherness that had woven the fabric of our marriage, but I had won Joseph one more chance. I ran my hand lightly over Hal's veined knobby hand and he patted my back consolingly.

We both lay awake that night. Hal was my life compass, but what if he pointed in the wrong direction? What if I was right? Did we have to destroy our son to save our family? What did it all mean? Hal's little mutterings and tossings helped me to realize he felt unsure, too. He used to say, "The best CEO is only right 52% of the time." He knew his own fallibility and we weren't gambling with dollars but with a precious life.

That week we informed our NAMI group of our decision. They applauded it. Dr. Ericson called it "Tough love." What if tough love killed somebody?

When Dr. Trotter, our pediatrician, told us, "I think I've found the right psychiatrist for Joseph," my hopes soared again. Perhaps Hal's strong stand could bring Joseph to health and wholeness. I prayed frantically every day that Joseph and the new psychiatrist would bond and that under careful supervision, Joseph would become himself once more.

Hal, speaking slowly and leaving plenty of space for processing, explained our position to Joseph. "Understand...you are welcome to live here as long as... you visit Dr. Martin once a week...and take the medication he prescribes. If you refuse to see him or to accept the medication... our deal is off. You will still be our son. We will love, but we won't take care of you."

Joseph did not answer. I prompted him. "Do you understand what Dad means?"

"Yes. I have to see Dr. Martin and take meds to live here. That's the deal."

"That's the deal," I answered.

Hal extended his arm. "Let's shake hands on it." We pumped each other's hands more than once. We three had a deal.

We scheduled Joseph's appointments with the psychiatrist for 5 pm, so I'd be home from school and he could take my car to the doctor's office. The first session seemed to go well. Joseph returned at 6:30 and tossed the car keys on the table. "How'd it go?"

"Fine. Dr. Martin's okay."

That night, Joseph agreed to accompany Hal and me to Harbor High to watch Laura march in the band at half-time, second clarinet, where Joseph had once been first clarinet. He showered and looked sharp in a blue polo shirt and clean slacks. The three of us sat on the hard bleachers and wore out our lungs cheering for Harbor High. Even Joseph cheered. In Washington, he had painted a striking picture of cheerleaders and now the sight cheered him. I drew the comforter of family love about me and enjoyed the evening.

On his second visit to Dr. Martin, Joseph returned home at five-fifty. Had Dr. Martin cut him short on time? Joseph needed his privacy so I didn't mention the ten minutes or ask about his medication. That night, I sought reassurance from my husband. "Honey, Joseph is doing better, isn't he?"

"He's better dressed. He's eating dinner with us. He's quieter now, so I don't know what he's thinking. Dr. Martin ought to be a help." Not much reassurance in those words.

"Joseph enjoyed the football game and watching the band march. We can do that again," I enthused. Hal had nothing more to say.

The third session, Joseph arrived home at 5:30, tossed me the keys and stretched his mouth in a tiger's grin---fierce, not friendly. A deep black feeling of impending disaster numbed me. I tried to use a normal voice. "How was Dr. Martin?"

"Okay. Psychiatrists are all alike. They want to control your brain waves."

"Maybe so. But maybe you need some help." He didn't appear to hear me as he brushed past me on the way to his bedroom. When he was out of sight, I raced to the phone. That grin. Unreal. A warning! I dialed Dr. Martin's office. I could barely hold the phone it felt so slippery. "Did Joseph keep his appointment today?"

"We've saved an hour for him three times, and he's never showed up once. We do apologize, but we have to bill you for those appointments."

I slipped the phone back in its place. Numbness crept up my legs and arms and moved into my chest. How could I evict my son? He'd never survive on the streets. Why had I shook hands with Hal on this? In a flash, I saw myself as a silly, optimistic mother, fooling herself, trying to make pretty.

When we met for our usual kitchen conference before dinner, the news devastated Hal. He slammed his fist on the wooden counter. "By God, how I hate this disease. Joseph never lied to me before. We've lost our son."

Hal's strong sense of personal integrity focused his attention on the lie itself and separated him from Joseph. I wanted to cry out, "Give him one more chance!" but I didn't. The normal guidelines of life disappeared in clouds of uncertainty. Good, bad, evil, benevolent—these labels didn't apply. Joseph might die living on the street. Depression might overcome Laura with Joseph at home. The shock of eviction might bring Joseph's personality together, or might lead him to drug addiction. No one knew the answers, not Dr. Ericson, not Doctor Martin, not our mental health system and God wasn't speaking to me. Hal had determined a course of action and I agreed, because Hal was my compass, my rock and I needed to trust him. I nodded. "We made a deal. We gave him his one last chance," I whispered.

As Hal walked toward Joseph's bedroom, I noticed how the erect posture of the young lieutenant I married had changed. His shoulders stooped. He looked defeated.

A tense and pale Laura materialized in the kitchen and slipped her arms around me. "Mom, do you remember when I was little, and Joseph used to call me his 'little pink rabbit'? We loved each other so much when I was little." I peered into Laura's face. She wasn't a child any more but a young woman facing tragedy. We blended our tears. At that moment, Mother and Daughter were one organism, joined in grief.

No sounds came from the back bedroom. Had the cork door Geoff installed smothered the sound, or were my men speaking in quiet tones?

Finally, the door opened. Joseph, a backpack on his back, strode past me toward the front door. Hal paused at my side. "Joseph wants to take a trip. He's packed his rucksack. I'm driving him to the bus station."

"I'm coming with you, Honey. You can't drive back alone. I need to say goodbye to Joseph."

"You and Laura, stay where you are. Your tears and regrets will make matters worse. Joseph is ready to try a new life style for a while."

Before I could move, Hal had closed the door between us. No chance for me to hug Joseph goodbye, but I understood Hal. He took this suffering upon himself to save Laura and me from as much pain as he could. But the decision might be a death penalty for Joseph.

Exhausted, Laura and I cuddled on the couch, each of us trying to sustain the other. Our weeping gave way to silence with occasional shudders and then emptiness. We had no sense of time so we startled when the front door opened.

Hal strode over and managed a grin. "Come on, girls, we're going out to dinner. The Crab Cooker."

I felt the only skill I had was to keep going. "Laura, let's wash our faces and comb our hair. Dad wants to take us out." Hal, too, was just holding on.

That night as we lay in bed wide-awake, staring at the ceiling, he reached over and squeezed my hand. "Don't worry. He'll be all right, Honey. He's stronger than you think."

His words didn't reassure me. His grasp felt weak, the bed sheets strangely cold and depressing. The ground beneath me was turning to dust. I might slip into the abyss left by this emotional earthquake.

CHAPTER 26

The Lost Tooth

When a tooth is missing, the tongue continually probes the space that it once held. When a family member disappears, the mind continually probes the space he held and focuses on absence. Days, weeks, months passed with no word from Joseph, who became unreal to me -- a ghost or an unresolved hope. The weather where we lived in Newport Beach constantly changed. Fog, wet and cold, slapped you in the face one day; on another, the ocean showed its teeth and black clouds walled off the horizon. At times, a breach in the clouds or fog let in stray beams of light.

Such an opening occurred in my mental fog at a clambake on the beach of South Laguna. Bill Saylor, my husband's business partner, and his wife Rosemary, who lived on this private pristine cove, annually invited the Major Data staff to a party. This year, a tangy, fishy steam rose from the sand where clams and crab cooked beneath layers of sand and burning charcoal. Rosemary and I sat together in the Saylor's luau shack, watching our crowd play beach volleyball a few yards away. This gave me some time alone with a very clever woman. She worked tirelessly with the League of Woman Voters and with Orange County government to provide services for the mentally ill. She packed an amazing amount of energy and wisdom inside her petite figure. Leaning toward me from her canvas colored chair, she inquired in a low husky voice, "What's the latest on your son, Joseph?"

"We tried tough love. Accept medical treatment, or get out. Now we don't even know if he's dead or alive."

She lit a cigarette, inhaled deeply, and her words flowed. "Martha, it's time for you to learn something new. The mind has its own place and you can stock it with new information instead of filling it up with your son's illness. Remember when my son, Richard, had valley fever?"

"Of course I do. That awful fungus in his body nearly killed him! They traced the fungus to a pile of hay in Colorado. What a terrible time that was."

"It was. But do you remember what I did?"

"You found a hospital in Fresno to treat valley fever."

Impatiently, she snuffed out her cigarette in an abalone shell that lay on the shack's floor. "True enough, but that isn't what I meant. I studied Russian—and I did so to train my brain to think of something besides valley fever and my son."

Just then, Hal, a short man, made an incredible leap and smashed the ball over the net. "Yea for our side!" I applauded. He turned and grinned. The game continued and Rosemary and I chatted. "I can't exactly see how learning Russian would help me."

Her short twenties' bob transformed her into the flapper she'd once been. "Hal wasn't thinking of Joseph when he smashed that ball. The mind can only think of one thing at a time. Valley fever and Russian don't room together. I chose to think about Russian. Learn something new, not Russian, not volleyball, but something new to you and for you." The ball game ended and the players ran across the sand, heading for the tub of iced drinks. Before they filled the shack, Rosemary added, "Learn something new. It will change your life."

When wildfires burn the hills of California, new seeds buried deep in the soil spring up with green landscape to cover the blackened soil. The wildfire of change seized me. A week later, I told my husband, "Honey, I've enrolled in a summer class at Orange Coast College. It's Wednesdays at 6. I'm going to learn BASIC computer language and then I'll program computer lessons for my students."

He turned down the volume of a football game on TV. "You're going to learn—what? You had a tough time with statistics when you got your credential. Maybe you should take creative writing, instead."

"No! Now that there are these minicomputers, we can afford to buy one for me. And I can build new synapses in my brain by making up learning programs for students."

His eyes twinkled as if he'd heard a good joke. "Okay. You just surprised me. That's a great idea. In fact, I'll take Basic with you."

That scared me! Who'd want to compete with Hal, an engineer? "You don't need to come. You already know Pascal and hard stuff. This is for beginners."

"It'll be a refresher course for me."

Almost immediately, my life changed. Every Wednesday at 5 p.m., Hal and I met in the OCC quad where we breathed air redolent with popcorn and feasted on juicy Polish sausages roasted in a little barbecue cart. As we ate, I studied my notes trying to make sense of this alien computer language.

"Honey?"

He looked up from his notebook. "Yes?"

"I'm really glad you come to class with me. But I just don't exactly understand what we're supposed to do."

Happiness spread across his face like jam on toast. "Thought you might need a hand."

I bristled a little. "The problem isn't just me. Our instructor's accent makes his directions unintelligible. He repeats over and over 'Press A-dolah' and I can't find a computer key like that anywhere on the keyboard." Hal chuckled. "If you'd had the advantage I did of growing up in a barrio where everyone had an accent, you'd understand him. He means tap on an A key and a dollar sign."

Diligently, I plugged away day after day trying to master logic and odd symbols like A\$. As I battered my head against the wall of computer language, I made a great discovery. I didn't have to be a passive victim. I could take control of my melancholic mind and force it to learn Something New. And the Something New had a room of its own where Joseph and despair and suffering did not gain admittance.

When I grasped the teaching potential of computers, my enthusiasm spilled over into Prince of Peace Day School. Parents caught the fever and the Parent Teacher Association, with no prompting from me, donated money to purchase computers. The Moms and Dads actually built twenty walnut cubicles to house them in my classroom. Proud Dad and professional programmer for NASA, John McCoy and my husband Hal, computer engineer, pulled me through the intricacies of keeping ten Radio Shack computers working smoothly while all the students, except kindergarteners, learned to program. Hal worked out a way for the little ones to participate by learning binary arithmetic. Grouped in a circle, the kindergarteners learned to stand or sit on the floor when a number was called out. 0 meant sit. 1 meant stand. The kids were happy and learning. My principal awarded me a new title, "Director of the Learning Center."

Creativity ran rampant. Hyperactive kids, who'd refused to write, now banged away on computer keyboards, creating wild stories of fierce pizza ovens and aliens and poems spattered with asterisks and exclamation points. They fought over a chance to play a computer game where you shot ghosts to learn multiplication.

A new electric spirit invaded our cozy classroom when I persuaded Prince of Peace Lutheran Day School to admit Mike Lewis, a wheelchair-bound eight-year-old, into the Learning Center. Mike's eyes danced when he saw the faces of the kids who would be his companions for the next five years. Mike talked with his eyes, not his mouth.

Howard, a kid with a shock of butterscotch hair falling in his face, bent over Mike. "Listen up. There are three possible answers. Blink once for answer A, twice for answer B, three times for answer C. Ready?"

Mike's *yes* nod sent ripples from his head through his core muscles and rocked his chair.

Howard spoke clearly and loudly. "Who was the third president of the United States? A: Andrew Jackson; B: John Adams; C: Thomas Jefferson?"

"Blink, blink!"

Howard shouted "Right on! Gimme five!" Mike's wobbly arm slowly rose from his chair and touched Howard's sturdy palm. Both boys grinned. There were no words then, and there are no words now, fit to describe the deep satisfaction the students and I shared as we communicated with Mike. His slender freckle-speckled face reddened with delight, as he understood he had a method to show off his knowledge.

Mike had a giant soul trapped in a body he couldn't control. He especially loved Friday Chapel, when students and teachers worshipped together. No matter how mischievous or rebellious a student might be, something in Mike touched the other child.

Now, I maintained in my brain three refugees from the stress of Joseph's disappearance: The Logic room where I learned to program, the Director's Hideout, and the Michael Spirit room. I might not be able to help my own son, but I could help these kids, especially Mike. His presence transformed the lives of everyone around him.

Teaching was so engrossing that I was nonplussed when Laura begged, "Mom, let's adopt a Japanese exchange student."

Why can't she be satisfied with her rabbits, hamsters, and guinea pigs? Why a Japanese student when I'm in the middle of learning computer language? Let J=Japanese student! Maybe Laura and I can write Japanese haiku. But a live-in student in our home? "Oh gosh, Laura, how in the world could I add one more thing to my day?"

She put on her billy-goat stare that meant, "I won't give up!" and turned to her father. "Dad, how about it? A Japanese student! I'd like a boy."

"It's up to your mother. She runs the house." By this statement, Hal was admitting that he'd like a Japanese student, too, but didn't want to load any extra tasks on me.

"Why a boy? Wouldn't you prefer a sort of sister?" I asked.

"The exchange students' counselor says all the families want girls because girls are easier. But I'm used to boys. I've always had two brothers."

"I'm at work all day and one extra person, male or female…"

"Dad and I will take care of him. The house is too quiet. I want to change *something.*"

Hal's and my glances collided. Laura needed a brother. I needed a son. Look at the changes BASIC and Michael brought me. Now it was time for the fires of change to blow through the house.

Two weeks later, we met Toshihiro at the John Wayne Airport and drove with him directly to Harbor High School. We gestured wildly with our hands and desperately passed an English-Japanese dictionary back and forth in our attempt to explain we were on our way to Harbor High School theatre where our daughter Laura, Director of Lighting and Special Effects, awaited us. "Hal, he can't understand you. Do you think it's jet lag?" I asked from the back seat.

"He sure as heck doesn't understand spoken English. Maybe he can read it." Toshi clapped and smiled his way through the play and hid any confusion and exhaustion he felt. So on our first evening together, he became the big brother that Laura needed.

Every week, with a ritual bow, he presented us a handmade gift from his relatives; pincushion dolls, a small jeweled tree, a delicate clay rose with open petals, a swatch of silk cloth with the inked outline of a fish. We always exclaimed, "Oh, it's so Japanese!" and that became his first understandable phrase in English. He used it to tease us, pulling on his eyes and laughing, "... so Japanese."

Rarely did Hal express his emotions in words, but when Toshi called him "My American Daddy," Hal clapped the young man on his shoulder and called him "My son." Toshi refused to leave our house at night without Hal's permission. Many evenings he sat cross-legged on the floor beside Hal's recliner chair, content to be near his American Daddy. They shared an underground wordless river of friendship. I saw that sorrow and joy could live together in one person, under one roof.

This was the seventies. My son, Geoff, was working on a PhD in clinical psychology at Fuller Graduate School of Psychology. His wife, Sarah, was also working on a PhD track that would lead to a degree in English, linguistics and rhetoric from USC. Julie had finished a Master's degree in psychology and was working as a family-planning administrator for Seattle.

"Hal, we have the most amazing family," I told my husband as we crawled into bed one night.

Hal murmured, "Do you remember, before we married, how I was afraid marriage would be boring? Gee, I'd love to have one boring day!" We fell asleep laughing.

CHAPTER 27

Return

"Too many stories start with a phone call," my writing teacher warned; yet, before texting and after telegrams, how else did news spread? Too often, a ring heralded disaster, but I could not resist the impulse to answer, even when my pile of homework towered to the ceiling and the laundry to fold formed a pyramid atop the dining table.

So, one evening, I reluctantly laid aside my red correcting pencil to answer a persistent ring. To forestall any wrong numbers, I answered, "Sarkissian residence."

"I'm calling from a Quaker organization in Washington D.C."

A memorized reply rolled off my lips. "I'm sorry but I'm not able to contribute to anything at present." It took guts to hang up on such an eager girlish voice, but I didn't have time or money for Quakers at this point.

On the verge of hanging up, the words "Do you have a son named Joseph Sarkissian?" suddenly stabbed my heart.

"Do you have news of my son? Is he alive?"

Her voice smiled. "Your son is alive and well. Every morning he comes to our Quaker Greenpeace Center for the homeless. He showers, eats breakfast and reads the newspaper. He's a good man. I have been trying to help him find work, but with no success. Yesterday, I asked him, 'Isn't there anyone who would help you?' and he answered, 'I guess my mom and dad would.' He gave me your number."

Blood rushed through my body and made my body tingle. My pulse beat to a joyful refrain, "Joseph is alive. Joseph is alive! Miracles happen. Lazarus is come out of the grave." Then I grasped the need for action—he might disappear again.

"What should I do? How do I bring him home?"

"Purchase a Greyhound bus ticket from Washington, DC to Santa Ana. You'll need to give Greyhound enough extra money to pay for meals on the way home. The driver will dole out money for food at each stop, so your son won't slip away. We've done this before and it works smoothly. Bring your son home as soon as possible. If you go to Greyhound today, he'll be home in three days."

"Thank you for figuring that out for me. This is really a miracle! Did you know Joseph has schizophrenia?"

"No. I only know Joseph is a fine gentleman and it's my joy to help him find his way home."

Her goodness flew through the telephone wires. The God I had such difficulty trusting spoke through her. My emotions overwhelmed me and my voice disappeared in sobs of fear and joy. As she hung up, I hoped she felt my gratitude.

Three days later, Hal, Laura, and I waited at the Transportation Station, a gracious Spanish style building with a blue tiled floor and the smell of chili peanuts. Laura, a gift-box of See's chocolates in hand, led the way to the bus area. Hal and I followed her. I felt dizzy and uneasy. Would Joseph hate us? Who would he be? Could we restructure our family to cherish and care for this 'fine gentleman' with schizophrenia?

With a loud screech of brakes and a cloud of carbon monoxide, the bus pulled up to the cement platform. The faces of the passengers were visible through the windows, but I couldn't make out Joseph's face through the window. The bus door, like a giant mouth, opened wide and a mass of people flowed onto the cement platform. We spun around searching for a muscular 160-pound man with a rucksack on his back. That awful sense of defeat I knew so well crept up my spine. "He's not here. We'll have to talk to Greyhound."

Then Laura let out a shriek. "I see him! He's here!" She darted in and out of the crowd like a radar beam and squealed with delight as she hugged a frail 85-pound man hidden in a giant overcoat. She pressed her gift of See's chocolates into his hands. His voice sounded rusty. "Thanks, Laura. Thanks."

We crowded around him now and dared to hug his frail body. He passed his box of chocolate and we each took one. We stood, marveling at the sight of each other and the taste of the sweetness of chocolate.

"Welcome home, Son," Hal said. I saw tears caught in Joseph's thick black lashes. The *Pals forever* were together again, but none of us knew what to do next. The empty bus moved away with another cloud of carbon monoxide. Soon, we stood alone on the platform, an awkward foursome.

"Where's your rucksack?" Hal asked.

"I was rolled. They got my ID. Everything."

Tears clogged our throats. We shifted our weight foot to foot. Then Laura sang out, "Let's get a hamburger. I'm starving." Our pert littlest was in charge and we sighed with relief. As we traipsed into Denny's café, a warm cloud smelling of fried chicken enveloped us. "Welcome to Denny's," chirped a uniformed waitress, whose sincere smile cracked her pancake makeup. Joseph responded with a broad grin to the generic greeting. Then we all smiled. Her welcome implied we were a *regular* family, not outcasts. The forest green and brown color scheme soothed us, too, as did plates with hamburgers, towers of fries and continually refilled coffee cups. Here we could meet each other on a common ground. Hal managed a casual voice to inquire, "Joseph, would you like to share your adventures with us?"

"Rented a cabin near Weed, California. Strange neighbors. Not friendly. Didn't like me."

Hal nodded. "What a bummer!"

Now Joseph's words from an unused voice streamed out in a turbulent rush. "Hitch hiked to Washington DC...rode in a truck, joined war on poverty... lived in tent city... it went bad." His face clouded over. The waitress lubricated his rusty voice with another cup of coffee.

Hal leaned forward for eye contact. "What happened?"

"Big guys rolled me. Took ID—took everything. Look." He dug in his pocket and laid a wrinkled check on the table. "I had my SSI check...no one would cash it. No ID."

I smoothed out the check and stored it in my purse. "Tomorrow, I'll see if SSI will cash it and I'll get your checks started again."

Joseph put his elbows on the table, chin in hands and whispered, "Bad news. I think I'm going blind. I can't read the menu. Just figured a hamburger and fries were okay."

"Where are your glasses?" I asked.

"Glasses?" He shook his head, puzzled. "I lost my glasses a long time ago...." His voice trailed off.

"That's it. You aren't going blind. You just need your glasses. Maybe stronger ones than you had, but you can see okay. Isn't that true, Hal?"

Overwhelmed by emotion, Hal slumped on the booth cushions. "Yes, get new glasses."

Joseph confessed in a bashful voice, "It's hard for me to tell what's what! I don't know if they've sent me a hallucination to mix me up, or if something real...like lost glasses...is going on."

In a pondering manner, Hal answered, "Yes, that's very hard to tell. Tomorrow you must see an optometrist and he'll figure it out."

Joseph drew back wary and sly as a fox. "No, I won't. An optometrist may be part of—the conspiracy."

"Remember how you liked your pediatrician Dr. Trotter taking care of you after your scooter accident? I bet you'd like Doc Isaac, who made your glasses. Do you remember him?"

"Of course I do. He went to our church. His son Rob was my pal." Anger edged his voice.

"Would you like him to check your eyes in case you have a vision problem?"

"Maybe."

Hal drew a deep breath and jumped into our dialogue. "So, it's settled. A trip to Dr. Isaac's tomorrow. Now it's time to shift gears. We don't eat desserts much anymore, but tonight I feel like having tutti-frutti ice cream with chocolate sauce. How about the rest of you?" When we dug our spoons into the dessert, our brows relaxed and our tics stopped ticking. Hal had an unrivaled sense of timing.

The next morning, we found the SSI check too old to be cashed, but we got Joseph re-enrolled for SSI. Dr. Isaac was happy to have Joseph as a patient once again and the new glasses worked. At least he wasn't blind. But he was still lost.

For over thirty-three years, Joseph's journey led Hal and me in and out of three jails, through five apartments, ten hospitals, five independent living homes, and ten board and care facilities. Throughout those trials, Joseph preserved his spirit of independence and his determination to survive, and Hal and I kept alive our determination to assist him. We never again withheld our home from him, and he never again stopped taking medication. But as we learned the nature of his severe neurobiological disease, we learned when to tack, when to let out the sail, and when to shorten it, and when to hide in a safe harbor.

Our journey took us to many county-approved homes recommended by his caseworker. Unfortunately, no licensing is required for homes for the care of the mentally ill, so while some board and cares were excellent, some were fraught with danger. If a patient recovered, he was moved to another placement, which immediately took away his sense of security. After many phone calls, I wrote a letter to bring to his caseworkers' attention the housing problem.

California Health Clinic
Santa Ana, California
Attention: Caren Leath — Caseworker

Dear Miss Leath,

As you know, our son Joseph Hunter Sarkissian is a cooperative, kind and shy man, stable on his new anti-psychotic medication. He has had the misfortune of living in a series of board and care facilities that have been below the standards set by California law. I am writing you to beg for a better living situation for my son and for more oversight of the board and care facilities. Here is a partial list of the board and cares Joseph has endured:

Restful Towers had violent patients. I witnessed one man throwing a TV through the window. There was loud swearing and fistfights. Tenants carried knives and robbed each other. This environment sent Joseph into a depression. How could anyone's mental health improve in such a place? We had to remove Joseph.

Garden Homes, Costa Mesa, his next board and care, had a manager in her seventies. She loved the clients and held Sunday afternoon musicals with talented clients. It appeared to be a perfect place for Joseph. We borrowed a clarinet and encouraged Joseph to practice. Every time we asked about the Sunday concert, he told us the manager had fallen and was injured.

Twice she was hospitalized. One Monday evening Joseph called us. "The manager's alcoholic. She's been hospitalized and they're closing the home. Can you come and get me now?"

Santa Ana Village, Santa Ana, had a wonderful manager, Mrs. Morgan, a black woman and a fabulous cook who sometimes even prepared fried chicken for the clients. We appreciate the life skills Joseph learned there; how to do his laundry and keep his room clean and his hair cut. He had made too much progress to stay with Mrs. Morgan and was required to move on.

Atlantis Home came next, at your recommendation, Ms. Leath. Here the manager told "the boys" to walk to South Coast Plaza, have a hamburger at McDonald's there, and not to return home until six. When they returned to their home, they found the door locked. One client, a former sneak thief, managed to wriggle his arm through a dog door, reach inside and unlock the door. The clients could not take their medications because they were locked up in a metal box. Joseph phoned the police, who came, opened the box, and passed out the medications. The police calculated the manager stole $300 from the clients, most of it in small bills hidden in mattresses and underwear drawers. He also stole any valuable objects, the house microwave and my son's TV. The police discovered that the manager had a record for drug usage. Why is the government hiring managers "off the street" without conducting an investigation before hiring? We are very proud of Joseph, who showed great leadership in organizing the men and calling the police. Please find Joseph a safe and healthy place to live.
Sincerely yours,
Martha Sarkissian, Joseph's Mother

After this letter, Ms. Heath moved Joseph to Tustin Place #2, which had won an award as the most outstanding board and care in Orange County. A Filipino husband and wife turned an ordinary house into a loving home. Joseph now had a driver's license and drove clients to doctors' appointments and picked up their medications at the pharmacy. He drove Zonia and Emile, his caretakers, to the market and to church. After a few years, he took his medications without supervision and Zonia and Emile declared him independent. That led to his being evicted from board and care.

By now a widow, the thought of handling a life-change for Joseph aroused my anxiety. Where could Joseph live? He announced firmly, "It's time for me to be independent. I don't need anyone fixing my meals or taking care of me. I don't want to live with you, either, Martha."

"I need to find a good independent place for Joseph," I told the caseworker.

"Please trust me. I have a wonderful place for him in Garden Grove."

I never had the opportunity to check out his new housing; Joseph felt eager to be on his own and his caseworker insisted she was the person to decide. "You sit back and rest, Mother," she told me. Though angry and anxious, I gave up. Maybe it was time for a caseworker to take over.

After Joseph had moved, I visited his new home. There I found men sleeping in the living room on couches, on the floor, and outside on cement next to an empty swimming pool.

Two of his three roommates openly used drugs. When one man attempted to rape a woman, Joseph called the police. Later, the manager warned him, "Never call the police, no matter what happens. That gives us a bad reputation in the neighborhood."

Clients paid $750.00 for room and board, but after a few days, no food was forthcoming. Many of the residents began begging at churches for food. "Joseph, I don't want you to go with them. The government has given sufficient money to pay for room and board. I don't want you begging."

I was bringing Joseph food, but he had to be careful because other hungry residents might steal it. Someone at the house stole $300 from an older woman who had been saving for years to get her belongings out of storage. Joseph slept with his trousers on and his wallet in his pocket. "Come home and live with me, Joseph," I pleaded.

"I want to be independent."

With each change in housing, Joseph developed an added skill. His first place taught him to keep his room clean. At Zonia's, for example, he learned to be helpful in caring for the other residents, and with a car purchased by an underpayment of SSI, he worked on his chauffeur skills.

Joseph progressed steadily toward health and wholeness; and yet now that he was officially recognized as an independent mentally ill person, able to direct his own life, he lived in the most squalid conditions ever, among thieves and rapists, many recently released from prison.

Without my Hal, and in my eighties, I did not know where to turn. I told my therapist, "Miriam, I'm past 80 now. I've spent most of my life trying to find a safe place for Joseph to live and now due to some idiotic licensing laws, Joseph has been evicted from his safe place."

"You need to remember that Joseph prefers his independence over the restrictions of a board and care. You and I can work on finding the right place for him to live while appreciating his independence and determination."

She kept the candle of hope alight inside of me.

CHAPTER 28

Going Home

*O*n a day in May, at the age of 84, I flew up the stairs to Miriam's office like a charmed spirit, not with a load of guilt and anxiety, but with a bucketful of joy. I waved a sheaf of papers. "Something wonderful has happened. I can hardly believe it!"

She glanced at her now overweight folder of notes concerning my life. "Since I've known you, many wonderful things have happened to you. Trips to China, India, Russia. You've won writing contests and found a lovely friend and companion. You've lived to see your two-pound grandson play baseball with the Junior Giants." Each joyful syllable from her lips delighted us both.

"This is even more wonderful!" I waved my papers again. "Last week, my friend Linda told me, "Open the website I sent you from NAMI." I ran to my computer and read, 'For rent. Costa Mesa apartment for independent mentally ill person. Mother must live in Newport Beach and volunteer.' The ad read as though it had Joseph's and my name on it.

That Saturday, Joseph, Geoff and I attended an open house and braced ourselves for the interview that would determine if Joseph could live there.

While Geoff talked to the fathers, Joseph and I took seats by ourselves against the wall. A cheerful girl with spiky hair, punk clothes and a small dog on a leash, bounced over beside me. "Do you have a dog?"

"Oh, yes, I do; a beautiful collie named Kristen."

In a few magic moments, we were telling each other our trials and joys of dog ownership. Alice suddenly jumped to her feet. "Mom!" she called in an urgent voice, "Take these people as tenants. I love them."

I told Miriam, "Last week, on the second of May, Joseph became a member of the Pepper Tree Lane community and I've brought you a photo."

Miriam did not need to be a vessel to hold my grief now. Instead, she shared my emotions of happiness and so increased my delight. She wanted to know every detail of Joseph's new home. I told her how eight families met for five years and after much prayer and discussions, joined together to buy property and convert houses into apartments for their independent mentally ill children. Miriam noticed every little detail of the Pepper Tree Lane Community as she studied the photos of the house, garden, gazebo, and especially Joseph's apartment. You have completed one of your life goals," Miriam commented.

Two days after Joseph moved in to the new community, I found myself running errands nearby and decided to drop in. I followed the curved path past the fountain and pressed my head against the windowpane to see if he was home. A contented man sat in a forest green easy chair, sipping from a cup of coffee, and reading the morning newspaper.

I rapped on the door and he opened it up. "Come on in. Want some coffee?"

We grinned at each other as he handed me a cup.

I took a sip. "Great coffee."

He smiled modestly. "I grind my own beans."

"It's delicious. I was doing errands in the neighborhood and thought perhaps you'd like to come out to lunch with me?"

"Martha, when we signed the rental agreement, you talked with Marilyn about my being *independent*. Am I independent?"

"Yes, you are. That means you can manage your own medications and don't need your medications monitored as they do in a board and care."

"So you agree I am independent."

"Yes, I do."

His old worried expression disappeared and he grinned broadly.

"Then, if that's true, no thank you to lunch in a café. I'll fix my own lunch in my own home.

I continued on my way, rejoicing. Joseph had reached his goal and I had reached mine.

Five months later, once again I almost flew up the stairs to Miriam's office, bubbling over with joyful words. "Miriam, do you remember my telling you Joseph wouldn't acknowledge me as his mother?"

"I do indeed. And how Dr. Ericson said that was his attempt to prevent me from suffering the stigma of his brain disease."

"Yes, and despite his interpretation, I've felt bad because I want to be valued as a Mom."

"I believe you had some good news when you arrived. Can you tell me what has happened?"

"Yes. At our Pepper-Tree-Lane Valentine parent-resident luncheon last week one mother suggested, 'Let's go around the table and tell who we love the most.'

"Some residents mentioned a dog, a brother, a counselor. When she came to Joseph, he answered, 'My mother. She loves me and everybody in this organization.'"

Happy tears filled my eyes. Joseph had opened his heart and welcomed me in as his mother. This was as proud a moment as when the doctor laid a very red-faced baby with curly reddish brown fuzz on his head and told me, "Here is your son, Mother."

The greatest challenge in my life lay in my belief that I caused the tragedies in my life, including my father's and my baby's death and my son's schizophrenia. A sense of guilt clung to me and I was always eager to say, "It's my fault." When my husband Hal died, I didn't believe I deserved or wanted a life on my own. I flirted with the thought of death.

I looked intently at my therapist, Miriam. Had I never really registered the violet-blue of her eyes? Had it really been seven years since our therapeutic relationship began? Over that time, Miriam's hair had several incarnations from spiky salt and pepper to today's gentler silver waves. Miriam still wore sporty clothes, open and ready for action. She greeted me as usual with a luminous smile.

Under her tutelage and non-judgmental comments, I became more adept at expressing my anger, disappointment, and sadness. Today, I wanted to express my appreciation. "Miriam, when we started therapy, I saw myself primarily as a mother and widow, almost buried in the debris of emotional earthquakes. I carried rocks of guilt as I trudged through a devastated landscape. As we explored the labyrinth of my childhood, I became aware of how I first gathered up guilt in my attempts to save my father. Your interpretations of my experiences and attitudes, and your unwavering belief in my value led me to express my creative voice in my memoir. Along the way, I dropped my heavy load. The rocks became markers, sign posts, on my life's journey."

Miriam responded, "I've always loved your metaphors. I hope you understand I have been happy to be your companion on your journey. You also need to know that *you* have done the work, and *you* have earned your sense of self-acceptance and peace. I truly hope that you will no longer quote me but realize any insights I may have had, you have internalized and are a part of you now."

"You'll be quoted in my memoir, but as you say, your insights are a part of me so I'll try not to begin a sentence with 'Miriam says...'."

We laughed in unison. I sighed, feeling the intimacy of this exchange. Then I added, "I also believe I've been guided not only by you but by a heavenly presence I cannot put into words."

"Martha, some matters are beyond words and meanings. I would never deny the work of the spirit."

This would not be my last visit with my therapist, though at this moment it felt as if we were celebrating the distance I'd come, the guilt I'd overcome.

I've turned eighty-eight. It's been twelve years since Hal died and I think of him every day. Many mornings I look in the mirror and ask him, "How am I doing today?" I seem to see him just behind me, in the mirror. He holds up his thumb. "Atta girl, Honey, you're doing just fine."

A Journey to Joy

A widow of 88, I live alone but am surrounded and supported by a network of children, their spouses, grandchildren, nieces, friends, a therapist, and a ten pound poodle. A strong sense of the presence of my husband Hal encourages me. Alone on Lido Island, I am never alone.

The words of **Hrant Harold Sarkissian** live on in my heart. He advised me, "Don't waste your tears on a dysfunctional appliance or a broken plate. Those are only minor irritations, not a major disaster." He suggested, "Picture everyone you meet with a sign around his neck saying 'I need attention.'" He comforted me with "Tragedy is not unique to us; knock on any door, you'll find sad events have visited there, too." He counseled me, "Treat mental illness as any other disease. Don't blame yourself, or others, or the victim. Accept the one with the brain disease while seeking scientific help." As a young man, he didn't believe in love, but as an older man, he defined love as "the glue that holds a family together." Sometimes I look in a mirror and see his reflection just behind me and I ask him "How'm I doing, Hal?" I see his grin and his thumb up sign. "Atta girl!"

Our oldest daughter **Julie,** her husband **Ron Stanke,** and their son **Danny,** live on Mercer Island, Washington. Julie recently retired from Seattle Public Health and now devotes her energies to organizing and sustaining a Farmer's Market on the island and to traveling with her husband, Ron. Their son Danny is a member of the cheer squad at Eastern Washington University. He tosses beautiful girls sky high and always has a positive attitude. He won the "Unsung Hero" award in high school for enduring football injuries with a grin and helping younger boys in athletics. Our family comes together for Christmas dinner and I enjoy asking each family member a question, "What is one thing more you would like from life?" Ron replied, "I have everything I want: my wife Julie and my son, Danny." He has volunteered in Danny's classrooms and on the soccer field and now enjoys traveling with Julie.

When I think of **Geoffrey Sarkissian**, his wife **Sarah Post**, and their children, **Julie and David,** I recall the year and a half that Hal and I shared our home with them and I bonded with the children. The house they built in Modjeska Canyon is surrounded today with a garden of native California plants and blends into the mountain landscape. If I close my eyes, I can visualize the western redbud tree aflame in the front yard, wisteria dangling from the porch beams, cactus blooming with a background of roses, and I hear the strum of Geoffrey's guitar, the music of songbirds and the welcoming bark of their vizsla, a robust but sensitive dog. Geoff, a computer sales person and builder of six garden bridges, is the same type of loving mediator and father as Hal once was. He and Sarah married when she was eighteen, and she has always given physical and emotional support to her extended family, both Posts and Sarkissians. Today she is a dedicated high school English teacher and master gardener of their private Eden.

When I had a bout of double vision, only my grandson **David** Sarkissian recalled my severe fall a year earlier. This enabled my neurologist to diagnose and cure the problem. I asked David "How did you remember I fell?" "Grandma, don't you know that's what I'm here for?" Today, he works in computer sales and lives in Pasadena. This year, 2013, granddaughter **Julie Sarkissian** returned to California from New York to hold a book signing for *Dear Lucy,* her novel recently published by Simon and Schuster. Presently, she is a nominee for the Dylan Thomas award for young writers. **Julie** began her book signing at her hometown library in the canyon with the words, "My first public presentation of my writing was in this library when I read aloud my third grade poem." The small library bulged with her elementary school teachers and canyon friends. This event celebrated not only her novel but also her loving spirit as she honored the library and her teachers. September 21, 2013, she married **James Fitzpatrick** by the sea in Montauk, Long Island. They reside in New York. I anticipate new adventures for Julie in both writing and married life.

Joseph Sarkissian, our second son, president of the Harbor High School Marching Band and assistant to the instructor, played first-clarinet in the Pasadena Rose Parade, 1972. At Evergreen University, Washington, he majored in art and chemistry. The ceramic pots he created adorn my house today. While working as a lab assistant to Dr. Kutter, a brain disease struck him down. Today, his apartment is filled to bursting with his many paintings. His ceramics, one of which won third place in a Seal Beach art contest, decorate his shelves. He faithfully drives me to market on Saturdays and to church on Sundays. In the community where he lives, his friends know he is always ready to drive a friend to the market or to a fast food café for a snack. He grinds coffee beans to make his own special brew. Mornings he and his friend Amy enjoy sipping his coffee together in the gazebo.

Our youngest child, **Laura Sarkissian,** an audio engineer, married **Bob Boyd** in 1992. Bob graduated from Golden West University and passed the California Bar exam on his first try. He established a law practice in Oakland. Some years later, they settled in Ukiah, California, where he is known as the leading criminal defense attorney. He is on the list of the 100 top trial lawyers in America. Bob and Laura's lives altered when their son, **Jesse Boyd**, born prematurely on December 19, 1994, weighed-in at the Oakland hospital at just 2 pounds. The parents became a family dedicated to Jesse. To bridge communication for their infant, they learned sign language. They studied laws and services for children with cerebral palsy and soon had a team of physical therapists, speech therapists, and vocational therapists working with **Jesse**.

Laura took part -time employment as a social worker, aiding other mothers to find assistance for their handicapped children. Jesse flourished. One day, after searching several years for a cure for Jesse's legs, Laura had a new insight. "Jesse is Jesse—not his legs!" Today Jesse, a miracle child for sure, is knee-deep in academic awards. He's a teaching assistant in PE and always a candidate for gifted classes. Jesse once told me, Grandma, I'm a celebrity in Ukiah." It's not only Jesse who is. Laura also is known as a school volunteer and an artist. She and Bob manned the snack wagon for the Giant Junior Baseball team, of which Jesse was a member. On Halloween, Bob and Jesse set up a stand on the street near Bob's office and pass out candies—a Ukiah tradition. Bob is a prominent criminal lawyer, also respected for legal work he performed for children who are wards of the state. No wonder when I walked along the streets with the Boyd's, cars slowed down, hands waved, and people called out "Hi, Bob! Hi, Laura! Hi, Jesse!" They are all celebrities.

About the Author

Martha Sarkissian began writing as a third grader splashing blobs of ink from a dip pen on her stories and poems. Her teenage dream was, "To go to Paris and be a writer." Instead, she married Hrant Harold Sarkissian in June 1947, the same month she graduated from Berkeley. She had five babies, and taught school until she was 80. As teacher, she was director of the Learning Center, where she worked equally with the highly talented and learning disabled. Through years crowded with activities, she managed to write children's stories, curriculums, articles, poems and novels. In her later years, she came to understand and delight in the unique capacity of the aging brain to grow. At age 88, having finished her memoir, *Living on a Fault*, she teaches a writing class and is working on the next project, a children's novel.

Questions for Discussion

01. Martha felt inadequate and self-conscious throughout her childhood and much of her life. What factors contributed to these feelings?
02. How did Martha's parents contribute to the feelings of guilt she carried with her?
03. How do you feel about Martha's decision to see a psychotherapist at the age of eighty? What role does the therapist play in the structure of the book?
04. Why did Martha's therapist suggest she spend forty-five minutes a day thinking about her husband's death?
05. Why was Martha's brother better able than her mother to accept Martha's inter-cultural marriage?
06. How did the culture of the fifties shape Martha's life and her self-image? Did Martha consider herself an equal to her husband? Did her husband consider Martha his equal?
07. What motivated Martha's humorous attempts to be an ideal wife? How did they affect her relationship with her husband?
08. In what ways did Martha's relationship with her father shape her relationship with her husband?

09. What is your reaction to Martha's response to the loss of her daughter? What restrained Martha's friends and family from showing more compassion at that time in her life? Did you consider the minister's assistance helpful?
10. What is your explanation of Martha's vision in the rose garden?
11. How do you assess Martha's decision to remain in Washington to work for her son's release? Was it the best decision for her family?

12. Did the Sarkissians make a wise decision when they evicted their son from their home?
13. How had Martha's confidence and self-assessment changed by the end of her memoir? What factors contributed to that change?
14. Why is Martha's memoir sub-titled "A Journey to Joy"?